Reimagining Contract Law Pedagogy

AF716375

Reimagining Contract Law Pedagogy examines why existing contract teaching pedagogy has remained in place for so long and argues for an overhaul of the way it is taught. With contributions from a range of jurisdictions and types of university, it provides a survey of contract law courses across the common law world, reviewing current practice and expressing concern that the emphasis the current approach places on some features of contract doctrine fails to reflect reality.

The book engages with the major criticism of the standard contract course, which is that it is too narrow and rarely engages with ordinary life, or at least ordinary contracts, and argues that students are left without vital knowledge. This collection is designed to be a platform for sharing innovative teaching experiences, with the aim of building a new approach that addresses such issues.

This book will have international appeal and will be of interest to academics, researchers and postgraduates in the fields of law and education. It will also appeal to teachers of contract law, as well as governmental and legal profession policymakers.

Warren Swain is Professor of Law in the Faculty of Law, University of Auckland, New Zealand, and Visiting Fellow, Clare Hall, University of Cambridge, UK.

David Campbell is Professor of Law in the Law School at Lancaster University, UK, and Visiting Professor, Auckland University of Technology Law School, New Zealand.

Legal Pedagogy

Series Editor

Kris Gledhill
Auckland University of Technology, New Zealand

This series consists of high-quality monographs, each of which explores best practice in an aspect of the law school curriculum. Books will cover teaching methods and curriculum design in the main areas of law, how to integrate themes and areas of jurisprudential thought, and wider questions about legal education more generally. With contributions from around the world, this series explores innovative thinking and practice within the context of a generally conservative branch of academia, with the aim of promoting discussion as to how best to teach the various aspects of the law degree and ensure the ongoing validity of the law degree as a whole. Typical topics addressed include the value of variety in teaching methods and curriculum design, how best to incorporate educational research, the role for more practical courses, and the need to ensure that law schools provide degrees of relevance to the needs of students and of society.

The books in this series will be of great interest to academics, researchers, and postgraduates in the fields of law and education, as well as teachers of law who may be interested in revising curricula and need guidance in doing so. In addition, the legal profession and in particular those who regulate entry into the profession will find much to interest them within the series.

Books in this series:

Re-thinking Legal Education under the Civil and Common Law
A Road Map for Constructive Change
Edited by Richard Grimes

Reimagining Contract Law Pedagogy
A New Agenda for Teaching
Edited by Warren Swain and David Campbell

For more information about books in this series, please visit www.routledge.com/law/series/LEGPED

Reimagining Contract Law Pedagogy

A New Agenda for Teaching

Edited by Warren Swain and David Campbell

Routledge
Taylor & Francis Group
LONDON AND NEW YORK

First published 2019 by Routledge
2 Park Square, Milton Park, Abingdon, Oxon OX14 4RN
52 Vanderbilt Avenue, New York, NY 10017

First issued in paperback 2020

Routledge is an imprint of the Taylor & Francis Group, an informa business

© 2019 selection and editorial matter, Warren Swain and David Campbell; individual chapters, the contributors

The right of Warren Swain and David Campbell to be identified as the authors of the editorial material, and of the authors for their individual chapters, has been asserted in accordance with sections 77 and 78 of the Copyright, Designs and Patents Act 1988.

All rights reserved. No part of this book may be reprinted or reproduced or utilised in any form or by any electronic, mechanical, or other means, now known or hereafter invented, including photocopying and recording, or in any information storage or retrieval system, without permission in writing from the publishers.

Trademark notice: Product or corporate names may be trademarks or registered trademarks, and are used only for identification and explanation without intent to infringe.

British Library Cataloguing-in-Publication Data
A catalogue record for this book is available from the British Library

Library of Congress Cataloging-in-Publication Data
Names: Swain, Warren, 1973– editor. | Campbell, David, 1958– editor.
Title: Reimagining contract law pedagogy : a new agenda for teaching / edited by Warren Swain and David Campbell.
Description: Abingdon, Oxon [UK] ; New York, NY : Routledge, 2019. | Series: Legal pedagogy
Identifiers: LCCN 2018045793 (print) | LCCN 2018051231 (ebook) | ISBN 9781315178189 (E-book) | ISBN 9781138036925 (hardback)
Subjects: LCSH: Contracts—Study and teaching. | Contracts. | Consumer contracts.
Classification: LCC K103.C64 (ebook) | LCC K103.C64 S93 2019 (print) | DDC 346.02/20711—dc23
LC record available at https://lccn.loc.gov/2018045793

ISBN 13: 978-0-367-66258-5 (pbk)
ISBN 13: 978-1-138-03692-5 (hbk)

Typeset in Bembo
by Apex CoVantage, LLC

Contents

Contributors

Rick Bigwood, Professor, TC Beirne School of Law, University of Queensland, Australia.

Brian H. Bix, Frederick W. Thomas Professor of Law and Philosophy, University of Minnesota, United States of America.

Roger Brownsword, Professor of Law, The Dickson Poon School of Law, King's College London, Professor, Bournemouth University, England.

David Campbell, Professor, Lancaster University School of Law, England, and Visiting Professor, Auckland University of Technology Law School, New Zealand.

David Capper, Reader, School of Law, Queens University, Belfast, Northern Ireland.

John Cartwright, Official Student (Fellow and Tutor) in Law, Christ Church, Professor of the Law of Contract, University of Oxford, England.

Paul J. Gudel, Professor, California Western School of Law, San Diego, United States of America.

Martin Hogg, Head of School, Professor of the Law of Obligations, Edinburgh Law School, University of Edinburgh, Scotland.

Richard Hyde, Associate Professor, School of Law, University of Nottingham, England.

Jonathan Morgan, Senior University Lecturer in Law, Fellow of Corpus Christi College, University of Cambridge, England.

Marcus Roberts, Senior Lecturer, Faculty of Law, University of Auckland, New Zealand.

Warren Swain, Professor, Faculty of Law, University of Auckland, New Zealand, and Visiting Fellow, Clare Hall, University of Cambridge, England.

Jessica Viven-Wilksch, Lecturer, Adelaide Law School, University of Adelaide, Australia.

Sally Wheeler, Dean, Professor, College of Law, Australian National University, Australia.

Paul Wragg, Associate Professor, School of Law, University of Leeds, England.

Chapter 1

Rescuing contract law pedagogy from the nineteenth century

Warren Swain

Introduction

Writing in the *Law Quarterly Review*, in 1886, Frederick Pollock set out his philosophy of legal education (Pollock 1886: 454–455):

> Most chiefly we can help him [the student] to fix in his mind that there are such things as general principles of law; that the multitude of particulars inevitably be versed as a practical student and worker are not really a chaos; and that, if he sets out with good will and good faith, he need have no fear that the search for a true art founded on science.

Pollock was one of a number of the new breed of university law professors who put their minds to the purpose of legal education around this time. His fellow Oxford jurist, AV Dicey, wrote a book with the title, *Can English Law be Taught at the Universities?* (Dicey 1883). The concern with legal education at this time wasn't a coincidence. There was a long tradition of civil law teaching in universities. The teaching of the common law on the other hand was a relatively recent development if one discounts Sir William Blackstone's lectures – which were not part of a degree syllabus. In earlier times the common law was exclusively learnt in the Inns of Court. Cambridge only introduced the Law Tripos in 1858 (Searby 1997: 193). Oxford had a joint degree of law and history from 1850, but a separate law degree did not appear until as late as 1872 (Lawson 1968: 34–60). Law was a novel academic discipline, and there were many in universities who doubted that it deserved to be taught there. At the same time there were many in the profession who thought that law should be learnt in practice and in the Inns. The subject only began to be taken seriously by many at Oxford within living memory (Simpson 2011). Against a background such as this it was understandable that academic lawyers felt compelled to defend their discipline.

Pollock was also a well-known writer on contract. His *Principles of Contract at Law and in Equity* was the standard work on the subject, but it was not a book written with law students in mind (Pollock 1876). Pollock's treatise was different from what had gone before. Earlier works on contract like the one by Joseph Chitty were written by practitioners (Chitty 1826). Earlier books on contract law, whilst no doubt useful to practitioners were, with a few exceptions, unsophisticated in their structure and methodologies. The first true contract textbook produced for students was Sir William Anson's *Principles of the Law of Contract* (Anson 1879). Anson wrote in his preface that he had sought to "delineate the general principles which govern the contractual relation from its beginning to its end" (Anson 1879: v). Anson was not just saying that the law could be reduced to general principles. He was suggesting that contract law has a clear narrative structure. It was implicit in this view that all contracts irrespective of the nature of the parties or the type of contract could be fitted within his general framework.

Anson admitted in a letter to Lord Justice Thesiger that he had oversimplified a complex picture for the sake of exposition (Waddams 2011: 211–212).

> I took a great deal of trouble to arrange the various parts of the subject in due proportion & order, but it wasn't until I began to fill in my outline that I realised how much labour was needed & how much more learning than I possessed. Some parts of the subject are very interesting, and here and there it seems . . . that the law is still unsettled even on rudimentary points, and in such matters one feels the excitement of an explorer.

Despite the opinions he expressed to his friend, the vision of contract law that Anson promoted in his textbook was quite different from the one in his letter. The simplified textbook version is the one that has come to form the basis of the way that contract law is taught in universities. The traditional contract course is taught in a particular way which is reflected in its structure, in the subject matter that is included and excluded, and in the way in which contract law fits within the overall curriculum.

Traditional pedagogy

There cannot be many other university courses, whether in law or any other discipline, which have changed so comparatively little since the days when Queen Victoria was on the throne. The traditional structure favoured by many contract courses looks something like this: contract formation; contractual enforceability; terms and contractual interpretation; vitiating factors; breach and remedies. This arrangement has some attractions. It shows the process of contracting as if it were a story with a beginning, middle and an end. Presented in this manner the subject appears coherent and logical and even based on principles. This has advantages for those learning the subject. It gives students a sense of security. They are left feeling that contract law has a pattern rather than just existing as a random collection of authorities and rules.

The idea that the law of contract has some coherent substructure has value in pedagogical terms. It provides a ready-made structure to student learning or what the learning and teaching literature calls instructional scaffolding. There are other benefits as well. It helps to give the law of contract explanatory force. This is a good thing which is capable of producing something like the recent elegant restatement of English contract law (Burrows 2016). There are also dangers. Dagan and Heller have recently examined the legacy of American classical legal thought and the role played by Samuel Williston. They point out that "Williston replaced the unprincipled multiplicity of the common law . . . with the unprincipled uniformity that dominates American contract law today" (Dagan and Heller 2017: xi). In England, Pollock and Anson were involved in similar projects to Williston. From the point of view of contract theorists the lack of principle is clearly undesirable. Nor does a single uniform law of contract reflect reality. Williston, Pollock and Anson present the law as though there was a general law of contract which applies irrespective of the subject matter or the type of contract. It is doubtful whether this model of contract law ever reflected reality even in the nineteenth century. It is certainly not an accurate representation of the modern law, particularly with the rise of the statutory regulation of contract law.

Not only does the traditional approach fail to reflect reality in large ways by promoting a general law of contract, but also in smaller ways as well. It places emphasis on some features of contract doctrine at the expense of others in a way which fails to reflect the character of most contract disputes. It is, for example, comparatively rare to find a modern authority on contract formation. Whilst formation is sometimes contested particularly in cases of tendering and the "battle of the forms", it is quite difficult to justify taking up large parts of the syllabus with the doctrine of offer and acceptance. Most contracts are after all conducted on simple standard form terms. The idea that contracts are individually negotiated by the parties is, to say the least, a very long way from normal practice when one of those parties is a consumer. There is an added reason for dissatisfaction. In the absence of a large body of modern authorities on contract formation, those used to illustrate these principles are of considerable antiquity and do not reflect modern practices. A leading case like *Adams v Lindsell* ((1818) 1 B & Ald 681) has some merit as an authority in showing an exception to the rule that an acceptance must be received. The more important point though is that a case such as this only operates as a default rule where no provision is made. Ultimately it depends on the expectations and intentions of those who are contracting. The postal rule is remote from modern life at a time where a contract is much more likely to be concluded by an exchange of e-mails than a letter. As Brownsword demonstrates, the point is not just that contracts are more likely to be concluded by e-mail than letter, but that new technology has a growing role in the business of contracting in a whole range of ways.

Because of the way that the traditional contract syllabus is structured it becomes difficult to devote sufficient time to two issues that *are* incredibly important in practice: contractual interpretation and remedies. This need not be the case. As Campbell points out, remedies are generally, though not universally, taught first in contract law courses in the United States. Elsewhere they are often tagged on to the end of the syllabus when in fact the topic deserves to be central. The traditional course also leaves a lot out altogether. Its focus is unduly narrow on cases that go to trial. This is not to say that elements of the content of traditional contract course have no value. The nature of agreement and bargain does raise profound and important questions about the very nature of contractual liability. Yet even such fundamentals are not always easy to discern when seen through the prism of decisions such as *Carlill v Carbolic Smoke Ball* [1893] 1 QB 256 no matter how entertaining. Legal doctrine sits at the heart of contract pedagogy and merits separate consideration.

One of the main features of the traditional approach is that the subject is taught using the case method. For many students who study contract law early in their degree, contract law serves as an introduction to legal method. In its purest form this pedagogy utilises casebooks. As Capper explains, there is a long tradition of using casebooks, often combined with the so-called Socratic method. In modern times the father of the case method was Professor Christopher Columbus Langdell (Langdell 1871). Langdell's casebook was a collection of materials and nothing else. There was no commentary. In England Professor Sir John Smith and his former colleague at Nottingham University Professor JAC Thomas pioneered this method in the 1960s. Casebooks are usually associated with the United States, but they are still used in various jurisdictions. Roberts's chapter, for example, gives an account of teaching using the casebook method in New Zealand.

Capper and Roberts give rich accounts of the strengths and weaknesses of the traditional pedagogy. A few can be highlighted. As Roberts points out, "The benefits of the casebook method and forcing students to read a large number of cases is probably increasing, since students in the second decade of the twenty-first century are so ill-equipped to concentrate and read for long periods of time". The old adage, "You can lead a horse to water but you can't make it drink" seems particularly apposite. There are other dangers in this type of approach. Capper and Roberts both observe that the cases alone, whilst essential, are likely to confuse students unless supporting material is provided. In Langdell's original casebook there is nothing to help or guide a reader beyond the way in which the material is arranged. Students need more of a structure than this. Arguably the most important contribution of the lecturer to their students' learning is to provide their audience with an intellectual road map. Without it the law of contract just becomes a procession of cases. The case law remains central to the way that legal practitioners view the subject even in a jurisdiction like New Zealand where so much of the law is included in the contract statutes. Yet the law isn't just about cases. A student who only understands the case law is likely to be left with a very partial view of the subject. This is not just the old debate about whether the study of law in a university should prepare a student for legal practice. Merely studying the case law gives an unduly narrow view of the subject. All but the most able students are likely to be unable to make much of the authorities without a great deal of guidance. If cases appear in a casebook in abbreviated form it might not even be a good training for reading cases. But if cases are not the end of contract pedagogy they are a necessary beginning. It is almost possible to think of that some aspects of the law curriculum could be taught without case law or at least a bare minimum of authority. Public Law at least outside hard core administrative law, probably falls into this category. Contract law without cases is scarcely a subject at all. Even contract theory is rather difficult to teach in the abstract.

Contract pedagogy and contract doctrine

A number of writers in this volume concentrate on particular contract doctrines or subject matter. This approach is usually overlooked in the pedagogical literature, which tends to focus on generic methods of teaching delivery. Even when the focus is on law teaching the discussion rarely gets sufficiently fine grained to talk about the way that a particular topic can be taught. Legal doctrine remains a central part of the student learning experience. It provides the building blocks of the subject. Even here the traditional way of teaching the subject is unsatisfactory. The leading English work on contract law (Peel 2015: 1) begins with the following definition of a contract: "A contract is an agreement giving rise to obligations which are enforced or recognised by law". Statements of this kind can be found at the beginning of many of the other contract textbooks. The idea that a contract is an agreement is often linked to the notion that a contract is a bargain. These ideas are examined in Hogg's and Morgan's chapters. Hogg and Morgan both conclude that agreement and bargain still have very important parts to play as underlying principles but they also conclude that neither provides all the answers. Hogg warns that "we need to take greater care that we do not over-egg the agreement pudding". Morgan points out that there are clear instances where the concept of bargain is "redundant".

Contract law remains largely a "black letter subject". It does not follow that a particular doctrine can only be taught in one way. There is room for innovation in ways that are both fundamental and would improve pedagogy. Some areas of contract doctrine have lacked a satisfactory intellectual framework for a long time. Bigwood's chapter discusses a striking and difficult to cure example of the problem which concerns the vitiating factors of duress, undue influence and the unconscionable bargain doctrine. He suggests that rather than exploitation what is needed is "a more complete and nuanced conceptual account of '*victimization*' in connection with the procurement or receipt of contractual benefits, 'victimization' including 'exploitation' but not being exhausted by that particular concern". As Bigwood's discussion shows, one of the challenges facing lecturers is to provide a coherent conceptual structure but an even bigger obstacle to explaining the material involves marrying good pedagogy with the actual practice of the courts.

Contract law and context

A major criticism of the standard contract course is that it is too narrow. It is rare to find a contract course which engages with ordinary life or at least ordinary contracts. In his humorous piece on legal education, James Gordon gave what he called an "honest" course description for contract law (Gordon 1991: 1696):

> *Contracts*. Study rules based on a model of two-fisted negotiators with equal bargaining power who dicker freely, voluntarily agree on all terms, and reduce their understanding to a writing intended to embody their full agreement. Learn that the last contract fitting this model was signed in 1879.

There is a good deal of truth in the caricature. Part of the problem is the way in which students are left without even a flavour of everyday commercial realities. This can make the subject matter feel remote and abstract. But the consequences are more serious than that. An account without context is incomplete. It fails to explain why contract doctrine is applied in the way that it is, in a particular context. It is possible to promote a formalist view of the subject but still regard context as playing an important role in pedagogy. This is reflected in the way that in England at least commercial contracting is central in practice and also in the way that the subject is taught. Yet at the same time it presents a partial picture.

The context of a transaction is potentially more than just about the background against which contract doctrine is applied. There are a number of different contexts highlighted by a number of the contributors. One of these is the prevailing commercial and intellectual context within which the law operates. Jessel MR famously said in *Printing and Numerical Registering v Sampson* (1875) LR 19 Eq 462 at 465 that:

> [I]f there is one thing which more than another public policy requires, it is that men [sic] of full age and competent understanding shall have the utmost liberty of contracting, and that their contracts when entered into freely and voluntarily shall be held sacred and shall be enforced by Courts of justice.

This statement doesn't reflect the way that contract law operates today. In modern times there are many more limits on what the parties can agree to. There are numerous restrictions on unfair terms including: Unfair Contractual Terms

Act 1977 (UK); Fair Trading Act 1986 (NZ) and Australian Consumer Law 2010 (Aus). The point is a larger one, however. As Brownsword shows, the law of contract sits within a complex regulatory framework. Public policy whether statutory or at common law is not a major feature of many contract courses. Perhaps it should be.

Students come to contract law with their own experiences of contracting. Those experiences can be utilised in the learning process. This gives an advantage to contract teachers as opposed to, say, those teaching company law or intellectual property. It is a source of insight that is not always very well utilised. A possible blueprint for using students' own real life involvement in the contract process is provided by Hyde in his chapter on teaching consumer contracts. There are lessons here for making the contract syllabus more accessible. At the opposite end of the spectrum are large-scale commercial contracts. Whilst the emphasis of most contract courses is on business contracting for the most part, even commercial contracting may not always be well understood. The traditional syllabus treats contracts as one of discrete one-off transactions. In fact, where commercial parties are involved they are more likely to be in a continuing relationship. Gudel's chapter explains how contract law can be taught from a relational perspective. Even if the syllabus isn't completely torn up, it isn't difficult to imagine how relational contracting should form at least a part of the modern contract syllabus.

These ways of thinking about the law of contract seek to consider the process of contracting from the point of view of actors in the process. The traditional contract course doesn't say very much about the law of contract as it is understood and applied by businesses and consumers. As Wheeler demonstrates a law in action approach can provide a useful perspective on the traditional doctrinal structure of contract law which after all only describes a small number of exchanges. The great merit in this approach is that it allows students to understand that contract law is used in different ways and is underpinned by a range of social norms. Contract law is a subject that many students find dull; in part this is because of the way that it is presented as a series of abstract rules. A law in action approach provides a valuable antidote.

Contract law is, of course, a product of wider society in ways that go beyond economic and regulatory perspectives. Following the Human Rights Act 1998 a human rights discourse has become a much more central part of the legal landscape, at least in the UK. There are instances where it may even have had an impact on contract law itself. Wragg identifies collateral reasons for making reference to human rights in the contract syllabus. He suggests that introducing these ideas better aids conceptual thinking and gives the subject greater relevancy; according to Wragg, human rights theory and doctrine, "provides a parallel to aid them through the unfamiliar".

Private law theory more broadly is often squeezed out of the law curriculum. The focus is largely on contract doctrine. Where theory appears at all it is in small elective courses. Even courses on jurisprudence or legal philosophy tend to cover broader questions of the "what is law?" type than engage with private law theory. This is not because there is nothing to say. On the contrary there is a vast and sophisticated body of theoretical literature. Bix argues that there is clear merit in teaching contract theory and that without it the teaching of the subject is incomplete. As he observes, "Legal practice should be learned in a way that connects it to history, economics, morality and justice, and practical reasoning". It is important to acknowledge that a particular theoretical perspective may be taught even if it is not always taught knowingly. For example, someone who is sympathetic to legal realism will inevitably teach the subject quite differently from someone who sees value in law and economics.

Finally, there are rich parallels to be drawn by introducing some comparative perspectives into the contract syllabus. Cartwright makes the important point that, "Not only can it give in short order a picture of the extent to which English law is similar to, or different from, our European neighbours, but it can give food for thought about the approach taken by English law". The traditional syllabus is nothing if not insular.

Contract law pedagogy: a future agenda

There are many ways to teach contract law. The way in which the content of the contract syllabus is been delivered is changing. In the next decade the old style lecture and tutorial is likely to be, if not obsolete, then a rarity. Technology is likely to be increasingly important. Content can be delivered using blended learning in which some content is delivered online and some face to face. As Viven-Wilksch shows, technology is already quite widely used in universities. It can be used to supplement learning but also as a means of encouraging the desirable deep learning and promoting skills-based learning. It is difficult to predict what will come along. Ideas like the flipped classroom which a few years ago were seen as innovative are likely to seem dated.

There may be things that are worth preserving from the traditional contract course even if the mode of delivery shifts. Case law will still be important. Contract law is likely to remain a core part of the legal syllabus and a means of teaching legal skills more generally. This volume provides a range of suggestions from the quite specific with a focus on a particular area of contract doctrine to quite broad questions of course delivery. There are a lot of options. The challenge lays in making the subject relevant to students and giving them a broad-based educational experience whilst at the same time not making the syllabus so heavy with content that it topples over.

References

Anson, W., 1879. *Principles of the Law of Contract*. Clarendon Press, Oxford.

Burrows, A.S., 2016. *A Restatement of the English Law of Contract*. Oxford University Press, Oxford.

Chitty, J., 1826. *A Practical Treatise on the Law of Contracts Not Under Seal*. S. Sweet, London.
Dagan, H. and Heller, M., 2017. *The Choice Theory of Contracts*. Cambridge University Press, Cambridge.
Dicey, A.V., 1883. *Can English Law Be Taught at the Universities?* Palgrave Macmillan, London.
Gordon, G.F., 1991. How Not to Succeed in Law School. *Yale L.J.*, 100, 1679–1706.
Langdell, C.C., 1871. *A Selection of Cases on the Law of Contracts*. Little, Brown and Company, Boston.
Lawson, F.H., 1968. *The Oxford Law School 1850–1965*. Oxford University Press, Oxford.
Peel, E., 2015. *Treitel The Law of Contract*. 14th ed. Sweet & Maxwell, London.
Pollock, F., 1876. *Principles of Contract at Law and in Equity*. Stevens & Son, London.
Pollock, F., 1886. Oxford Law Studies. *L.Q. Rev.*, 2, 453–464.
Searby, P., 1997. *A History of the University of Cambridge 1750–1870*. Cambridge University Press, Cambridge.
Simpson, A.W.B., 2011. *Reflections on the Concept of Law*. Oxford University Press, Oxford.
Waddams, S., 2011. *Principles and Policy in Contract Law*. Cambridge University Press, Cambridge.

Chapter 2

Agreement

Martin Hogg

Introduction

Agreement lies at the heart of our understanding of contract law, and most teachers begin with this topic when structuring any course of contract teaching. This is reflected in most of the contract texts. *Chitty on Contracts* (Beale 2012, para 2–001) states: "The first requirement for the formation of a contract is that the parties should have reached agreement". That was not always so: in classical Roman law, consensual contracts were merely one of a number of forms of contract. In the other recognised forms, the agreement (or *consensus in idem*) of the parties was not a necessary component. Even by the time of post-classical Roman law, the standard student text – the *Institutes of Justinian* – treats of consensual contracts (Inst 3.22) only after the reader has first been treated to an explanation of real contracts (Inst 3.14), oral promises (stipulations) (Inst 3.15–19), contracts of surety (Inst 3.20), and written contracts (Inst 3.21). Form was the crucial matter, the agreement of the parties merely being one (restricted) form. In early English law too, agreement was not central to the various forms of action that would one day be grouped together into the modern, unified law of contract, and so would not have been central to studies of the law: other actions, including assumpsit and debt, were as important as that of covenant, an agreement-based action which might have furnished, but did not, a general law of contractual enforcement. In the common law, agreement came relatively late to be accepted as a central explanation of the validity of contracts, though given the need for mutual consideration in all contracts other than those by way of deed or seal, bargain also featured as an explanation for many contracts; moreover, given that contracts by way of deed or seal are unilateral in form and effect, promise also served as an explanation for some contracts. So, in the common law at least, while agreement is the dominant explanation for the majority of contracts, some contracts require or may have other explanations. In legal systems which lack a generally applicable requirement of mutual consideration, and which treat unilateral promises as a different species of voluntary obligation to contract, there is the possibility of agreement becoming *the* normative explanation for contract (this is seen, for instance, in my own legal system of Scotland).

Agreement as a concept has an intuitive, easily understood explanatory force, hence its enduring popularity with courts, academic writers, and teachers. But it also has a vagueness about it – how can I know if and when we have agreed, and the details of what we have agreed? (problems which are particularly acute with oral contracts) – such that it requires an extended explanation when teaching the concept to students, and it continues to produce a healthy body of legal disputes and concomitant case law. This, of course, furnishes many opportunities for engaging teaching, and students seem perennially to enjoy the debates which arise in this aspect of contract law.

The past, present, and future of teaching contractual agreement

In looking at how agreement is taught within contract law, it will be useful to look at three timeframes. Drawing on my own experience as both student and teacher, I want to examine first the teaching of contract law in the recent past, before moving on to looking at teaching at my institution at the present time. I shall then offer some suggestions for future development of agreement-based pedagogy.

The past

The quality of the teaching of contract law was, in the past, of variable quality, something which has been personally narrated to me in conversation with alumni who graduated in the 1960s. Teaching standards have, however, improved immeasurably at most institutions since that time.

If the quality of teaching contract law has improved, the medium of doing so has not altered drastically over the last fifty or sixty years. The traditional large lectures (albeit enhanced by features such as PowerPoint, on-screen reference to internet resources, and libraries of recorded lectures) enhanced by small group tutorials (at which problem scenarios are discussed) remains, in my institution at least, the format for delivery of the introductory course in contract law; in the advanced (Honours) course, small group seminars, at which topics are analysed in depth and students encouraged to present and debate their views on the law (rather than just to identify the "correct" answer) also remain the format (as was the case when I was a student in the late 1980s). One thing that has changed is the greater ease of accessing study materials. When I was a first year student, the first short textbook on Scots contract law (Woolman 1987) had only just been written by my contract tutor, Stephen Woolman, an inspiring teacher and now a judge at the Court of Session. In the same year as Woolman's textbook appeared, the first edition of the standard modern academic treatment of the law, McBryde's *Law of Contract in Scotland* (McBryde 2007), also appeared. These two books provided students with, respectively, introductory and advanced treatments of contract law. Prior to this, students were required to have recourse to a few chapters of Gloag and Henderson's general work on Scots law (MacQueen and Mackay 2017), to outdated texts (such as Gloag's *Contract*, the last edition of which had appeared in 1929), or to English textbooks (an unsatisfactory resource in areas in which the law was not identical in Scotland). Learning contract thus became much easier for students studying in my legal system from the late 1980s, as accessible materials became available and as teaching standards dramatically improved.

But what of the substance of what was, in the past, taught about contractual agreement? Much, of course, was the same as it remains today, given that agreement was and remains the cornerstone of the normativity of contracts. But a few differences are noticeable. There was little, if anything, taught about the role (such as it is) of good faith in concluding contracts; there was a much greater emphasis on contractual freedom, with little discussion of counterbalancing external restraints on that freedom; and there was a greater focus on the mechanics of offer and acceptance, and less on the theory and general considerations surrounding agreement. When I took up my appointment as a lecturer (in 1995), the first tutorial problem in the course plunged the students straight into an offer and acceptance analysis of agreement. It raised problems of whether an "anticipated" (rather than firmly stated) price is enough for an offer, the status of a mass-circulated advertisement, the effect of an enquiry concerning delivery contained within what otherwise looks like an unqualified acceptance, what sort of conduct might convey contractual intent, the postal acceptance rule, and the effect of a revocation of an offer and an acceptance arriving together. It was only later that the law school added an additional tutorial problem exploring more general issues around agreement. This new tutorial problem remains in use today.

The present

As mentioned above, the format of how we teach contract and, in particular, agreement has not changed much since my student days or even the 1960s: lectures and tutorials for the introductory course and seminars at the advanced level. The style of teaching has changed quite a bit, however, with more emphasis on developing students' oral and research skills, working in groups, and reading a range of materials (including cases, commentaries, law reform reports, and comparative material). The substance of what is taught has also changed, as the discussion immediately following will show.

Having had a taster of contract law in a more general course on the legal system, in Edinburgh's first year Contract & Unjustified Enrichment (CUE) course lectures begin with a section entitled "The Structure of Private Law" in which the law of obligations is set within the wider structure of the law (the chart of the law provided to students illustrates the difference between public and private law, and between property law and obligations), a distinction between voluntary and involuntary obligations is introduced, and contract is then introduced as a form of voluntary obligation. There is a brief description of the main characteristics of the principal classes of obligation. In taking this approach, we are doubtless reflecting the characteristics of an institution teaching within the traditions of a mixed legal system in which taxonomy and principles are traditionally stressed. What is missing presently from the introductory Edinburgh treatment of the field is anything about the variety of contract theories that can be found across the common law world (e.g. promissory theory, bargain theory, reliance theory, relational theory, economic theories). Discussion of such theories is left over to the more advanced "Honours" contract law course which is an optional offering for students in the latter stages of the LL.B degree.

Freedom of contract is explained near the very beginning of our introductory course, with quotations from Adam Smith's *The Wealth of Nations* (specifically the passage from Book I, Chapter 2, in which the desire to contract is explained as self-interest motivation) and from the remark of Sir George Jessel MR in *Printing and Numerical Registering Co v Simpson* (1875) LR 19 Eq 462 that "contracts, when entered into freely and voluntarily, shall be held sacred and shall be enforced by Courts of Justice". Importantly, the idea of agreement is taught alongside a number of other guiding principles. First, it is explained that there is a principle concerned with "discrimination and refusal to contract" (Edinburgh Law School 2016) –

> While in general people are free NOT to contract, there are many exceptions in modern legislation which forbids refusal to contract in certain situations on the grounds of the sex, racial group, disability or age of the other party (see now the Equality Act 2010, replacing Sex Discrimination Act 1975, Race Relations Act 1976 as amended, Disability Discrimination Act 1996, Employment Equality (Age) Regulations 2006). Even at common law, innkeepers and common carriers are not entitled to refuse to accommodate a would-be customer without sufficient excuse. But private clubs may discriminate.

There is also initial explanation of the ideas of extortion and inequality of bargaining power, and the role of good faith and fair dealing. This scene-setting is important, as it helps to ensure that from the very beginning students appreciate that contractual freedom is not absolute or unconstrained, and that not everything that is agreed may be enforceable at law.

The students are then introduced to a definition of a contract, which they are told is:

> an *agreement* between two parties having the capacity to make it, in the form demanded by law, to perform on one side or both, acts which are not

> trifling, indeterminate, impossible or illegal, creating an obligation enforceable in a court of law. Agreement is usually analysed as an *offer* made by one party (a proposal for a contract) *accepted* by the other party.

So, a performance-related agreement is taught as *the* defining feature of contract, albeit one which is constrained by considerations such as its trifling, indeterminate, etc., nature, and requirements of capacity and form. The agreement so defined is said to give rise to obligations. Its analysis is said *usually* to take the form of an offer and acceptance. Note that in this explanation no alternative definition is given in promissory or bargain terms, but as this is a peculiarly Scots law definition such alternative definitions would be unhelpful, given that in Scots law mutual consideration is not required for a contract, and a unilateral promise is a separate species of voluntary obligation.

The objective position the law takes when assessing agreement is explained, with citation made of the remark of Lord Dunedin that "commercial contracts cannot be arranged by what people think in their inmost minds. Commercial contracts are made according to what people say" (*Muirhead & Turnbull v Dickson* (1905) 7 F 686). Reference is also made to the position adopted in the *Draft Common Frame of Reference* (DCFR) that "[t]he intention of a party to enter into a binding legal relationship or bring about some other legal effect is to be determined from the party's statements or conduct as they were reasonably understood by the other party" (Article II. – 4:102). The DCFR is quite often quoted in the first year contract law class, which I suspect would not be the case in many common law introductory classes on contract law. In our teaching materials there is then a brief section on "intention to create legal relations", which stresses that not all agreements give rise to contracts: it is only those which disclose a common intention on the part of the parties to the agreement that it should be binding at law. A reference to the slightly different concept of parties "consenting to be bound" might have appeared in the materials at this point, though it does not.

There then follow several pages of materials on offer and acceptance, which is introduced by a section on the "role of offer and acceptance". In delivering this section, my colleague Professor Hector MacQueen (who teaches the introductory contract law course) strikes a note of warning, by telling students that the approach of the law to the problem of "cross offers" arguably allows the offer and acceptance dogma to override the basic principle that contract is about agreement (Edinburgh Law School Contract Lectures, delivered on 4 October 2016). So students are taught not to be overly reliant on the offer and acceptance analysis and to question whether its application allows one invariably to reach the right conclusion on formation questions. I shall return to this point when considering future pedagogy.

The materials presented to Edinburgh students on offer and acceptance follow what I imagine will be a familiar pattern to contract law teachers: (1) *Offer*: requirements for a valid offer; distinguishing offers from other pre-contractual statements, particularly invitations to treat; the status of various sorts of communications – advertisements, tenders, auction bids, promises of reward, undertakings to accept the highest of any offers, and (bringing the historical analysis up-to-date) website communications; the time when an offer takes effect; termination of offers; (2) *Acceptance*: requirements for a valid acceptance; distinguishing acceptances from requests for clarification; cross offers; acceptance by conduct; time when an acceptance takes effect, including discussion of the postal acceptance rule. Again, in the material on offer and acceptance, there is occasional reference to the provisions of the DCFR. As Professor MacQueen was lately a Commissioner at the Scottish Law Commission, he is also well placed to refer to possible law reform in the area of formation of contract (for instance, of the postal acceptance rule) when giving his lectures, though in an introductory course law reform can be touched upon only briefly given the need to cover the entirety of contract law in the limited number of lectures available (things are, of course, different in advanced courses of contract law: so, for instance, in my Contract Honours course, I regularly discuss with my students various law reform proposals and ask them for their views on how they think the law ought to be reformed). Students at the lectures are encouraged to make comments on, and ask questions about, the lectures as they are being given.

The weekly tutorial problems which students analyse and discuss in small groups include three on formation of contract: the first (added at the close of the 1990s) looks at the elements necessary for a minimally sufficient agreement; the second (mentioned earlier as the formerly first tutorial problem in the course) looks at the rules of offer and acceptance; and the third at formalities applicable to certain types of contract. In the new first problem the students are guided by the facts of the problem to consider how an arguably enforceable contractual agreement may be affected by virtue of its being discussed on the golf course by two business parties (is it by virtue of this setting a mere social agreement?) and by virtue of the parties agreeing to leave to a later occasion the question of price (never agreed, despite performance on the other side – is a *quantum meruit* appropriate, or ought the solution to lie in unjustified enrichment?). The new first problem was inserted at the start of the course so that students' attention was directed more clearly to the notion of agreement in the round, rather than asking them to focus simply on the mechanics of offer and acceptance as a means to reaching agreement. That strikes me as a sensible and welcome development.

How does our teaching of agreement differ from what was on offer in the past? There is I think more discussion of law reform; there is greater reference to comparative materials and supra-national projects (like the DCFR); and there is more by way of warning that the offer-acceptance paradigm is only one way of viewing contract formation, albeit one that is still readily applicable to back-and-forth negotiations between distant parties. Also, I think students are encouraged to be less reverential of judges', commentators', and their teachers' views. We generally encourage students, even in their preliminary studies, to be reflective of what they study, and to consider whether the law surrounding matters like agreement of contract could be improved. Moreover, the fact that students see a lot more of practitioners and judges during their study than they did of old helps them to think of themselves as emerging lawyers rather than just as the passive recipients of the wisdom of distant and unerring sages.

The future

Turning to the future of contract pedagogy, the obvious central question is how we might want to do things differently in the future. In this regard, there are a number of questions and issues that I believe it would be useful for contract teachers to consider.

First, there is, I think, much sense in beginning any introductory contract course with a mini-introduction to the law of obligations generally, thereby setting contract within the wider obligational field. Of course, students who take an introductory Roman law course in their first year (as I did) will have the advantage of being presented with the institutional scheme of the law at the very start of their legal studies, and of being able to use that scheme as a foil against which to compare the current law of their own legal systems. But for those students who do not take Roman law, a little scene-setting of the place of contract within the wider law of obligations can be very helpful (as mentioned earlier, such scene-setting is a feature of Edinburgh's first year contract course). Such an approach allows students to better understand why voluntary agreements between two or more parties have a connection with other forms of voluntary obligation, it enables them to assess the significance accorded to the human will as a medium for consenting to the imposition of obligations, it facilitates an assessment by them of the continuing relative significance of agreements in the face of growing external regulation of such agreements, and, of course, it demonstrates to them that contract law has connections to other parts of the law of obligations (and beyond).

Second, there would be value in some reflection by contract teachers on the desirable balance between teaching principles and cases. The common law's traditional antipathy for general principles has been diminishing somewhat during my career as a student and teacher, and the recent acceptance by most present-day scholars of the benefits for pedagogy of recognising a general law of obligations, and of explaining the various types of obligation by reference to taxonomies, general rules, and principles, has been noticeable in textbooks and the courses of study offered by universities. Of course, this does not mean that cases cease to be of interest, far from it. But in making sense of an ever-growing body of case law, it is useful to set out principles and schema for explaining the law, an approach which scholars of comparative law have been particularly quick to apply in their teaching of domestic law.

Third, the movement towards recognising the utility of principles and rules of law has been evident in the emergence of the first Restatements of English obligations law (Burrows 2012, 2016). I have found using these especially helpful when teaching the common law to students. They provide a natural starting point for discussing areas of complex law, where the right answer often has to be teased out from a plethora of judgments. I expect to make increasing use of such Restatements as more of them appear, as I imagine the courts will too.

Fourth, the examples which comparative lawyers have found useful when developing their approaches to teaching English law raise the question: Should common lawyers be drawing upon more comparative materials from civilian and mixed legal systems? I would suggest so, even if it is just to show that the common law has a distinctive way of looking at something, and thus to inform students that there are other ways of addressing legal issues. So, in my own teaching of contract law, including that relating to the concept of agreement, I certainly intend to continue drawing on comparative observations. It is worth adding that contract students at my own university have for generations been exposed to both Scots and English cases and materials, ensuring that they benefit from the perspective of both the common law and a mixed legal system (with its civilian influences). I believe that this gives them an advantage in understanding and applying the law.

Fifth, I think we must make efforts to update our case studies of contract problems by reference to modern facts and examples. This will necessitate getting rid of some of the hoary-old cases, unless there really are no other examples to illustrate the point in question. Many of the agreement-based disputes arising these days involve electronic communications by parties, standard form disputes, contracts prepared by legal agents, or consumer contracts involving much greater degree of state regulation. Textbooks tend still to rely on nineteenth-century cases when explaining fundamental points, and authors (and teachers) appear to be loathe to give up using the original authorities in the field. I am not sure that students are always best served in their study of contract law by explanations of carbolic smokeballs (*Carlill v Carbolic Smokeball Co* [1893] 1 QB 256) and postal exchanges between countesses and their prospective servants (*Countess of Dunmore v Alexander* (1830) 9 S 9), especially where the reports of such cases are often defective or in challenging prose. Modern disputes regarding factory production lines (*RTS Flexible Systems Limited v Molkerei Alois Müller GmbH* [2010] UKSC 14) and whose terms govern contracts concluded by an exchange of brief emails (*Baillie Estates v Du Pont* [2009] CSIH 95) can be just as useful in explaining the rules surrounding agreement and formation of contracts. The pressing problems of the nineteenth century are not always those of the twenty-first. This is in no way to decry the value and fascination of legal history, merely to suggest that – especially in introductory courses – utilising factual scenarios which are as relevant as possible to the future legal careers of our students is desirable, and that using (where possible) modern case law assists that goal.

Sixth, as is already being done in teaching at my own institution, we need to stress to students that, while offer and acceptance analysis offers a useful way of analysing some contract formation disputes, it is not the only analysis, and can be positively unhelpful in cases which do not conform to a simple back and forth exchange of communications (e.g. the document prepared by a third party for both contracting parties to sign). We must emphasise to students that the offer and acceptance paradigm is merely one paradigm among others for understanding the notion of agreement and the process of contract formation.

Seventh, as contract teachers we need to reflect more in our teaching on the way in which our fondness for particular theories of contract law affects the way we present the law to students. So, we should reflect on the extent to which we stress the need for "intention" to contract as opposed to the need for an objective "consent to be bound" to agreements, a point to which I return in the final section of this paper; a similar point could be made of other issues, such as whether it is the objective perspective of the reasonable party in the shoes of the other party which defines the traditional "objective approach" of our contract law, or whether it is the objective position of the reasonable third party observer. As well as such self-reflection, an early exposure of students, even briefly in introductory courses, to differing theories of the normative force of contracts would have value in their understating of the basics of the law, as well as provide a good basis for later more in depth study of the law.

Eighth, in an age of increasing state interference in private law relationships, we should be attuned in our teaching to the need to draw the attention of our students to the external controls on agreement, emphasising what this means for the ability of outside actors to police contracts. The impending departure of the United Kingdom from the European Union is unlikely, despite what politicians may believe, to reduce greatly demands for such external controls.

Ninth, assuming that we are not to abandon the traditional teaching framework of lectures and tutorials, we need to find ways to continue to improve the practical negotiation skills and oral argumentation of students. One way to do this would be to use a contract scenario between specified imaginary parties as the basis for writing a course of tutorial problems. Such a course could thus begin with imagined negotiations between parties for a contract, before proceeding to the contract's formation, its content, its performance, its breach, and the subsequent remedying of the breach. Students could be divided into groups acting for the various parties, and could be encouraged to meet outside class and develop ideas for deployment in class debate. This sort of programme could be peppered with one or more mini moots, during which students could present oral arguments about the ongoing legal relationship of the parties. Some institutions doubtless use this sort of programme already.

Last, we need to consider the extent to which the agreement-related issues which arise in practice resemble the ones we teach in classrooms. Part of this relates, of course, to my fifth point about the need to update the case law which we use to teach contract to our students. But it is also about being attuned to dispute avoidance and the way in which contract drafters are responding to legal developments. In this respect, it can be helpful to show students examples of contracts during lectures (my colleague Professor MacQueen has recently shown the first year contract class his contract for the purchase of a new home) and also to include classes on contract drafting (such a session features in my advanced contract class). Building and maintaining a connection between law and practice is essential to good contract law teaching.

Is agreement still important?

A final, overarching question about how we ought to teach agreement to contract students relates to an existential question about the concept itself: does agreement really matter that much to contract law and practice? If it doesn't, then perhaps we ought to ditch it, or at least downplay its significance, in our teaching of contract law.

In asking the question whether agreement really matters that much, let me attempt to assess a number of arguments tending to the view that agreement is not very important to contract law. First, there is the old argument of Patrick Atiyah that contract is not really about enforcing agreement (or promises) at all, but rather about protecting detrimental reliance and the conferral of benefits. I have commented on this view before (Hogg 2009), so shan't repeat my views in detail here. Suffice to say that I do not think that Atiyah's grand detriment-benefit theory is capable of explaining the corpus of contract law as we have it. In particular, it cannot explain the enforcement of executory contracts where neither party has yet performed, or the enforcement of unrelied-upon unilateral promises. It seems clear to me that the law does indeed sometimes enforce contracts and unilateral promises simply because they are the voluntary undertakings of parties disclosing an intent to give rise to binding obligations.

Another old argument is that it is the appearance of agreement which really counts, rather than agreement itself – in other words, that it is the conduct of parties objectively assessed rather than their agreement subjectively assessed which founds contracts. This point is essentially true, in so far as it reflects the perspective of courts in the common law tradition. But this is no bad thing, quite the contrary: it is a practicable and realistic approach. None of us, judges included, can read minds. Moreover, a subjective approach could be exploited in bad faith by a party which had changed its mind and subsequently alleged a lack of subjective agreement. Perhaps the most decisive riposte to this argument is that agreement is itself not an entirely personal, internal matter: any concluded "meeting of the minds" requires, in the words of the seventeenth century writer and judge Lord Stair, "engagement", not merely "desire" or "resolution", and "engagement" (Dalrymple 1693: 1.10.2) – conduct showing a commitment to be bound – is necessarily an objectively manifested, external, public declaration.

A more challenging argument is that agreement is heavily regulated by courts and by statutes, each of which can interpose or strike down obligations. That being so, the "agreement" reached by parties quite often will not reflect their actual obligations. However, as I have previously commented (Hogg 2013: 25):

> will-based theories, whether promissory or agreement in nature, need not attempt to explain the whole content of contracts as stemming from the will of the parties. All they need do is (1) to demonstrate that the existence of the contract was the result of a voluntary exercise of the will, and (2) to explain the content of the express terms of the contract, in so far as these are not struck down or over-ridden by statute or public policy.

If this point is accepted, then all that it means is that we should recognise the parties' agreement as *a* source of obligation, but not the only one.

A practical concern is that, not infrequently, negotiating parties seem not to worry overly about whether they have reached agreement on more than the basic points necessary to identify their expected mutual performances and their respective timings. There are various reasons why this relaxed approach may be so. They may view details as "legal niceties" which are unnecessary to doing business; they may be so focused on a successful conclusion that they ignore potential pitfalls (what can be called "optimism bias"); they may hope that any problems which do arise can be resolved amicably without the need to revert to contractual rights and remedies; they may be too busy to attend to the details, and keen to start performing as soon as possible; they may be willing to forego elements of the agreement in order to get the job done and to perpetuate the relationship over the long term; or they may have decided simply to leave matters about which they have been unable to agree to one side, hoping that they will prove unimportant. These sorts of observations are the bread and butter of relational contract theory, a constant observation and argument of which has been that the actual agreement may well have much less significance than traditional contract theory *and teaching* gives it. If this is true – and I think there is merit in much of it, even if relational theory cannot provide a general normative theory for contracts – then we need at least to point this out to students when teaching contract law.

If we accept, even in part, the validity of the concerns raised by relational theory, then we need to take greater care that we do not over-egg the agreement pudding, by giving too much emphasis to the relative significance of the agreement on paper and neglecting external forces operative upon the content of the contract and the behaviour of parties in practice. That said, agreement is likely to, and ought to, remain at the core of contract law pedagogy. It is a golden thread that runs through not only formation of contract, but mistake, contractual content, agreed damages, remedies, and other crucial aspects of contract law. Continuing to emphasise its importance provides an important anchor for contract law, one necessary to ensure that external interference in contracts does not increase to such an extent that contractual obligations become swallowed up by the non-voluntary, imposed liability of tort law.

References

Beale, H., 2012. *Chitty on Contracts: General Principles*. 32nd ed. (Vol. 1). Sweet & Maxwell, London.

Burrows, A.S., 2012. *A Restatement of the English law of Unjust enrichment*. Oxford University Press, Oxford.

Burrows, A.S., 2016. *A Restatement of the English Law of Contract*. Oxford University Press, Oxford.

Dalrymple, J., 1693. The Institutions of the Law of Scotland: Deduced from Its Originals, and Collated with the Civil, Canon, and Feudal Laws, and with the Customs of Neighbouring Nations. In *IV Books*. 2nd ed. Printed by the Heir of Andrew Anderson, Edinburgh.

Edinburgh Law School, 2016–17. *Contract & Unjustified Enrichment: Lecture Handout*. Unpublished.

Hogg, M., 2009. Perspectives on Contract Theory from a Mixed Legal System. *Oxford J. Legal Stud.*, 29, 643–673.

Hogg, M., 2013. Competing Theories of Contract: An Emerging Consensus? In: DiMatteo, L.A., Zhou, Q., Santier, S., Rowley, K., eds., *Commercial Contract Law: Transatlantic Perspectives*. Cambridge University Press, Cambridge, pp. 14–40.

MacQueen, H.L. and Mackay, R.D., eds., 2017. *Gloag & Henderson: Law of Scotland*. 14th ed. W. Green, Edinburgh.

McBryde, W., 2007. The *Law of Contract in Scotland*. 3rd ed. W. Green, Edinburgh.

Woolman, S., 1987. *An Introduction to the Scots Law of Contract*. W. Green, Edinburgh.

Chapter 3

Bargain

Jonathan Morgan

Introduction

Clearly most contracts made, and litigated, are bargains or exchanges. But are the categories entirely coextensive? Are all legally enforceable contracts bargains, and all bargains contracts? My suggestion is that those teaching contract law should pose these questions about its basis directly and not merely obliquely, if at all, in the course of expounding "consideration (and related doctrines)". In order to do this effectively, we should formally separate teaching the creation of contractual obligation from modification of existing contracts. The result, hopefully, would be more open engagement with two important issues: first, the proper province of the law of contract; second, the correct approach for courts, and contracting parties, towards regulating contractual modification.

How the subject is currently taught: "consideration (and related doctrines)"

How is the "bargain theory" of contract currently taught? I have taught (and been taught) contract law for much of the past 20-something years at Oxford and Cambridge Universities. I do not think the approaches at those institutions differ (fundamentally, in kind) from the curricula followed at other English universities, to judge by the content and organisation of student textbooks. Thus (conscious of the possibility of error) I will generalise my personal experience.

A full week's teaching (i.e. one tutorial/supervision out of eight or nine in total) is invariably spent examining "consideration (and related doctrines)". The satellite matters being (invariably) promissory estoppel and (usually) "intention to create legal relations" (sometimes squeezed into a different week). The focus is heavily doctrinal. As with much else in contract law, these doctrines have developed through and must be taught through the leading cases. Some of these are Victorian or earlier (e.g. *Eastwood v Kenyon* (1840) 11 Adolphus and Ellis 438, *Carlill v Carbolic Smoke Ball Co.* [1893] 1 QB 256). Others range through the Twentieth Century (the "intention to create" doctrine crystallised only in *Balfour v Balfour* [1919] 2 KB 571, and promissory estoppel only in *Central London Property Trust Ltd v High Trees House Ltd* [1947] KB 130). The "topical" question, which tends to consume most of the time for discussion, is "one-sided" modifications to existing contracts. The venerable law on this topic (stated in *Pinnel's Case* (1602) 5 Coke's Rep 117a, *Stilk v Myrick* (1809) 2 Campbell 317 and 6 Espinasse 129, and *Foakes v Beer* (1884) 9 App Cas 605) received an electrifying challenge from the Court of Appeal's invocation of "practical benefit" consideration in *Williams v Roffey Bros & Nicholls (Contractors) Ltd* [1991] 1 QB 1. The *Roffey* decision side-stepped the absence of (orthodox) consideration to enforce a promise to pay more than was originally due. Compare the earlier recognition (in promissory estoppel) of a defence when promises to accept less than was owed are withdrawn. The Court of Appeal was recently willing to extend *Roffey* into the "promise to accept less" situation (*MWB Business Exchange Centres Ltd v Rock Advertising Ltd* [2016] EWCA Civ 553; [2017] QB 604).

These overlapping doctrines about the modification of contracts are complex and subtle. Their development, and interrelation, demand careful explanation by the teacher. Examined in isolation, the doctrines remain controversial. The propriety and wisdom of using "practical benefit" consideration to circumvent *Stilk v Myrick* (and now also *Foakes v Beer*) is hotly contested. Whether promissory estoppel is merely a contract that dare not speak its name (as Atiyah (1978) alleged), or a fundamentally different kind of obligation, is also contested. We must bear in mind Milsom's historical observation: counsel who advanced the arguments in the seminal cases certainly did not do so in order to create new species of obligations. They were interested only in winning the dispute on the facts. If that involved abuse of the common law's elementary categories then it would not be the first time (Milsom 1981). However, it is not clear whether judicial *acceptance* of such transformative arguments can be explained similarly by sheer forensic pragmatism. In particular, Lord Denning's determination to develop promissory estoppel could be viewed as another bold law-reform campaign from the bench (a successful one, according to Lady Justice Arden: *Collier v P & M J Wright (Holdings) Ltd* [2007] EWCA Civ 1329; [2008] 1 WLR 643, [42]).

A pedagogical difficulty is that (to quote Lord Denning himself in *McIlkenny v Chief Constable of the West Midlands* [1980] QB 283, 316–317) estoppel is "a big house with many rooms". The contract teacher cannot hope to cover its many sub-categories. Thus promissory estoppel is analysed in a more or less isolated way. One bravely hopes that when the students study proprietary estoppel in land law, especially the relief granted, they will reflect again on arguments such as Atiyah's (albeit *mutatis mutandis* – since the main problem in the property cases is failure to comply with statutory formalities rather than absence of consideration). Some familiarity with the conscious Australian departure from the confines of English promissory estoppel is expected from stronger students (at least), but this tends to begin and end with *Waltons Stores (Interstate) Ltd v Maher* (1988) 164 CLR 387. The judgments there remain stimulating, but *Waltons Stores'* afterlife and the considerable literature surrounding it cannot decently be required knowledge, even as further reading.

As stated, the controversial complexities of modification consume most teaching time. This is inevitable (given its topicality), although arguably distorts the focus since modification has its own set of problems to which consideration provides a very questionable solution. It is also necessary to cover (albeit briskly) the basic, uncontroversial points: consideration must be *sufficient* (e.g. past consideration is not), but it need not be *adequate* (herein "peppercorn" or nominal consideration). Deed promises are enforceable irrespective of consideration. Business parties are strongly presumed to have "intention to create legal relations"; the contrary presumption governs family agreements, collective bargaining between employers and trades unions, and other non-commercial situations.

The contours of contractual obligation are in this way broadly indicated, but they do not usually receive much attention – let alone extended discussion, criticism or defence. Analysis usually amounts to the following. Any system of law needs to have some test for deciding which promises or agreements constitute legally enforceable contracts. In English law that badge of enforceability has long been "consideration" (for the creation and modification of contracts alike). While venerable, that doctrine can be adapted to meet "new problems" (as the *High Trees*/*Roffey* sagas show). Here lies the genius of the common law, especially when shaped by Lord Denning.

This is about the level of theoretical sophistication that most students of the law (or rather their teachers) can hope to reach in the time available, in my experience. Often it is reached after reading the set-piece debate between Professors Atiyah (1986) and Treitel (1976). Whoever is adjudged to have the better in that exchange, the ground-rules of their scholarly dispute required close attention to judicial decisions and doctrinal developments, the soundness of these to be assessed against doctrinal orthodoxy. (For general criticism see Campbell 1992.)

Yet much of that orthodoxy is misleading. How "uncontroversial" are the basic rules about consideration? The sheer complexity of the rules on contract modification indicate the need for a first-principles reappraisal. The assumption that consideration has the pivotal role in policing modification should be questioned; a permissive regime (which permits the parties to self-impose limits on possible modifications) may function better. A total separation between creation and modification of obligations is needed to see this clearly. If my "re-imagination" has a general theme, it is that we need to step back and look at the wood as well as the trees. Two quite distinct "woods" need to be mapped: first, the initial creation of contractual obligation; second, modification of contracts.

Creation of obligations

At heart the doctrine of consideration requires a valuable exchange as the definition of an enforceable contract. But *should* contract law be so defined? Should bargain be both necessary and sufficient? Should any non-bargain ("gratuitous") undertakings be enforced? And when (if at all) should reciprocal bargains *not* be enforced (assuming that a sufficiently certain agreement exists, and the absence of pathologies such as fraud or duress, etc.)?

In addressing these vital questions about the province of the law of contract, an exclusive (or overwhelming) concern with the technicalities of consideration doctrine may obscure the inquiry (although grasp of the principles is, naturally, necessary) – partly because the big picture dissolves into a welter of detail, but also because other doctrines/principles are germane. These can be crowded out, or sometimes ("public policy") deferred to another part of the course or entirely omitted from the curriculum.

Creation of obligations: necessity of bargain?

We teach students that (deeds aside) contracts must be supported by consideration. I suggest that this is seriously misleading. In reality, commercial contracts are enforced irrespective of consideration (sometimes by creating a formal exception, sometimes by recognising that apparent "gifts" are in business inherently reciprocal). The corollary (discussed in the next section) is that non-commercial promises are usually unenforceable even when they are supported by consideration. The frontier of the law of contract is (more or less) that between commercial and non-commercial agreements.

It is sometimes suggested that consideration is evidence of "serious intention to be legally bound", but that is quite incorrect. Gift promises are unenforceable even when the surrounding circumstances show that the promisor had good reason to make one, and thus they were seriously intended. For example, family obligation, or gratitude for a past service (e.g. rescue; money spent schooling one's wife). These circumstances provide good reasons to promise payment for which nothing (or nothing further) is to be given in return. But from the doctrine's early days in the Sixteenth Century, "natural love and affection" has not been good consideration and neither has receipt of a past valuable service (except where it was always understood that the promisee would be remunerated). These venerable rules show beyond any doubt that consideration is *not* evidence of serious intention (compare the civilian *causa*, understood as "the reason for making the promise"). Consideration defines contracts as a *subset* of seriously intended promises: i.e. reciprocal agreements, bargains or exchanges. This embarrasses theorists who assert that all seriously intended promises should be legally enforceable (bargain or no).

Consideration requires bargain. This is the stuff of trade. It rules out gift promising, irrespective of serious intention. Is this apparently amoral distinction defensible? Arguably yes: there is good reason not to enforce *true* gift promises. But that argument becomes pernicious (and the legal rules shakier in application) when extended into commercial law. Contract teachers should attempt to draw out the important distinction between true benefaction and pseudo-gratuitous business promises.

Eisenberg (1997) argues that "the world of gift" would be tainted if it were absorbed into that of enforceable contracts. Eisenberg defines a gift promise as one made "for affective reasons like love, affection, friendship, comradeship, or gratitude, or to satisfy moral duties or aspirations like benevolence or generosity, and which is not expressly conditioned on a reciprocal exchange". As he proceeds to argue, making such promises legally enforceable would "impoverish" them by "submerging" the relationship between the parties. First, enforceability might lead to a smaller number of gift promises (and perhaps therefore gifts) being made, for people might not be willing to commit themselves legally (rather than just morally) to the fulfilment of gift promises. Second and more fundamentally, if gift promises became enforceable contracts, it would no longer be possible to ascertain whether their ultimate performance by fulfilling the gift was really motivated by the socially valuable concerns mentioned above (love, gratitude, benevolence, etc.) or under the threat of legal liability. Thus it is precisely because the law values donative promises, and wishes to preserve their distinctiveness, that it does *not* enforce them.

Posner (1977) points out that it certainly may be beneficial (for both promisor and promisee) to enter into a binding contract today to make a gift next year, because this creates *present* value for the future gift (compare waiting until next year and then just making the gift). Posner therefore suggests it is doubtful whether the law should distinguish sharply between bargains and gratuitous promises. Of course, this is susceptible to the critique that Eisenberg subsequently advanced: the risk of inappropriate takeover of gift-giving by the norms of contract law. Eisenberg asserts that the costs of this "impoverishment" would exceed any benefit from enforcing gift promises.

English law follows a *via media*. When a promise is made in a deed, there is no need for consideration to support it. This historical survival (from the old writ of covenant) retains great utility today. The deed facilitates legally enforceable gift promises. Thus the determined promisor can transfer the value of the promised gift in advance of actually making it (Posner's point). Moreover, this practice does not founder on Eisenberg's objections. A gift promisor who deliberately makes use of legal formality in this way is quite consciously going outside the realm of personal relations (love, generosity, etc.). The promisor deliberately opts to take the promise outside the "world of gift" and into the legal realm, so there is nothing "impoverishing" about its being legally enforceable. That is precisely what was intended. Provided that the usual run of gift promises is (as a default matter) not enforceable, but only those deliberately cast in a specific legal form, the separation between Eisenberg's two spheres is maintained. The same could be said about the legally advertent promisor who casts (effectively) gratuitous promises in reciprocal form by stipulating for some nominal counter-performance (the "peppercorn" rent and similar stratagems). This makes use of the rule that "consideration need not be adequate"; as with use of a deed, this tactic is readily available given legal advice (or awareness), but unlikely to be done accidentally or inadvertently.

If the point of the bargain principle (consideration) is to mark out contract law as the enforcer of *commercial* agreements, the doctrine faces an obvious difficulty when confronted with "gratuitous" business agreements. For instance, an undertaking in commercial negotiations to hold an offer open for a certain period; a promise by an owner of shipped goods to exempt stevedores unloading the goods from liability in negligence; a bank's undertaking in a documentary credit to pay a party which has not paid for that credit to be opened in its favour.

There is a strong sense that these promises should be enforceable. They are all made for clear commercial reasons. Many such agreements are enforced by the courts (but not all). Sometimes consideration is dispensed with by a formal exception. Sometimes consideration is "found", even if this means the court forcing the case onto the Procrustean bed. But sometimes the promise is indeed held unenforceable for want of consideration, and this inevitably attracts criticism. Important examples of each can be given by the contract teacher. They shake the supposed centrality of the consideration doctrine.

Many payment obligations are enforceable without consideration; they are the lifeblood of commerce. A documentary credit is enforceable against the bank even though the payee provides no consideration. Goode (1991: 218) argues that various "ingenious" attempts to reconcile documentary credits with consideration "[all] fall to the ground as being inconsistent with the practice and understanding of the parties". Commercial parties simply expect the promise of payment to be enforced, irrespective of consideration (or indeed of reliance, or formality (deeds)). And they are enforceable, precisely because of the commercial necessity for binding documentary credits.

Goode (1991: 219) noted that there was no direct legal authority formally waiving the requirement of consideration; "This is scarcely surprising, for any bank which sought to take the consideration point would destroy its commercial reputation overnight". Recently a bank came close to taking the explosive point, although counsel ultimately did not rely on it: *Taurus Petroleum Ltd v State Oil Marketing Co of Iraq* [2015] EWCA Civ 835 [13] (Moore-Bick LJ); [2017] UKSC 64, [25] (Lord Clarke), [95] and [100] (Lord Mance). Yet even the hint of a suggestion that lack of consideration could prevent enforcement of a bank's abstract payment obligation (Goode's apt term) brought firm denunciations. Goode's prediction that any such argument would "receive short shrift at the hands of the judiciary" proved entirely correct.

As is well known, Lord Mansfield's suggestion that written commercial promises should be enforceable irrespective of consideration was overruled as heretical by the House of Lords (*Pillans v Van Mierop* (1765) 3 Burr 1663; cf. *Rann v Hughes* (1778) 4 Bro PC 27). The general proposition has never been judicially revived (although cf Law Revision Committee (1937), para 29–32). But the sense of *Pillans v Van Mierop* lives on in some of the most important categories of "commercial paper" (now mostly electronic). Where commercial practice requires it, English law has had little hesitation in dispensing with the supposedly fundamental requirement of consideration.

There is a widely shared sense that commercial contracts should be enforceable irrespective of consideration. Teachers should invite students to consider whether this actually contradicts the bargain principle. Are commercial promises (apparently) lacking consideration really gratuitous? As Goode notes (1991: 209), documentary credits (etc.) "cannot be treated as a gift-promise; to the contrary, those who issue such promises are hard-headed financiers who do so for that most sound of commercial reasons, profit". (Of course, such credits *are* paid for, but the promising bank "looks for [its] reward from a party other than the promisee"). The same point was famously recognised by Lord Wilberforce in *The Eurymedon* [1975] AC 154, 161. The Privy Council waved aside the objection that the promise to absolve defendant stevedores from negligence liability was unsupported by consideration. The entire passage repays careful study. The central proposition was that there was "little doubt . . . in commercial reality" that this was a bargain and not a gratuitous promise. All the parties enjoyed "commercial relations entered into for business reasons of ultimate profit".

If anything, Lord Wilberforce pulled his punches describing it as "prima facie implausible" to see these undertakings as gratuitous. It would be quite unreal. Businesses are not motivated by love, gratitude, generosity or the other fine human feelings that mark out the "sphere of gift" (cf Eisenberg 1997). If a particular commercial promise seems "gratuitous" in isolation, that is because it is being examined away from its context of ongoing reciprocal relations. In business there is no such thing as a free lunch. A "gift" is promised when, and only when, there is firm expectation of reciprocal benefits being conferred in turn or when, as in *The Eurymedon* and with the issue of documentary credits, there is a web or chain of commercial contracts where promises to "non-privy" parties are the basis for the wider transaction(s).

Businesses exist to make profits. They are not charities. They are not rich uncles dispensing gifts to nephews who cease smoking. They do not feel the moral obligation to reward a past service (a life saved, a wife educated). It is not obvious that companies would be permitted to engage in truly bountiful behaviour, consistent with their duties to their shareholders. So if the doctrine of consideration concludes that commercial agreements are truly "promises to make gifts" it has gone wrong somewhere.

Should the teacher declare redundancy or advocate abolition? The courts have characteristically preferred to sideline the issue quietly. It would be more intellectually satisfying to abolish consideration as a requirement for the creation of commercial contractual obligations. This would realign doctrine and practice. Is such reform necessary? Notwithstanding the circumventions of consideration described above, it can sometimes still bite commercial parties. Promises to hold a commercial offer open are unenforceable unless paid for (i.e. embodied in an option contract). This is given as a leading example of the commercial inconvenience of the consideration doctrine by Nathan Oman (2016) (note that LRC (1937) para 38 recommended removal of the consideration requirement for such offers, noting their enforceability in "most foreign countries"). Oman would abolish consideration outright. Instead he proposes that the law should enforce every promise supporting a market-based transaction. This would be consistent with judicial scepticism about consideration from Lord Mansfield, Lord Wilberforce and Sir George Leggatt. In a review of Professor Burrows' *Restatement of the English Law of Contract* (2016), Mr Justice Leggatt (the leading contract theorist on the English bench today) questioned the space devoted to consideration given that "the doctrine has become almost entirely irrelevant in practice" (Leggatt 2017: 523).

So far this essay has assumed that the common law of contract is right to concern itself primarily with commerce. Pedagogically that will not do. A strong case can certainly be made for the descriptive correctness of the position, i.e. that as a matter of fact English contract law *is* near exclusively commercial in practice, with its heart and soul in the Lloyd's Reports (cf. Beale 2012, p105). But that is not a complete answer. What *should* be the focus of the law of contract? Oman (2016) has provided a strong defence of the moral virtues of market transactions, including the civilising effects of trade (Montesquieu's *doux commerce*), the co-operative spirit it engenders, modern trade's openness to strangers (i.e. those outside the clan or tribe) and the global economic benefits of free trade since 1800. Thus we can argue that the law of contract not only does support the market in fact, but that it is *right* to focus on commercial transactions.

Against this, it should be noted that Hanoch Dagan and Michael Heller (2017) powerfully argue that contract lawyers should not dismiss non-market agreements as the proper concern of "other disciplines" (e.g. labour law, consumer law, family law). This is to deny the *contractual* nature of non-commercial agreements. Contract law can expand choice across such a wide range of consensual activity by supplying transaction types (sets of default contract rules), and not just for commercial law. At the level of theory there is (of course) much to be said for this. It might seem an impossible task pedagogically, however – at least in a basic compulsory "contract law" course. Dagan and Heller's work still might caution us against claiming that the general law of contract *just is* commercial (and vice versa).

Creation of obligations: limits of the bargain principle

Should *every* bargain be legally enforceable? Is every (non-pathological) agreement supported by consideration a binding contract? The answer, of course, is no. But a doctrinal tangle obscures the nature of the inquiry. I suggest that teachers should cut through by engaging with the crucial underlying question: What are the limits of the markets that contract law should support? This question is currently addressed, obliquely, through the doctrines of "intention to create legal relations" and public policy. The former (in my experience) does form a minor staple of the contract curriculum, but the label (intention) is unhelpful. "Public policy" (as an obscure, perhaps quaint, aspect of the illegal contracts doctrine) is often not taught at all as part of a basic contract course. Given this partial (and misleadingly labelled) doctrinal coverage, it is not surprising that contract law teaching rarely engages directly with the substantive limits of contract law: Which bargains should fall outside its jurisdiction altogether?

Briefly, the teacher should discuss two further possible "limiting" doctrines: formality and reliance. But neither has a significant role in policing the jurisdictional boundaries of contract law. Certain kinds of agreements must satisfy a particular *formality* before they are legally enforceable. Formality requirements are statutory, sporadic and unsystematic. They attract complex common law exceptions, revealing a very longstanding judicial unease about their strict enforcement (in particular, once agreements have been performed, in whole or in part). Usually, the detailed study of formalities is (reasonably) allocated to other subjects such as land law, where they are centrally important (being required for transactions to create and transfer interests in land). Thus contract teachers deal with them barely at all. Arguably, however, formalities stipulated by contracting parties themselves should be seen as uncontroversial and enforced according to their terms (i.e. stripped of the complex exceptions that surround statutory formality rules). Examples include clauses in pre-contractual negotiations stating that no contract comes into force until signed by both parties, or clauses in written contracts requiring that modifications to the contract must be made in signed writing. The latter seem common in commercial practice, yet the underlying theoretical issue is unsettled and repays study (i.e. should freedom of contract extend to parties contracting-out of the common law's normal *absence* of formality requirements?) (Morgan 2017). The Supreme Court's recent acceptance that parties can create binding "no oral modification" clauses will draw scholarly and pedagogical attention to this neglected question: *MWB Business Exchange Centres Ltd v Rock Advertising Ltd* [2018] UKSC 24; [2018] 2 WLR 1603.

While it has sometimes been suggested that action in reliance is an essential element of a binding legal contract, the position is no longer (if it ever was) seriously advanced. It is associated with Grant Gilmore who (wrongly) prophesied the Death of Contract (1974), and with Patrick Atiyah. Few can doubt that, as Gilmore and Atiyah emphasised, an important function of the law of contract is to protect reliance on promises. Hence for Atiyah, a relied upon promise should be seen as the paradigm of a contract and not relegated to some other category as "promissory estoppel" because of the absence of consideration. Contract teachers should emphasise the good sense of Atiyah's insight. Reliance is a submerged, but vital, factor in difficult disputes about the formation of contracts by conduct (including when the parties required that the contract be formed only upon signature – but then went ahead with its apparent performance in the absence of a signature, e.g. *RTS Flexible Systems Limited v Molkerei Alois Müller GmbH* [2010] UKSC 14) or whether there is a certain enough agreement to be legally enforceable (e.g. *Foley v Classique Coaches Ltd* [1934] 2 KB 1). It is much harder to convince the court that no contract was formed when the parties' conduct strongly implies the presence of a contract (i.e. what they did, not what they said). All of this is an important challenge to orthodox, where an agreement lacking consideration "logically" cannot be a contract, nor "logically" can the parties' subsequent conduct help determine whether they were initially *ad idem*.

But Atiyah's emphasis on reliance can be carried too far. In particular, it is carried much too far if taken to entail that executory contracts are unenforceable. Practicality shows why. It would be disastrous for commercial certainty to require reliance as a precondition. Many contracts themselves become items for sale in markets (e.g. futures and derivatives trading), which presumes that the underlying contracts are from their inception enforceable. Having to investigate the degree of performance (or other reliance upon) the underlying contract (of sale, loan etc.) would make such markets impossible. They are hardly new commercial phenomena (see e.g. Simpson (1991)). More broadly (and even more disastrously) it would make the enforceability of every contract depend on the court's assessment of whether (and precisely when) there had been "reasonable" reliance upon it. This inquiry could fairly be described as discretionary; in the equitable estoppel jurisdiction, the degree of reliance must make it "unconscionable" for the promisor to revoke its undertaking. This should not become the rule across the board. For very good reason, it is elementary in English law that contracts are fully binding from the moment of formation, irrespective of reliance (Direct authority for such a basic principle is characteristically, if paradoxically, rather hard to find, but see *Centrovincial Estates plc v Merchant Investors Assurance Company Ltd* [1983] Com LR 158. For rejection of a "reliance theory" of documentary credits' enforceability, see Goode (1991: 224–225).)

The "reliance" school might salvage some pride by accepting that contracts are enforceable from the moment of formation precisely because contracts *tend* to be relied upon (even if they are not in fact, in every case, relied upon) from the outset. But the invocation of a presumed tendency (rather than actual proof of reliance) considerably weakens the argument. The teacher would note the echoes of the convoluted reasoning of Fuller and Perdue (1936), the pioneers of contract-protecting-reliance theories (who defended "expectation" damages as a tractable proxy for foregone opportunities, which is a species of reliance loss that would be very difficult to prove and assess directly). Reliance should not be elevated into a necessary condition for legal enforceability, i.e. its absence should not obstruct the formation of a binding contract, even though its *presence* furnishes highly significant evidence that a contract has come into being.

Thus neither formalities nor reliance can be seen as important jurisdictional limits on the categories of enforceable bargains. But clear limits are imposed by two other doctrines: first through the deemed absence of "intention to create legal relations"; second through miscellaneous heads of "public policy".

Unfortunately, the rational teaching of the matter is hampered by the arrangement (and content) of the standard contract curriculum.

From *Balfour v Balfour* onwards, the courts have held that parties to various kinds of non-commercial agreements do not intend them to be legally enforceable. (By contrast, business agreements are strongly presumed enforceable without any need for positive evidence of intention to that effect.) The basic contours of the doctrine reaffirm the bargain principle (or rather the *commercial heart* of the bargain principle, explored above). Commercial bargains are without more presumed enforceable. Non-commercial bargains, i.e. *even when reciprocal*, are not. The *Balfour v Balfour* doctrine is the corollary of consideration, underscoring the law's non-enforcement of non-commercial bargains.

For all the ostensible concern with "intention", it is quite clear that the doctrine is used as a tool to police the boundaries of contract law (see Hedley 1985). Certain kinds of agreements are deemed outside the law's jurisdiction. Collective bargaining agreements and (at one time) those between husband and wife, even when separating (*Balfour* itself), are examples. Needless to say, such line-drawing requires judicial value judgments which will often be controversial (e.g. Freeman 1996).

That those choices are semi-disguised under the rubric of "intention" does not help open engagement with the underlying question: When *should* contract law decline to enforce bargains? Students should not be misled by the surface appearance. Engagement with the real issue is required. The doctrinal form of this jurisdictional tool lends it porosity, which may be advantageous. Business parties wishing to avoid litigation may expressly deem their agreements "honour-only" commitments (relying on social sanctions for enforcement); i.e. businesses can explicitly disclaim the strong presumption that their agreements are to be legally enforceable (Rudden 1999). Conversely, parties to agreements presumed unenforceable can expressly declare their intention to be legally bound, or cast the agreement in specifically legal form, e.g. a deed, where it is hard to imagine that the parties could not intend legal enforcement, or why bother? (see *MacLeod v MacLeod* [2010] 1 AC 298, [36]). In the end, the jurisdiction-policing job done by *Balfour v Balfour* is presumptive only, with the boundary subject to express redrawing by the parties. This mutability is inherent in the doctrine's ostensible concern with intention.

For an incontrovertible jurisdictional rule we must look rather to public policy. The common law doctrine is a naked exercise in applied judicial morality. For example, English law long resisted the enforceability of pre-nuptial agreements on public policy grounds (ousting the jurisdiction of the divorce court; tendency to encourage divorce; likelihood of financially weaker party not fully appreciating the financial implications of divorce, etc.). This policy rule has now been judicially declared obsolete (*Radmacher v Granatino* [2010] UKSC 42; [2011] 1 AC 534). But others remain. A contract to pay for sexual services is unenforceable. (Victorian judges famously extended the taint of immorality to a contract for hiring out a carriage to a prostitute, in which she was to "advertise her wares": *Pearce v Brooks* (1866) LR 1 Ex 213.) Wider concerns about sexual immorality seem quaint if not ridiculous today (hiring a flat for a "kept mistress" was unenforceable in 1911 (*Upfill v Wright* [1911] 1 KB 506) but not by 1978 when Roskill LJ commented (*Heglibiston Establishment v Heyman* (1978) 36 P & CR 351, 361): "All I can say is that if [living together outside marriage] is to be interpreted as using premises for an immoral purpose there must be a great many breaches of [leasehold] covenant being committed in London and elsewhere today".) Yet common law public policy is not past the age of childbearing. In 2017, Jay J held that an "involuntary father" could not sue a fertility clinic which had allowed his former partner to use his sperm to bear a child, in breach of the clinic's contractual duty to obtain his consent for such use. The father's claim was barred by public policy, including the moral offensiveness of treating the birth of a child as compensable "loss": *ARB v IVF Hammersmith Ltd* [2017] EWHC 2438 (QB); [2018] 2 WLR 1223 (applying by analogy tort cases refusing to grant parents the cost of bringing up such "unwanted children": e.g. *McFarlane v Tayside Health Board* [2000] 2 AC 59).

Parliament has also made various contracts unenforceable. Examples include the Human Tissue Act 2004, s. 32 ("Prohibition of commercial dealings in human material for transplantation") and the Surrogacy Arrangements Act 1985, s. 1A ("Surrogacy arrangements unenforceable"). Sometimes Parliament rescinds an exclusion. Gambling contracts were long "void" under the Gaming Act 1845, but since 2007 contract law has resumed jurisdiction (Gambling Act 2005, ss.334–335). Davey (2013) comments, "This rebirth is likely to be painful, as wagering moves from the public law sphere of regulation by licensing to include the unfamiliar realm of consumer contract law".

This public policy material poses pedagogical challenges proportionate to its great theoretical interest. In my experience, "illegal contracts" are no longer routinely taught as part of the core contract curriculum, but left to (optional) advanced obligations courses (and/or to restitution courses concerned with the (previous) bar *in pari delicto potior est conditio defendentis*). Even there, the focus is on contracts which involve criminal behaviour (a difficult enough question notwithstanding *Patel v Mirza* [2016] UKSC 42; [2017] AC 467); little attention is paid to the difficult question of which contracts should be unenforceable even though no crime is involved (neither prostitution nor wagering are, or were, in themselves criminal). No doubt the ethics of enforceable surrogacy or organ-donation agreements are debated in seminars on medical law or law and economics (consider e.g. Becker and Elias (2007) and Purshouse and Bracegirdle (2018)), and the desirability of pre-nuptial agreements considered in family law, and so on. But should not contract lawyers spend some time analysing (and teaching undergraduates about) the outer limits of their subject?

If the argument of the previous section was correct, contract law is market-oriented. (This is at the heart of the bargain principle, and the consideration doctrine.) If so, students of contract law must consider the limits of markets. What things should not be bargained over and traded for money?

Nicholas J McBride's account (2017, ch 5) is an excellent introduction to the limits of markets and commodification, and thus the limits of contract law. Oman (2016, ch 8) also considers "pernicious markets" which contract law should not foster. These illuminating accounts will help students (and their teachers) make better sense of the rules which draw the boundaries of contract law. Undue focus on the technicalities of the consideration doctrine certainly will not. A pedagogical reorientation is needed.

Variation of obligations

Contract modification should be taught as a discrete subject. But the consideration doctrine ought not to dominate discussion here either. The substantive questions are quite distinct from those concerning formation. Parties modify contracts when faced with opportunism, change of circumstances or some combination of the two. This gives rise to difficult questions. To what degree should the courts excuse parties from further performance when circumstances change, or to what degree should it be left to the parties to provide for this (whether *ex ante* through a force majeure clause, or after the fact)? When parties make *ex post* changes, how should such variations be regulated?

Since the common law doctrine of frustration is so narrow, and when force majeure clauses may be absent or (inevitably) limited in scope, parties do frequently make ad hoc modifications to address changes of circumstances. But sometimes a modification is opportunistically sought by the party which benefits from it. Vulnerability to exploitation seems to be an inherent feature of sequential (i.e. non-simultaneous) contractual performance (see e.g. Judge Richard Posner, *United States v Stump Home Specialties, Inc.* (1990) 905 F 2d 1117, [12]:

> There is often an interval in the life of a contract during which one party is at the mercy of the other. . . . [Party] A can always refuse to renegotiate, relying instead on his right to sue [Party] B for breach of contract if B fails to make delivery by the agreed date. But legal remedies are always costly and uncertain").

The potential for exploitation is ubiquitous. The pressing question is how to distinguish genuine free modifications from those opportunistically extracted. It proves intractable. Unfortunately, teaching this set of issues rationally is obstructed by the current state of the law.

Arguably the bargain principle has nothing of value to say in answering the questions mentioned. I am naturally aware that consideration is, axiomatically, a requirement for the variation (as for the initial creation) of contractual obligations. But the axiom's effects have been unfortunate. English law long approached opportunism only obliquely, through the doctrine of consideration. Very belatedly a doctrine that at least poses the right question (i.e.

economic duress) has arisen to do the job. Unfortunately though, few English judges have been bold enough to suggest that duress should take over entirely, and so the requirement of consideration for modification be dropped (but see e.g. *The Alev* [1989] 1 Lloyd's Rep 138 per Hobhouse J; *Adam Opel GmbH v Mitras Automotive UK Ltd* [2007] EWHC 3205 (QB), [42]-[43] per David Donaldson QC).

Consideration thus remains as a requirement for valid modifications. Since the great problem concerning variations is opportunism, asking, "Is the variation a bargain?" is to ask the wrong question. It gives the wrong answer, or rather, two wrong answers. There can be variations which, although supported by valid consideration, are obtained opportunistically, which is why economic duress must also be considered. Conversely, there are variations which make perfect commercial sense but which cannot satisfy the rules on consideration because one party promises nothing additional to their obligations under the existing contract. There may be no opportunism. The variation should therefore be enforceable, as a commercial response to changed circumstances. But it will not be, according to orthodoxy, because consideration is lacking.

That orthodoxy, as everybody knows, has spawned a litter of additional doctrines, i.e. promissory estoppel and "practical benefit consideration". As noted, these rules currently absorb much of the contract teacher's attention. They are complex, controversial and either actively evolving or (at least) of comparatively recent vintage. It is understandable and inevitable that such contestable and topical developments attract considerable pedagogical attention. But it is regrettable too. Functionally, these developments move the law no closer to a sensible approach to the opportunism problem, absolutely no closer, than the classical law in *Stilk v Myrick* and *Foakes v Beer*.

The fact that a variation is relied upon tells us nothing about whether it was extracted by opportunism; inherently, most variations will rapidly generate action in reliance. So the *reliance* requirement characteristic of *High Trees* estoppel brings no advance in the analysis of the opportunism problem. (It is, of course, welcome that opportunism features in the "unconscionability" inquiry: *D&C Builders v Rees* [1966] 2 QB 617, but that decision now seems an *avant la lettre* recognition of economic duress, since the 1970s a general contractual defence and no longer confined to refusal of equitable relief.) Promissory estoppel's functional redundancy is underlined by its confinement to "defensive" use (i.e. in the *Foakes v Beer* situation); it cannot be invoked to enforce "increasing pacts" (i.e. in the *Stilk v Myrick* situation: see *Combe v Combe* [1951] 2 KB 215; *Baird Textile Holdings Ltd v Marks & Spencer plc* [2001] EWCA Civ 274; [2002] 1 All ER (Comm) 737). This limitation defies satisfactory rationalisation (cf. Halson 1999; Barnes 2011). There is certainly no rationale to be found based on differential incidence of opportunism in the "increasing" and "decreasing" scenarios.

Because of the "defensive" limits of promissory estoppel, commercially deserving "*Stilk v Myrick* cases" have required a different route around orthodox consideration, viz. "practical benefit" since *Williams v Roffey Bros*. But this exception threatens to swallow the rule. Commercial parties would only freely agree to adjust a contract when it is mutually beneficial to do so. To quote Lord Wilberforce again, it is (to say the least) "implausible" to postulate a *truly gratuitous* promise. Why would Roffey Bros promise to make a gift to their incompetent carpenter, Lester Williams? It is ridiculous to suggest that the company might have been motivated by benevolence, generosity, gratitude or any of the other fine motives behind true gift-giving (and gift promising). Simply, Roffey Bros promised to pay Williams more because it was in the company's self-interest to do so, as the least-bad solution. So long as Williams' unsatisfactory conduct is not impugned as opportunistic (i.e. his incompetence in doing the work, and his initial over-optimistic tender price), this is straightforwardly a commercial bargain that the law should enforce. Both sides benefit. *It is reciprocal* (as the Court of Appeal in *Williams v Roffey Bros* appreciated).

There is a shorter answer. Posing the consideration question again upon modification is redundant. In terms of the jurisdictional analysis proposed above, since the original contract between the parties was unquestionably a commercial venture, any variation of it is no less commercial (e.g. Gordon 1990: 999). The argument that consideration should be abolished as a requirement for formation of commercial contracts applies *a fortiori* to commercial contracts' variation.

For these reasons, it is suggested that the requirement of consideration for modification of commercial contracts should rationally be dropped altogether. That is the underlying logic of the *Roffey* case. It is equally applicable to the "*Foakes v Beer* situation" where the Court of Appeal has indeed recently applied *Roffey* (*MWB Business Exchange Centres Ltd v Rock Advertising Ltd* [2016] EWCA Civ 553; [2017] QB 604). The Supreme Court declined to rule on the point: [2018] UKSC 24; [2018] 2 WLR 1603, [18]. *Foakes v Beer* was "ripe for re-examination" (and potentially for overruling), but that was not to be undertaken in obiter comments by a five-member court. So the leading case limps on for now, eroded by exceptions. The practical benefit argument might be "somewhat forced" (per Lord Sumption, ibid) but it satisfies commercial expectations. Students should be invited to consider what remains in substance of the "consideration for variations" doctrine.

Should a laissez-faire approach to variation be welcomed? It would certainly be consistent with the radical argument advanced above: that all commercial agreements (including, therefore, agreed variations) should be enforced, irrespective of "consideration"; and that to characterise these as "gifts" is a category error. Doubts remain under two heads. First, *reliance*: should purely executory "gratuitous" variations be enforceable from the outset, or only once (and to the extent that) they have generated the expected benefits to the "gratuitous promisor"? Second, *opportunism*. Does consideration after all serve as a bulwark against it that the law would discard at its peril?

The reliance point may best be pedagogically explained by reflecting on the maxim that a bird in the hand is worth two in the bush; as Lord Blackburn famously put it,

> All men of business . . . do every day recognise and act on the ground that prompt payment of a part of their demand may be more beneficial to them than it would be to insist on their rights and enforce payment of the whole.
> (*Foakes v Beer* (1884) 9 App Cas 605, 622)

Naturally this depends on the single bird actually being in the hand (or the "prompt payment of a part" of a debt actually being made). It can scarcely be worth more to be only *promised* one bird in a bush than to be promised two therein. Quite the contrary. Hence it has been suggested that these "gratuitous" variations should become binding only upon performance; it is only when the debtor actually pays part of the debt that the creditor's promise not to enforce the balance becomes enforceable (LRC 1937: para 35). It equally is only when Williams actually completes the carpentry work that Roffey Bros' promise to pay more for its completion is enforceable (e.g. Chen Wishart 2010, 2016). This seems the clear meaning of these promises to pay more, or accept less. They are conditional on performance. Doctrinally they can be given effect as a unilateral contract (if and when the debtor pays, the creditor is bound not to enforce the balance, e.g. *MWB v Rock* [89]-[90] per Arden LJ, without the concurrence of Kitchin and McCombe LJJ); or as an entire obligation so that it is only when Williams completes the work can he claim the additional payment (note that the actual interpretation of Roffey Bros' promise on the facts is a matter of some controversy given the quantum awarded: Treitel (2002: 19). We have suggested above why it would be disastrous for commerce to impose a general requirement of reliance for *every* agreement to have binding force. But it makes sense of the variations agreed in these cases to require actual performance as a condition of their legal effect.

It should again be stressed by contract teachers that opportunism is an endemic problem in ongoing contractual relationships. But the consideration doctrine is not a particularly effective solution. *Foakes v Beer* apparently protects creditors against wily debtors who must realise that giving a bird in the hand (a voluntary payment of 95p in the pound?) is always worth two in the bush, given the cost of recovering debts. But the protection works only against debtors unscrupulous enough to use this insight to chisel off a proportion of what they owe, but *not* well-enough informed about the law of contract to perform the requisite formal bow to the doctrine of consideration. After all, it is not difficult to put the variation in a deed or, failing that, make some trivial alteration to the debtor's obligations which is economically immaterial (as perhaps Coke CJ's "hawk, horse or robe" in *Pinnel's Case* (1602) 5 Co Rep 117a, and certainly Jessel MR's satirical "tomtit" in *Couldery v Bartrum* (1881) 19 Ch D 394, 399). With that formality satisfied there would be a "reciprocal" variation in the orthodox sense (or a deed), despite the debtor's opportunism. The old rigid cases might send a signal that contracts are not to be varied for the benefit of one side only. But the signal is a weak one when the doctrine can be so easily circumvented. That it anyway has to be backed up by economic duress is an admission of defeat.

The student should consider whether economic duress is a wholly satisfactory solution. It is unfortunate that this is usually considered in a different part of the course from variations, because economic duress on formation is likely to be very rare (i.e. "coercive" refusal to contract at all). Economic duress is then primarily a doctrine policing opportunism in *variations*. At its core is an unimprovably vague question: whether the party in whose benefit the variation was made exerted "illegitimate commercial pressure". This is a non-definition. Judges believe that this can be distinguished (by them) from the "rough and tumble of . . . normal commercial bargaining" (*DSND Subsea Ltd v Petroleum Geo-services ASA* (unreported 2000) per Dyson J). Not everyone will share their confidence. Unpredictable value-judgments are written into the test.

Pedagogical attention should encompass the parties' own strategies to deal with opportunism and not confine itself to the doctrinal solutions. Prudent drafters should address the problem (rather than place all their trust in economic duress, let alone consideration). The law should respect the parties' choice. A number of possible mechanisms are available, such as a clause requiring renegotiation (on the failure of which an arbitrator is empowered to impose a binding solution), in the event of specified changes of circumstances (*Associated British Ports v Tata Steel* [2017] EWHC 694 (Ch); [2017] 2 Lloyd's Rep. 11). This brings an independent party's judgment to bear, therefore affording some protection from opportunism. Without involving a third party, the contract could stipulate that only variations made in signed writing are enforceable ("No Oral Modification" clauses). Such a formal requirement protects both parties against casual or ill-considered modifications. But the determined *opportunist* would have to ensure only that the pressured party put its signature to the variation, so the protection is weak (see per Judge Frank Easterbrook in *Wisconsin Knife Works v National Metal Crafters* (1986) 781 F 2d 1280, 1292:

> The modification-only-in-writing clause has nothing to do with opportunism. A person who has his contracting partner over a barrel, and therefore is able to obtain a concession, can get the concession in writing. The writing will be the least of his worries.).

The only clear way to prevent opportunistic renegotiations would be to have an entirely unmodifiable contract. Parties fearing a high risk of opportunism might include such a clause, judging that its value would outweigh the risk that the contract might need to be varied for benign reasons (e.g. unexpected change of circumstance). It is not clear that such clauses would be enforceable (see Davis 2006). In principle, if included by sophisticated and well-advised parties (who have decided that their value outweighs their costs), they ought to be enforced. But it is clearly a difficult question on which teachers should encourage debate.

In this section I have consciously sidelined much of the current law on variation of contracts. A more educationally coherent approach would focus on the special problems of contract modification. The central task is to distinguish welcome flexibility (in the light of changing circumstances) from damaging opportunism. Neither consideration nor promissory estoppel have much to offer. To pose the jurisdictional question again (viz. "Is this variation within the scope of the law of contract?") is redundant when the original contract was, by definition, within the jurisdiction. It is implausible to suggest, in any event, that there was truly gratuitous promising "within the realm of gift" in cases like *Foakes v Beer*. Estoppel in this area has transparently been a device to circumvent the narrowness of classical consideration doctrine, rather than a fully worked-out alternative theory (a separate obligation based on reliance not bargain). With the recognition that denial of consideration is redundant or incoherent or both, estoppel would be left with no role to play here.

Commercial drafters routinely insert force majeure clauses. These supplement the deficiencies of the common law frustration doctrine. Force majeure clauses offer superior clarity of definition (which events, precisely, amount to "force majeure" (i.e. a relevant change of circumstances?)) and superior flexibility of outcome (e.g. permitting more loading time at a discounted demurrage rate) compared to frustration bringing the contract automatically to an end. Force majeure clauses are a form of ex ante contract variation (catering for known unknowns). A coherent approach to teaching variation would look at change of circumstances, frustration and force majeure together the enforcement of *ex post facto* variations (in particular their policing through economic duress). Just as frustration cannot be understood without the context of force majeure clauses, teachers should pay prominent attention to parties' preferred solution to renegotiations. This would decisively tilt what infant contract lawyers learn towards "modern commercial practice", and away from "irrational rules from centuries long past" (Gordon 1990: 1006).

If I have any general philosophy of teaching this aspect of contract law, it is to identify the proper function of the "bargain principle" and the doctrine of consideration. Its role in delimiting the jurisdiction of contract law to commercial agreements is at least coherent. It is still open to scholarly debate, of course (and what are the proper outer limits of "commerce"?). But when extended to variations, consideration (and bargain) is functionally redundant. The baroque complexity of the doctrine today perhaps indicates the difficulty. Nobody can be a good common lawyer without a good grasp of its doctrinal history. Students must understand where doctrines have come from. But as a technique for understanding the modern law, rather than history for its own sake, our approach must be (as Holmes (1897) famously put it) to get the dragon out of his lair and decide whether he is a useful animal. If "non-useful" (given the functions that we need the law to perform), it may be necessary to slay rather than tame the doctrinal "dragon". Teachers should not shy away from teaching contractual modification with a much smaller role for consideration, as little more than an antiquarian survival. Sometimes we must break with the inheritance of the past, if the common law today is to function as well as it did when the doctrine of consideration was first worked out.

References

Atiyah, P.S., 1986. *Essays on Contract*. 2nd ed. Clarendon Press, Oxford.

Atiyah, P.S., 1978. When Is an Enforceable Agreement Not a Contract? Answer: When It Is an Equity. *L. Q. Rev.*, 95, 174–178.

Barnes, M., 2011. Estoppel as a Sword. *LMCLQ*, 372–392.

Beale, H., 2012. *Mistake and Non-Disclosure of Fact: Models for English Contract Law*. Oxford University Press, Oxford.

Becker, G. and Elias, J., 2007. Introducing Incentives in the Market for Live and Cadaveric Organ Donations. *J. Eco. Perspec.*, 21, 3–24.

Campbell, D., 1992. The Undeath of Contract: A Study in the Degeneration of a Research Programme. *Hong Kong L.J.*, 22, 20–47.

Chen-Wishart, M., 2010. A Bird in the Hand: Consideration and One-Sided Contract Modifications. In: Burrows, A. and Peel, E., eds., *Contract Formation and Parties*. Oxford University Press, Oxford, pp. 89–113.

Chen-Wishart, M., 2016. Reforming Consideration: No Greener Pastures. In: Degeling, S., Edelman, J. and Goudkamp, J., eds., *Contract in Commercial Law*. Thomson Reuters, Sydney, pp. 77–103.

Dagan, H. and Heller, M., 2017. *The Choice Theory of Contracts*. Cambridge University Press, Cambridge.

Davey, J., 2013. Gambling Contract Law: A Difficult (re) Birth? *J. Bus. L.*, 6, 614–641.

Davis, K.E., 2006. The Demand for Immutable Contracts: Another Look at the Law and Economics of Contracts Modifications. *NYUL Rev.*, 81, 487–549.

Eisenberg, M.A., 1997. The World of Contract and the World of Gift. *Cal. L. Rev.*, 85, 821–866.

Freeman, M., 1996. Contracting in the Haven: *Balfour v Balfour* revisited. In: Halson, R. ed., *Exploring the Boundaries of Contract*. Dartmouth, Sudbury, pp. 68–82.

Fuller, L.L. and Perdue, W.R., 1936. The Reliance Interest in Contract Damages: 1. *Yale L. J.*, 46, 52–96.

Gilmore, G., 1974. *The Death of Contract*. Ohio State University Press, Columbus, OH.

Goode, R., 1991. Abstract Payment Undertakings. In: Cane, P. and Stapleton, J., *Essays for Patrick Atiyah*. Clarendon Press, Oxford, pp. 209–235.

Gordon III, J.D., 1990. Dialogue About the Doctrine of Consideration. *Cornell L. Rev.*, 75, 986–1006.

Halson, R., 1999, The Offensive Limits of Promissory Estoppel. *LMCLQ*, 256–277.

Hedley, S., 1985. Keeping Contract in Its Place – *Balfour v. Balfour* and the Enforceability of Informal Agreements. *Oxford J. Legal Stud.*, 5, 391–415.

Holmes, O.W., 1897. The Path of the Law. *Harv. L. Rev.*, 10, 457–478.

Law Revision Committee, 1937. *Sixth Interim Report: Statute of Frauds and the Doctrine of Consideration*. HMSO, London.

Leggatt, G., 2017. Book Review. *L. Q. Rev.*, 133, 521–523.
McBride, N., 2017. *Key Ideas in Contract Law*. Hart Publishing, London.
Milsom, S. F. C., 1981. *Historical Foundations of the Common Law*. 2nd ed. Butterworths, London.
Morgan, J., 2017. Contracting for Self-Denial: On Enforcing "No Oral Modification" Clauses. *Cambridge L.J.*, 76, 589–615.
O'Sullivan, J., 1996. In defence of *Foakes v. Beer*. *Cambridge L.J.*, 55, 219–228.
Oman, N.B., 2016. *The Dignity of Commerce: Markets and the Moral Foundations of Contract Law*. University of Chicago Press, Chicago.
Posner, R.A., 1977. Gratuitous Promises in Economics and Law. *J. Legal Stud.*, 6, 411–426.
Purshouse, C. and Bracegirdle, K., 2018. The Problem of Unenforceable Surrogacy Contracts: Can Unjust Enrichment Provide a Solution?. *Medical Law Rev.* 07 Feb.
Rudden, B., 1999. Gentleman's Agreement in Legal Theory and in Modern Practice. *The Eur. Rev. Private L.*, 7, 199–220.
Simpson, A.W.B., 1991. The Origins of Futures Trading in the Liverpool Cotton Market. In: Cane, P. and Stapleton, J., *Essays for Patrick Atiyah*. Clarendon Press, Oxford, pp. 179–208.
Treitel, G.H., 1976. Consideration: A Critical Analysis of Professor Atiyah's Fundamental Restatement. *Australian L.J.*, 50, 439–449.
Treitel, G.H., 2002. *Some Landmarks of Twentieth Century Contract Law*, Clarendon Press, Oxford.

Chapter 4

Key themes in the teaching of remedies

David Campbell

Introduction

In this chapter I will argue that the general if by no means universal practice in the US of spending substantial time on remedies at the start of courses on the general principles of the law of contract should be adopted much more widely in the Commonwealth, where it is unusual if not unknown, and my impression is that remedies typically feature as the residuum of the contract course, if they are taught in any substantial way at all. My argument will, however, rest on a different ground than that on which the US practice typically rests, which is a belief that first obtaining a knowledge of what precisely the claimant can hope to gain from recourse to law – which is not justice, or vindication, or the like, but a particular remedy – aids the student in understanding the way that sophisticated legal advice can and should be structured so as to achieve the best possible actually available outcome. (For an account of this attitude, see Bix's chapter in this book.) I am of the opinion that this belief is overall true and very important, but even so of less importance than the belief that lies behind my own commitment to teaching remedies first, which is the following.

The principal problem facing the teacher of contract is that a student typically comes to the subject with a more or less simplistic version of the view of economic exchange and legal contract which in a more or less sophisticated form is taken in neo-classical economics and in the classical law of contract: in exchange and contract the parties pursue a self-interest which is so pure that we might call it solipsistic. This belief is mistaken, and there is no more important mistaken belief in the culture of liberal democratic society. It is impossible ultimately to understand exchange and contract on this basis because the essential feature of both is not solipsistic self-interest but co-operation between the parties, which is possible because the law channels the self-interest which the parties undoubtedly do pursue away from solipsism and into mutual respect. Recognising that contract is based on mutual respect allows the coherent understanding of both the positive doctrines of contract which are capable of being coherently understood, which is by no means all of them but certainly is most of them, and the normative basis of legitimate contractual action. The critique of the mistaken belief in solipsistic self-interest which this requires is best accomplished if the teaching of contract begins with remedies.

This chapter is not a direct reflection of my own teaching, and indeed it could not be because, save for one occasion in the US, I have never been able when teaching general principles to spend the time on remedies I think fit, which would be one semester of a two semester course (and so I have welcomed the opportunity to teach optional special courses on remedies to students who have earlier studied the general principles). Nevertheless, this chapter is a direct expression of what I would do had I the time. Rather than go into the doctrinal and theoretical issues in a depth which would detract from the pedagogical purpose of this chapter, I have decided to refer only to my own works in order to try to explain and to justify the approach I would take. Despite this, I hope that the reader seeing the consequent bibliography is not led to conclude that my argument against a solipsistic understanding of self-interest in contract is itself self-absorbed to the point of solipsism.

The conventional approach in the Commonwealth

When required to give some thought to remedies for breach of contract, the student's initial belief in solipsistic self-interest will take the form of some inchoate expectation that the consequence of a finding of liability ('conviction of the defendant' as it is sometimes put) will be that the court will compel the defendant to perform its primary obligation ('perform its promise' or 'perform the contract' as it is sometimes put), i.e. that the remedy for breach of contract is specific performance. This belief is not at all challenged in a conventional course which is focused on the establishment of liability and whether, liability otherwise being established, there is a vitiating factor, using this term very widely. Even when the student has been able to rise to an understanding of why it might be that liability was contested in the cases she is asked to study, she will not be led to go on to ask what the consequences of successfully establishing liability were. The inchoate belief that 'the contract will be performed' will obviously be left more or less intact if the contract course allows no time, or no real time, to be spent on remedies at its end. Even if some substantial time is allocated to remedies, the significance of the substitutionary remedy of compensatory damages being the default remedy may not emerge if the teaching is not properly focused. Compensatory damages may well be taught more or less entirely in terms of remoteness and may receive no more attention than specific performance. The expectation interest, if discussed at all, may appear merely as one of a large number of topics in remedies, such as non-pecuniary loss or loss of a chance, and its inherently substitutionary nature will remain obscure.

It is wrong that a student can pass a contract course and remain of the belief that establishing liability means that 'the contract will be performed'. This perpetuates a simple failure to understand the law. But it is even more wrong that this will leave the student believing that a claimant's 'rights' have been 'vindicated' when this happens. This perpetuates a mistaken belief in the solipsistic self-interest of the parties. Let us turn to how teaching remedies first can yield a superior outcome.

Compensatory damages and the expectation interest

I believe it is wise to directly confront a student's initial belief that the remedy for breach is specific performance by direct reference to some of the innumerable *dicta* to the effect that damages are the default, substitutionary remedy for breach, such as that of Lord Hoffmann in *Co-operative Insurance Society Ltd v Argyll Stores (Holdings) Ltd* ([1998] AC 1 (HL) 11F-G): 'Specific performance is traditionally regarded as an exceptional remedy, as opposed to the . . . damages to which a successful plaintiff is entitled as of right . . . the general principle [is] that specific performance will not be awarded when damages are an adequate remedy'. Mentioning that it is intended to return to the case when the student will better be able to understand why this is the position, one can turn to one of the simpler cases which illustrate the essential point, such as *Cohen v Roche* ([1927] 1 KB 169 (KBD)), in which a buyer's claim for specific performance of a sale of eight Hepplewhite chairs failed and damages were awarded.

Cohen v Roche has certain period features which impede its understanding by a student now, but the judgment does make it clear that specific performance was refused because 'the goods in question were ordinary articles of commerce and of no special value or interest [so] no grounds exist for any special order for delivery' (*Cohen v Roche* 181). (That this was an award under s 52 of the Sale of Goods Act 1893 can be noted, with further discussion of the Act reserved for later.) Having established the preference for the substitutionary remedy over compulsory delivery, it may be valuable to point out that, as the chairs were valued at between £70 and £80 and the contract price was £60, the damages awarded were £15, for by reflecting on this the student may develop a preliminary conception of the aim of substitutionary damages being compensation. It may also be thought worthwhile to pose, but at this stage to leave unanswered, the further question why the law not only does not compel the defendant to deliver the chairs, but leaves it to the claimant to take the active step of securing another sale if it wishes to obtain such chairs.

Development of this preliminary conception of compensatory damages requires the introduction of two important distinctions. The first is that between primary and secondary obligations (*Moschi v Lep Air Services Ltd* [1973] AC 331 (HL): 350C-E), in the former of which the parties promise to perform the terms of their agreement, whilst in the latter they promise to provide a remedy in the event of breach, though, of course, the performance of this promise remains latent until breach. (It would be more correct at this initial stage to say 'non-performance' rather than breach, for the law of contract has, of course, provided what can be called remedies against non-performance for reasons in addition to breach, of which common mistake and frustration are the most theoretically important. But it is probably wise to avoid drawing attention to this refinement at this stage.) I shall return to this distinction, but at this stage it is necessary only to show that the primary obligation has the *economic* purpose of expressing the parties' choice to enter into an exchange and the secondary obligation has the subsidiary *legal* purpose of providing security against breach. Drawing this distinction opens the conceptual space in which the student can see the possibility of a substitutionary remedy, there being no necessity that the remedy provided be compulsory performance of the primary obligation.

The second important distinction is between the expectation and reliance interests. Because other famous authorities on the compensatory aim of damages, such as *Livingstone v Rawyards Coal Co* ((1879–80) LR 5 App Cas 25 (HL) 39), fail to sufficiently distinguish between contract and tort, it is essential to set out compensation in contract by reference to the 'first rule' of contract remedies, the rule in *Robinson v Harman* (1848) 1 Ex 850; 154 ER 363 (Ex Ct)), stated by Parke B as: 'Where a party sustains a loss by reason of a breach of contract, he is, so far as money can do it, to be placed in the same situation, with respect to damages, as if the contract had been performed' (ibid 855; 365). Though again there are period features which impede its understanding by a student now, *Robinson v Harman* is itself a good illustration of the rule. The case concerned, of course, the lease of a dwelling for a term of 21 years at an annual rent of £110, which the vendor breached when it emerged that its interest in the property was not sufficient to allow this disposition of it. Speaking more than a little anachronistically, the significance of *Robinson v Harman* is that it established one of the exceptions to the now abolished rule in *Bain v Fothergill* ((1874–75) LR 7 HL 158 (HL)), which limited to reliance loss the liability of defendants who failed to complete sales of interests in land because of defects in title. By not normally compensating the purchaser for lost expectation, the conveyancing practice of the time was to in this way share the risks of establishing title, which, prior to general land registration, were unavoidably considerable, often requiring investigation of documents which were, in the famous words attributed to Lord Westbury, 'difficult to read, disgusting to touch, and impossible to understand'. But the defects in title in *Robinson v Harman*, arising from the terms on which the defendant had recently inherited an interest in the property, were of a sort that the defendant should reasonably have known and the claimant could not reasonably know, and the general rule was not applied. Subsequent case law and commentary has generalised this into the rule now central to the law of expectation, but let us look back at the case itself.

The defendant did not dispute liability but, no doubt in reliance on the rule in *Bain v Fothergill*, paid £25 into court, which would have met the reliance loss represented by the claimant's legal expenses, which were found to be something in excess of £15. But in the event £200 beyond the payment into court was awarded, which, deducting the £15, meant that expectation damages were *circa* £210. The distinction clearly emerges between the reliance award which, confined to £15, would have returned the claimant to the position it was in before the contract was made, and the £210 expectation damages which put the claimant in the position it would have been in had the contract been performed.

The point may be hammered home, and the theme established by discussion of the damages awarded in *Cohen v Roche* continued, by asking how the £210 was quantified. Although liability for expectation at all was the crux of the case, we cannot directly know from the case itself how these damages were quantified, which was not discussed, no doubt because it was not in dispute. However, the wording of the conclusion of Alderson B's judgment in *Robinson v Harman* (856; 365) – 'The defendant, having undertaken to grant a valid lease, not having any colour of title, must pay the loss which the plaintiff has sustained by not having that for which he contracted' – and the citation of the case in other authorities of the time, of which *Engell v Fitch* ((1869) LR 4 QB 659 (Ex Ct): 668) is the most important, make it as certain as one can ever say absent direct evidence that the market damages of obtaining a similar property for a similar term were awarded.

It is possible to explore the difference between expectation and reliance by addressing the 'bad bargain' problem associated with *Anglia TV Ltd v Reed* ([1972] 1 QB 60 (CA)) (Campbell and Halson 2015). The case has the instructive incidental aspects of turning on the claimant's inability both to secure a substitute and to prove its lost profits (*Anglia TV v Reed* 63C-D), and showing the strengths and weaknesses of Lord Denning MR's *dictum* that a claimant which has suffered no loss of profits or cannot prove such loss can claim wasted expenditure 'in the alternative' (ibid 64A) takes one to the heart of the bad bargain problem and the relationship of expectation and reliance when quantifying loss. The leading case indicating the correct solution to the bad bargain problem is, of course, *Commonwealth of Australia v Amann Aviation Pty Ltd* (1991) 174 CLR 64 (HCA): 80–82, 84–86, 99–101, 104–108, 126–128, 134–135, 154–156, 163, but the, with respect, regrettably excessive complexity of this judgment makes it all but impossible for the student to relate the instructive *dicta* to the *ratio*, whatever it is, of the case. A more comprehensible statement of the correct position may, of course, be found in *CCC Films (London) Ltd v Impact Quadrant Films Ltd* [1985] 1 QB 16 (QB).

It is essential to draw the discussion of compensation of expectation to a close by underlining the difference between the economic and properly legal aspects of a contract. The aim of any economic exchange is to realise a surplus, which may, of course, be non-pecuniary when a party is an end consumer, but for a commercial party will be a profit. The key to understanding the law of remedies is that, though the parties enter into a contract in the belief that their surpluses will be realised by the exchange of the economic goods, i.e. by the performance of their primary obligations, in a case of breach, remedies are by default focused, not on performance, but on profit, which is protected as the expectation interest.

Causation

Having established that damages are by default compensation of lost expectation, it is necessary to turn to causation. A student coming to the subject typically may find it easy to accept that a defendant should be liable only for such loss as it has caused, but will have an expansive view of what compensable loss encompasses. The aim of teaching should be to make the student understand the serious limits the default rules of causation place on a claimant's liability, and that understanding will initially be resisted because the belief the student brings with her, even after accepting that damages are the default remedy, is that damages should mulct the defendant who, after all, has breached (is 'guilty' of committing a 'wrong' as it is often put). At some cost of concealing the confused or even vexed quality of the doctrines relevant to causation, it is possible to bring some conceptual coherence to the subject by saying that there are three such doctrines which constitute successive stages of the argument which the claimant must successfully make in order to be awarded substantial damages. They are set out in the following table:

Stage	*Losses not compensated*	*Losses compensated*
1 cause in fact	speculative losses	certain losses
2 cause in law	remote losses	proximate losses
3 mitigation	avoidable losses	unavoidable losses

Cause in fact

The claimant must first prove that the breach in fact caused the loss. The but-for test applies in contract as well as tort (*Borealis AB v Georgias Trading SA* [2010] EWHC 2789 (Comm); [2011] 1 Lloyd's Rep 482 [43]-[47]), but it is of the nature of a contractual relationship that a question of whether there was any causal link at all will tend to arise only very rarely. The most intriguing problem thrown up by the but-for test is the one posed by the decision in *Cory v The Thames Ironworks and Shipbuilding Co Ltd* (1867–68) LR 3 QB 181 (QB) which was drawn to wide attention by being discussed in *Victoria Laundry (Windsor) Ld v Newman Industries Ld* ([1949] 2 KB 528 (CA) 538–539). The loss which the claimant actually suffered from its inability to make an 'exceptional and unnatural' (*Cory v Thames Ironworks* 190) and undisclosed use of the hull of a vessel bought from the defendant being remote, the claimant was awarded the loss which would have been caused by an inability to use the hull for its normal purpose. But, as reported, it does not appear that the claimant would ever have made this use of the hull, and this loss therefore should not have survived the but-for test. A reluctance to award nominal damages seems to have been the main motivation of the court in reaching its decision (ibid: 189–190). This is highly interesting, but perhaps not appropriate to a student first coming to the subject, who must be led to awards of nominal damages as a normal consequence of breach. Explaining why this is the case is, I am arguing, a major task of the teaching of remedies.

The important problem which arises in contract is not a flat denial of causation but the quantification of the loss which the breach has caused. Though it is incontrovertible that a relaxed attitude is taken towards the precision with which claims must be quantified, and in some sense provable, as opposed to merely speculative, quantification of loss must be made, and it is valuable to refer to a loss of profits claim not being made either in *Anglia TV* (63D) or *CCC Films* (29D-F). Though the reasoning on this point in the cases is lacking as, anticipating the difficulties they would face, the claimants in both cases can hardly be said to have made such a claim, it is easy to imagine why they both took this course. Though it has by no means achieved universal currency in the law of England and Wales, I believe the best antonym of speculative is 'certain', so that the standard of proof of compensable losses is certainty.

Certainty is not, of course, intended to convey a requirement that losses must be certain in the sense of inevitable. It rather is intended to convey a requirement of definiteness or precision at a level appropriate to the facts of the case. When market damages are being claimed for the extra expense incurred in, say, actually buying substitute goods (see the discussion below), documentary evidence should be able to be given of this liquidated sum. When profits are lost because a project has had to be abandoned because of the breach, it might be possible that, for example, lost sales are readily provable because the claimant has a full order book. But, in the absence of such evidence, proof can be far more difficult. Satisfactory proof should be of a sort that would meet relevant accounting, business analysis, banking, etc., standards, but it can readily be conceived that no such satisfactory proof is possible, as in *Anglia TV* and *CCC Films*. Going further into the detail of the litigation technique of proving contested losses is inappropriate in a general principles course, but a student may be referred with profit to the unreported (an ancillary decision of the Court of Appeal on the procedure for appointing expert witnesses providing the evidence of lost profits is reported) but illustrative *Vasiliou v Hajigeorgiou* ([2010] EWCA Civ 1475).

The advantage of describing the standard of proof as certainty is that it allows a clearer sense of what is required by contrasting the word certainty's connotation of definiteness or precision with its connotation of inevitability when inevitability is precisely what is not meant. The misguided claim that the 'loss of a chance' poses any particular problem should be discussed here. Though it is sometimes wrongly cited as authority for the claim that speculative losses may be compensated, and though the judgments are preoccupied with remoteness which, in a proper *Hadley* sense, was not really an issue, the outcome of *Chaplin v Hicks* ([1911] 2 KB 786 (CA)) is particularly instructive. It was not, of course, inevitable that the claimant would have been awarded one of the contracts, even though the Court of Appeal dwelt on the breach having occurred when the claimant, one of initially 6,000 competitors, had reached a stage in the competition when she had a one in four chance of winning (ibid: 791, 796, 798–799). But as the total value of the contracts may be determined from the report, quantification is a matter of the fundamentally simple and perfectly acceptable arithmetic operation of dividing that total by four, though the student who is led through it will find the loss of *circa* £150 to be some distance from the, no doubt rough and ready and rounded, £100 damages awarded at first instance. The lesson must be emphasised that no business project, such as *Anglia TV* and *CCC Films*, will ever certainly, in the sense of inevitably, succeed, and what distinguishes *Chaplin v Hicks* is that the loss in it was much more, not much less, certain than in cases such as *Anglia TV* and *CCC Films*.

Cause in law

The centrality of *Hadley v Baxendale* ((1854) 9 Exch 341 (Ex Ct)) to the teaching of remedies across the common law world makes it unnecessary here to do more than indicate the relative emphases which should be placed on its various aspects, though it must be acknowledged that doing so glosses over some abiding confusions in a number of influential accounts of the case. The first aspect that must be emphasised is, of course, Alderson B's famous – this is not strong enough a word – *dictum* which establishes reasonable contemplation as the basis of what has come to be known as the first limb of *Hadley* (ibid 855). To this must then be contrasted the second limb, which requires 'special circumstances [to be] known and communicated' to the defendant (ibid 356) – notice, it has come to be said, to be given of the possibility of loss outside of its initial reasonable contemplation – if the defendant is to be liable for losses within contemplation expanded by notice. A student should come to understand that this is a general disclosure requirement the purpose of which is to allow informed negotiations about the allocation of unusual liability by countering the defendant's initial informational disadvantage. Paradoxically, the very limitations of our knowledge of the facts of *Hadley* as reported, to which attention was drawn in *Victoria Laundry v Newman* (357–358), are a useful point to start discussion of the application of the second limb under different circumstances.

The teacher of remoteness has been placed in something of a quandary over the discussion of the reception of *Hadley v Baxendale* by the, with respect, terminological or conceptual confusion in the appellate decisions regarded as the centrepieces of that reception. Though it is drawn so briefly as to be almost *en passant*, the distinction between the loss of ordinary laundry business which 'Reasonable persons in the shoes of the defendants must be taken to foresee without any express intimation' and the loss of 'special . . . particularly lucrative . . . contracts' on which *Victoria Laundry* (543) turns is an excellent illustration of *Hadley's* two limbs. But though it is wrong to lay too much stress on single words (even assuming the words were correctly reported), the Court of Appeal's restatement of *Hadley* in terms of 'reasonable foreseeability' (ibid: 539–540), rather than the 'reasonable contemplation' exclusively used by Alderson B, inevitably invites treating the issues in contract and tort as essentially the same when they are indeed quite opposed. This misguided line is emphasised by the logomachy of elaboration on the possible synonyms of 'foreseeability', which is very largely equated with contemplation, in *Koufos v C Czarnikow Ltd, The Heron II* ([1969] 1 AC 350 (HL) 378D), which shows how far the reasoning of even the most outstanding of our judges can be undermined by the belief that essentially the same rules should accommodate both contract and *Donoghue v Stevenson* ((1932) AC 562 (HL)) negligence.

The, it is submitted, better line is exemplified in *British Columbia and Vancouver's Island Spar, Lumber and Saw-mill Co Ltd v Nettleship* ((1867–68) LR 3 CP 499 (CCP)), in which, though there is no great rigour in terminology, contemplation is rightly taken to connote, not what might be foreseen, but what the defendant had an opportunity to negotiate, something, of course, that is wholly irrelevant to the imposition of negligence liability by the state. *British Columbia Saw-mill* considers not what the defendant could have known, but for what it 'intended to become responsible' (ibid 506) or, looking at the matter from the opposite viewpoint, what 'advantage [the claimant] has . . . paid for' (ibid 508):

> The mere fact of knowledge cannot increase the liability. The knowledge must be brought home to the party sought to be charged, under such circumstances that he must know that the person he contracts with reasonably believes that he accepts the contract with the special condition attached to it.
>
> (ibid 509)

It should be recalled that, to be perfectly accurate, *Hadley* was a decision about the direction to be given to a special jury charged with deciding what was in the reasonable contemplation of a party in the defendant's position as a matter of fact. Though English civil procedure has eschewed the use of a jury in contract cases, this does not alter the nature of the decision which has to be reached by the court. No nicety of legal terminology or doctrine should govern decisions about proximity in contract cases. The court must determine, as a matter of fact, the liability a commercial party, having any special knowledge such a party in that situation should have, assumed because it was within reasonable contemplation during negotiations concluded at the time of agreement.

Whatever problems the running together of contract and *Donoghue v Stevenson* negligence were exposed in *The Heron II* have, of course, been made to seem relatively small by those posed by the attempt made in *Transfield Shipping Inc of Panama v Mercator Shipping Inc of Monrovia, The Achilleas* ([2008] UKHL 48, [2009] 1 AC 61) to introduce, in this context entirely novel, the 'scope of duty' refinement of the 'assumption of responsibility' test into contractual remoteness (ibid [14]–[16]). There is considerable difficulty of combining the judgments to yield a *ratio*; or of trying to reconcile what seems to be the best *ratio* with the, on the face of it perverse, conclusion reached by Lord Hoffmann, which reversed the views of all but one of the arbitrators and judges who had tried the matter closer to the facts. But even these are relatively minor obstacles to the student's understanding of the case by comparison to asking her to come to terms with how a negligence doctrine which, though it exceedingly misleadingly uses terminology appropriate to contract, has the very aim of producing in tort a result different to the one which contract would yield (Campbell 2015b, 2016c), is meant to assist in applying one of the fundamental rules of contractual damages. Though the hope one had that this regrettable decision would receive no support and so share the fate of *Junior Books v Veitchi* ([1983] 1 AC 520 (HL)) as it deserved have been disappointed, or certainly postponed, I still believe it is best to present *The Achilleas* as an anomaly which has no proper place, and hopefully no long future, in the law of contract.

Mitigation

Though it unarguably is a difficult case, *British Westinghouse Electric and Manufacturing Co Ltd v Underground Electric Railways Co of London Ltd (No 2)* ([1912] AC 673 (HL)) is, it is submitted, the best introduction to mitigation. Not only is the statement of the law of mitigation (ibid 689) in the case, to which I will return, extremely authoritative, but in coming to terms with the case's basic concern to avoid betterment, which the judgment and headnote help make clear by revealing the various sums at issue, the student should grasp the essential effect of mitigation, which is to keep the defendant's costs of protecting the claimant's expectation as low as is reasonably possible. The unarguably intractable difficulties about the case's precise *ratio* can be set aside and still leave the significance of this basic concern intact.

It is, of course, important to discuss the extent of what the claimant will be required to do in order to have satisfied the requirement to mitigate, and in this connection the requirement in *Payzu v Saunders* ([1919] 2 KB 581 (CA)) that the claimant deal again with the defendant, with which commercial relationships had obviously become fraught as a consequence of the breach which gave rise to the case, is instructive. The rationale of the, as it were, opposite policy of protecting reasonable attempts to mitigate even if they were very expensive or (to some extent) unavailing (*Banco de Portugal v Waterlow and Sons Ltd* [1932] AC 452 (HL)) must also be discussed.

But the most important issue to discuss is the perfectly normal working of mitigation in market damages. It is perhaps best to bring Pt VI of The Sale of Goods Act 1979 (c 54) directly into view in order to discuss the standard case in which market damages assist the buyer after non-delivery (ibid s 51) and the seller after non-acceptance (ibid s 50) to obtain substitutes. In appropriate circumstances, market damages show compensatory damages to work in a way upon which, it is submitted, it is, in its fundamentals, impossible to improve (Campbell 2005, 2016b). (The contrast with response to mistaken allocative decisions in non-market economies is stark (Campbell 2001).) In the context of the general principles of contract (on a truly major conceptual and doctrinal confusion that runs through Pt VI and all common law provisions for sales of goods based on it, including in this sense the Uniform Commercial Code, see Campbell 2016b: 309–310), the remedy is not the damages as such but what the Uniform Commercial Code calls 'cover': obtaining the substitute at, after the award of damages *prima facie* assessed as the difference between the contract price and the market price (Sale of Goods Act 1979 ss 50(3), 51(3)), no net cost. Reference should be made to the wonderfully accurate account of the way the rules work in *William Bros v ED T Agius Ltd* ([1914] AC 510 (HL): 530–531 emphasis added):

> the buyer . . . is entitled to recover the expense *of putting himself* into the position of having those goods, and this he can do by going into the market and purchasing them at the market price. To do so he must pay a sum which is larger than that which he would have had to pay under the contract by the difference between the two prices. This difference is, therefore, the true measure of his loss from the breach, for it is that which it will cost him *to put himself* in the same position as if the contract had been fulfilled.

The crucial point is that ss 50 and 51 market damages internalise mitigation. I have spoken of the use of market damages to 'assist' the obtaining of substitutes. It is better to say it normally requires this. By stating that damages will be awarded to compensate 'loss directly and naturally resulting, in the ordinary course of events', ss 50(2) and s 51(2) codify the first limb of *Hadley v Baxendale*. Stating that 'the measure of damages is *prima facie* [market damages]' makes mitigating by obtaining a substitute what, without further argument to oust the *prima facie* default, the Act requires.

It is by no means essential and it may be thought to prematurely introduce termination when it will not be properly discussed for some time, but I would nevertheless now distinguish between rejection for breach of condition and acceptance after breach of warranty so that s 53 can at this point be explained as market damages when the buyer (perforce) accepts defective goods. Some question about the remedy for breach of warranty as opposed to the remedy for non-delivery will arise in the mind of the good student even if s 53 is not discussed.

It is providential how often the decided law throws up very similar cases which have apparently contradictory outcomes, the explanation of which can be of great pedagogical value, *Krell v Henry* ([1903] 2 KB 740 (CA)) and *Herne Bay Steamboat v Hutton* ([1903] 2 KB 683 (CA)) being an obvious example. The core of mitigation is happily expressed in the contrast of this sort between *Charter v Sullivan* ([1957] 2 QB 117 (CA)) and *WL Thompson Ltd v Robinson (Gunmakers) Ltd* ([1955] Ch 177 (Ch D)), two cases of repudiation of an obligation to buy a car. In the former case, mitigation by sale to another buyer at the contract price (*Charter v Sullivan* 118) meant that loss was zero and damages were nominal. In the latter case, damages were substantial, but this is because mitigation was not possible, though this was not obvious because the problem was not an inability to return the particular car to the suppliers, for it was returned, but a loss of volume of sales in a market in which supply exceeded demand (*Thompson v Robinson* 187). Whatever the merits of the specific 'lost volume' argument, the background concern with the possibility of mitigation central to these cases is exemplary, and the vital point is illustrated in the most vivid way by the cost of breach in *Charter v Sullivan* being nominal. Breach at zero cost: what a scandal! It is best to rub the point in by claiming that *Charter v Sullivan* is the paradigm of what will happen following breach of a commercial sale of generic goods, when a substitute is available, the market price is (tantamount to) equal to the contract price and mitigation requires the substitute to be obtained (Campbell 2013: 177–181). This is what we are left with in *Charter v Sullivan* if the claimant's failed attempt to claim lost volume damages on the authority of *Thompson v Robinson* is stripped away. The acquired knowledge of normal consequences of the operation of the positive law should surely undermine the student's initial belief that the remedy for breach of contract is specific performance, for the remedy for the paradigm case of breach of contract is one in which no legal action will be taken at all!

Why has the law of remedies 'shown a marked solicitude for men who do not keep their promises'?

At this point the student is obliged to confront the central feature of the law of remedies that, as Farnsworth put it when summing up of the lesson of his magisterial survey of that law, '[it] has shown a marked solicitude for men who do not keep their promises' (Campbell 2005: 459). Having seen that this solicitude is central to the law she has now studied, the student should grasp that the remedies for breach of contract normally do not even try to prevent breach but allow it on the terms of the Holmesian choice: 'The only universal consequence of a legally binding promise is that the law makes the promisor pay damages if the promised event does not come to pass. [The law of contract] leaves [the promisor] free to break his contract if he chooses' (ibid: 461–462).

If the student can grasp that the Holmesian choice is the positive law, then a great deal has been done. But an explanation of why this is the positive law is needed to secure that grasp. This can be done quite briefly by referring back to the early distinction between primary and secondary obligations. Primary obligations, stating the terms of the exchange, are an economic, not a legal matter. The secondary obligation which is the properly legal component of a contract has the function of providing security against breach, and its form is derived from this function (Campbell 2005). The rule in *Robinson v Harman* is insufficient to explain the positive law. Compensatory damages do indeed seek to put the claimant in the position it would have been in had the contract been performed. But this in itself cannot explain the rules of causation. This requires the additional 'rule' that protection of the claimant's expectation is done at least cost to the defendant. The coupling of these two rules unites the parties' interests, channelling their self-interested action into a form of co-operation in response to breach. Of course, in any one instance the defendant would prefer to simply walk away at zero cost, but walking away is inconsistent with maintenance of the law of contract as a system for facilitating contractual exchange and so is morally inconsistent with the defendant's participation in that system. A hypothetical argument shows how the self-interested negotiating of the parties produces this co-operative outcome.

Though now cognisant of the Holmesian choice, the student will certainly initially think that prevention by a remedy of specific performance would be the best form of security. The first point that must be made is that, once it is recognised that primary obligations are economic exchange obligations, then complete prevention of breach is simply impossible because errors in exchanges are inevitable, as they are in any system of economic allocative decision-making. The goal of contract cannot be to prevent breach but to establish, using Professor Cooter's term, the optimal level of precaution (Campbell 2011: 1109–1114). It would be irrational to invest the same amount of resource to ensure that the carriage of generic tins of beans was as likely to be successful as the carriage of nuclear waste, and once the student appreciates this, then the most fundamental point must be addressed.

The very meaning of goods being generic being that they can be bought and sold on the market, the real security a claimant has when a sale of generic goods is breached lies in turning to the market in order to secure a substitute, so long, of course, as market damages allow her to do this at no net cost. The extra security of, for example, a remedy of specific performance for non-delivery is of no value to the buyer in generic sales, which therefore will not pay for it. Though the positive law of remedies for breach of contract initially appears to have 'shown a marked solicitude for men who do not keep their promises', this is only because those who on occasion find the promise broken chose to contract on terms which allowed this because the goods they therefore bought and sold were more attractive on a competitive market than goods which could have been bought and sold on specific performance terms. To require the student to confront the way that the free choice about the remedies of contracting parties has produced a positive law utterly at variance with her initial beliefs about that law is, I believe, a great pedagogical achievement.

Consequential loss and specific performance

The general principles of the law of contract (and the historically preceding laws) have, of course, from time immemorial recognised that a claimant may have a non-commercial interest in the defendant's performance of its primary obligation and that an award of damages will necessarily be an inadequate remedy for breach, in the sense that money awards are simply not relevant to the nature of the loss caused, for which specific performance (or injunction effectively leading to specific performance) therefore is the proper remedy. The student must be introduced to this and the *dictum* of Sir RT Kindersley VC in *Falcke v Gray* ((1859) 4 Drew 651; 62 ER 250 (Ch Ct): 252) that specific performance would be awarded when 'the contract is for the purchase of articles of unusual beauty, rarity and distinction, so that damages would not be adequate compensation for non-performance'. It accurately captures the law in an intriguing case in which the claimant's interest may well have been (I believe it was) commercial. But though some idea of uniqueness should be drawn from the non-commercial cases, those cases are almost incidental to the law of remedies, which should focus on the initially apparently senseless use of specific performance by commercial parties.

In what has been said so far of compensatory damages, it has been largely assumed that goods are generic. Though this is by far the prevailing case in the market economies in which most goods are almost always available in competitive supply, it need not, of course, be the case. The student should be introduced to the concept of consequential loss as, precisely, a consequence of a substitute, and so mitigation by obtaining a substitute, not being available. *Hadley* and *Victoria Laundry* illustrate the point perfectly. I believe it is again wise to refer to the Sale of Goods Act, where the *prima facie* assumption of market damages in ss 50 and 51 (and 53) may be ousted and consequential loss claimed under the s 54 provision for 'special damages'.

For the purposes of a general principles course, consequential loss can be made the link between compensatory damages and specific performance and other forms of literal enforcement. Section 54, of course, consolidates the second limb of *Hadley*, and *Hadley* and *Victoria Laundry* again themselves show that this can pose a serious problem for the claimant, for whereas market damages are, for the purposes of a general principles course, always proximate, it is of the nature of consequential loss that it can be remote, and even more that it can be speculative, as can be shown by reminding the student why no expectation claim was made in *Anglia TV* and *CCC Films*. But that a loss will not for these reasons be compensated does not mean it did not occur, and this should be made the central theme of the teaching of the use of specific performance by commercial parties.

The law on this point is, of course, now dominated by *Co-op v Argyll*. But before resuming discussion of this case, it is submitted it is wise to explore the issues through the concept of 'commercial uniqueness'. *Behnke v Bede Shipping Co Ltd* ([1927] 1 KB 649 (KBD)) is a very valuably instructive case, in which specific performance under s 52 of the Sale of Goods Act 1893 was ordered of delivery of a cargo vessel which was to be used for commercial carriage of goods by sea because the vessel 'was of peculiar and practically unique value' to the claimant (ibid 660). Given the ground for specific performance of sales of goods which had been established in non-commercial cases, the argument for such an award in respect of a commercial chattel was bound to draw on some idea of uniqueness, but it should immediately be stressed to the student that commercial uniqueness is an oxymoron as, in principle, a commercial party should always be able to be satisfied by an award of damages.

Commercial uniqueness is, in the first instance, an argument about the impossibility of mitigation. *Behnke v Bede* could arise only because the unavailability of a substitute vessel meant that market damages were not a possible remedy. The award of specific performance depended on the court finding that the vessel was wanted for 'immediate use' and that, because she possessed certain features which made her particularly fit for use in the waters in which she was to sail, there was 'only one other comparable ship [which] may now have been sold' (ibid 661).

But why, then, was no s 54 claim made for consequential loss representing the profits of the cargo business lost by not having available either the vessel which had been bought or a substitute? The reported case does not make this clear but it is submitted it must have been because, such lost business surely being within reasonable contemplation under the first limb of *Hadley*, the extent of that business could not be proven. If, for example, the claimant had agreed contracts with shippers on its books, it is impossible to understand why it would not have brought a s 54 claim rather than a s 52 claim for, even leaving aside the difficulties it had to overcome to make the s 52 claim successfully, damages which actually compensated it for lost profits would surely be at least as good a practical remedy as specific performance. The s 52 claim was motivated by the claimant's fear that an award of damages would not, in fact, compensate the loss suffered. The problem is one of fear of uncompensated loss.

This fear runs through all the attempts by commercial parties to, as it were, avoid the default rules of compensatory damages by seeking forms of literal enforcement of primary obligations (Harris *et al* 2005: pt 3). In addition to specific performance, and injunction effectively leading to specific performance (*Société des Industries Metallurgiques SA v Bronx Engineering Co Ltd* ([1975] 1 Lloyd's Rep 465 (CA)), these include actions for the total contract price after affirmation of a repudiated contract (*White and Carter (Councils) Ltd v McGregor* [1962] AC 413 (HL)) and commercial uses of cost to complete damages (*East Ham Corp* v *Bernard Sunley and Sons Ltd* [1966] AC 406 (HL)). The equitable discretion in specific performance, including defences such as undue hardship and problems of supervision, is fully considered in Lord Hoffmann's speech, with which all his brethren agreed, in *Co-op* v *Argyll*. This must be compared with the doctrines to similar effect in the common law forms of literal enforcement, of which the 'legitimate interest' is the most important, and the student should appreciate that it is unsatisfactory that essentially the same problem of the availability of literal enforcement is subject to different decision-making (Harris *et al* 2005: ch 15). Particular attention should be paid to the way that the weighing of undue hardship and the weighing of the legitimate interest, which unfortunately now must be discussed with reference to *Cavendish Square Holding BV v Makdessi; Parking Eye Ltd v Beavis* ([2015] UKSC 67; [2016] AC 1172 [28]-[32]), have served a similar function in regulating the availability of literal enforcement, but the law can produce quite different outcomes.

Just how far things can go wrong is, of course, demonstrated by the outcome of *White and Carter*, which is on its face outrageous and can be explained, to the extent it can be explained, only by the law as it stood, which the majority in the House of Lords reluctantly felt obliged to follow, giving the claimant a complete freedom to choose whether to terminate or affirm, and therefore to ignore the policy behind mitigation. (I myself do not believe this was the prior law.) Discussion of *White and Carter* requires some discussion of termination, but, it is submitted, this is to the good as termination should be introduced to the student as a remedy, for this this will give her some idea of the practical significance of distinguishing between warranties and conditions when this is taken up later in the course. The central importance of mitigation is usefully illuminated by this important example of a rule which, by excluding mitigation, and therefore the interests of the defendant, produced such an unsatisfactory result (Campbell 2016c), which Lord Reid therefore sought to abandon by his *obiter* introduction of the legitimate interest (*White and Carter* 430–431).

The problem is that whereas compensatory damages, exemplified by market damages, work well by uniting the interests of the parties, pursuit of literal enforcement by commercial parties seeking to avoid the quantification of compensatory damages is a zero sum game. Confining the claimant to damages leaves it with the uncompensated loss, but awarding specific performance transfers the loss to the defendant though, in the absence of the claimant negotiating an ouster of compensatory damages, the defendant reasonably would have thought it was contracting on the default basis of damages. Allowing the claimant to avoid the default rules when it did not negotiate an ouster in my opinion amounts to giving the claimant a remedy for which it failed to contract (Campbell 2002, 2004, 2011: 1114–1126, 2013), and whether this is wise is one of the principal issues now confronting the law of remedies. I am uncertain whether this issue is too difficult a matter for a general principles student to confront. I nevertheless would ask the student to confront one vital aspect of the issue.

In a case like *East Ham v Sunley*, when it is known that 'the building contracts rule' makes cost to complete damages widely available, the ouster of the normal compensatory principles is perfectly acceptable. It is what the parties agreed. The situation is terribly confused in other areas because of the persistence of the belief, even in the highest appeal courts, that the aim of remedies should be to guarantee primary performance. The student can, however, benefit from the guidance provided by one of the most outstanding judgments in modern commercial case law, the dissent of Millett LJ in the Court of Appeal hearing of *Co-op v Argyll* (299F-306D). The most important part of this judgment is the argument that, against a background of a settled practice of not awarding specific performance in circumstances like those in the case, the parties *had agreed* that the remedy for breach would be damages (ibid 305D-G). This should be contrasted to the mere dogmatism about performance in the reasoning of the majority. There can be no better place to stop the teaching of remedies than with this stark contrast between dogmatism about the aim of remedies and an understanding of remedies in terms of what the parties agreed (Campbell and Halson 2013).

Conclusion: self-interest in the law of remedies

It is obviously a matter of concern that even treatment of remedies at the length here contemplated leaves a great deal out, of which the unavailability of punitive damages and the very restricted availability of non-pecuniary loss and disgorgement damages (both the quasi-contractual awards of long provenance and the more recent attempts to correct a much wider range of what are claimed to be wrongs) are the most regrettable. I myself think the explanation of the way contract treats punitive damages and non-pecuniary loss (Harris *et al* 2005: 594–603) can be of great interest to the student, and the explanation of why mandatory disgorgement damages are wholly inconsistent with the purpose of contract (Campbell 2011) even more so. (This is a distinct point from the point that the quasi-contractual awards serve no useful purpose (Campbell 2015a).) There is, however, a limit to what can, or even should, be included.

I hope that the part of a course on general principles spent on remedies I have outlined begins to do the main work such a course should do. This is to show outright that the belief which the student brings to the start of her studies, which is that contracting parties are motivated by solipsistic self-interest, is quite wrong. Though the parties are indeed motivated by self-interest, they chose default rules of remedies for breach the essence of which is that they channel self-interest into co-operation. The very idea of compensation as the goal of damages and the rules of causation, and in particular mitigation, which guide quantification of compensation show that remedies are based on acknowledging the mutual interests of both the claimant and the defendant. Their co-operation yields a response to mistaken decisions upon which, in the form of market damages, it is, in its fundamentals, impossible to improve. The speech of Viscount Haldane LC, with which all his brethren simply agreed, in the *British Westinghouse* case (689), is an authoritative statement, not merely of the law of mitigation narrowly understood, but of the basis of the default law of remedies for breach:

> There are certain broad principles which are quite well settled. The first is that, as far as possible, he who has proved a breach of a bargain to supply what he contracted to get is to be placed, as far as money can do it, in as good a situation as if the contract had been performed. The fundamental basis is thus compensation for pecuniary loss naturally flowing from the

> breach; but this first principle is qualified by a second, which imposes on a plaintiff the duty of taking all reasonable steps to mitigate the loss consequent on the breach, and debars him from claiming any part of the damage which is due to his neglect to take such steps.

It should be the principal goal of the teaching of remedies to enable the student to understand the implications of this *dictum* for her understanding, not merely of remedies, but of the moral basis of contract law. When the general principles course moves on to formation and interpretation, and such other subjects as are included in the course, the student will be prepared to appreciate what those doctrines of the law of contract also fundamentally articulate: contracting parties are motivated by self-interest, but their self-interest is channelled away from unproductive expression in forms of force and fraud and into the immensely productive form of voluntary, because mutually beneficial, exchange. This can happen only because legitimate self-interest in contract is not solipsistic but is based on mutual respect (Campbell 2017).

References

Campbell, D., 2001. Breach and Penalty as Contractual Norm and Contractual Anomie. *Wis. L. Rev.*, 681–694.

Campbell, D., 2002. The Treatment of Teacher v Calder in AG v Blake. *Mod. L. Rev.*, 65, 256–269.

Campbell, D., 2004. The Extinguishing of Contract. *Mod. L. Rev.*, 67, 818–832.

Campbell, D., 2005. The Relational Constitution of Remedy: Co-operation as the Implicit Second Principle of Remedies for Breach of Contract. *Tex. Wesleyan L. Rev.*, 11, 455–480.

Campbell, D., 2011. A Relational Critique of the Restatement (Third) of Restitution § 39. *Wash. & Lee L. Rev.*, 68, 1063–1132.

Campbell, D., 2013. What Do We Mean by the Non-Use of Contract? In: Braucher, J., Kidwell, J. and Whitford, W.C., eds., *Revisiting the Contracts Scholarship of Stewart Macaulay: On the Empirical and the Lyrical*. Hart Publishing, Oxford, pp. 159–190.

Campbell, D., 2015a. Better Than Fuller: A Two Interests Model of Remedies for Breach of Contract. *Mod. L. Rev.*, 78, 296–323.

Campbell, D., 2015b. The Dog That Did Bark in the Night-Time: What Mischief Does Hedley Byrne and Co Ltd v Heller and Partners Correct? In: Barker, K., Grantham, R. and Swain, W., eds., *The Law of Misstatements: 50 Years on from Hedley Byrne v Heller*. Hart Publishing, Oxford, pp. 111–132.

Campbell, D., 2016a. The Absence of Negligence in Hedley Byrne v Heller. *L. Q. Rev.*, 132, 266–277.

Campbell, D., 2016b. Market Damages and the Invisible Hand. In: DiMatteo, L.A. and Hogg, M., eds., *Comparative Contract Law: British and American Perspectives*. Oxford University Press, Oxford, pp. 297–312.

Campbell, D., 2016c. Reply to Mark P Gergen, "The Right to Perform on Repudiation and Recover the Contract Price in Anglo-American Law". In: DiMatteo, L.A. and Hogg, M., eds., *Comparative Contract Law: British and American Perspectives*, Oxford University Press, Oxford, pp. 338–343.

Campbell, D., 2017. Adam Smith and the Social Foundation of Agreement: Walford v Miles as a Relational Contract. *Edinburgh L. Rev.*, 21, 376–404.

Campbell, D. and Halson, R., 2013. The Irrelevance of the Performance Interest: A Comparative Study of Keep Open Covenants in Scotland and England. In: DiMatteo, L.A. ed., *Commercial Contract Law: Transatlantic Perspectives*. Cambridge University Press, Cambridge, pp. 466–502.

Campbell, D. and Halson, R., 2015. Expectation and Reliance: One Principle or Two? *J. Cont. L.*, 32, 231–243.

Harris, D., Campbell, D. and Halson, R., 2005. *Remedies in Contract and Tort*. Cambridge University Press, Cambridge.

Chapter 5

Exploitation

Rick Bigwood

Introduction

How, if at all, should the exploitation concept be taught to law students within the subject of study known as "contract law"? In this chapter, I argue that, as an exculpatory reason in contract law, "exploitation" is both overused and under-analysed; it is overused in part *because* it has been insufficiently analysed by those who have seen fit to employ it in an attempt to describe and explain the law, or to justify a particular judgment issued in the name of the concept. This does little to advance the law student's comprehension of the exculpatory doctrines of contract law – duress, undue influence and unconscionable dealing especially. What is needed here, rather, is a more complete and nuanced conceptual account of "*victimization*" in connection with the procurement or receipt of contractual benefits, "victimization" including "exploitation" but not being exhausted by that particular concern. In transactional settings, at least, one "victimizes" another by using him or her "merely instrumentally", that is, by exercising interpersonal power over the person so as to subject him or her to an unacceptable reason for intentional action (here, entry into a contract). The consequence of such victimization is that any transactional consent resulting from the use (misuse, abuse) of such power cannot be considered genuinely "voluntary" or "legally responsible", such that any ensuing transaction cannot be regarded as just inter se. The only logical (minimal) way for the law to vindicate the formal equality of the victim is to recognize and support a corrective power of rescission in his or her favour, subject to defences available to the victimizer.

Even hoping for a more nuanced and complete account of victimization in transactional settings, however, may ultimately be to cry for the moon, for it is becoming increasing difficult to provide a coherent descriptive and normative account of the law relating to "valid-but-defeasible" contracts – the more so if one attempts a cross-jurisdictional approach in comparative perspective. This, I fear, augurs poorly for the teacher or (worse) student of modern contract law. Certainly, the exploitation concept is not capable of rescuing the situation. On the contrary, it is partly to blame for the present state of the law.

The exploitation concept and modern contract law curricula

Every teacher of contract law must at some point in the syllabus, after dealing with the principles by which contractual obligation is effectively assumed by parties who objectively intend as much (offer, acceptance, consideration, etc.), introduce the learner to various reasons that the law recognizes as sufficient to *dispense from* the assumption of obligation that has, at least in most cases, already formally occurred: "vitiating factors", "pleas in avoidance", "unjust factors" (or whatever). So, when it comes to the exploitation concept in contract law, for example, "exploitation" can be advanced as a reason for displacing our normal conviction that contracts should be binding on parties who have outwardly satisfied the formal ceremonies of contract formation. Barring some defence available to the "exploiter", we believe that a party should be excused from performing contractual commitments that have resulted from the other party's act of interpersonal exploitation. As to *why* we consider exploitation (or any other vitiating factor) to be a sufficiently weighty reason to override our ordinary devotion to contractual sanctity, that is a matter to which I must return later.

A review of leading texts indicates that the exploitation concept and indeed exculpatory reasons more widely appear to receive rather sundry treatment at the hands of those entrusted to educate the modern student of contract law. It is noteworthy that, bar one, none of the standard contract law texts (at least in my limited collection) contains a standalone chapter on "exploitation". The exception is the leading text on the law of contract in New Zealand, by Burrows, Todd and Finn, currently in its fifth edition (Burrows *et al* 2016). Previous editions of that work simply presented a series of discrete chapters on each of mistake (Chapter 10), misrepresentation (Chapter 11), duress, undue influence and unconscionable bargains (Chapter 12), illegality (Chapter 13) and contractual capacity (Chapter 14). In the fifth edition, however, Chapter 12 has been retitled "Exploitation", and the authors explain in the opening paragraph that the subject matter that follows is, broadly speaking, about "the attempted exploitation of one contracting party by the other", which is a problem that "[t]he courts have been familiar with . . . for a long time", and that they (the courts) "have developed three particular doctrines to deal with it" (Burrows 1993): duress, undue influence and unconscionable bargains. Thus, those authors clearly see taxonomic capital in the exploitation concept, realized by its perceived ability to inform, explain and order more specific exculpatory reasons within the law of contract. This is similar, too, to the use that restitution scholars have occasionally made of the exploitation concept within their own field of inquiry. For example, in his original work on *The Law of Restitution* (Burrows 1993), Burrows included a chapter titled "Exploitation" (Chapter 6), exploitation being used as an umbrella concept under which the law relating to presumed undue influence and unconscionable transactions was ordered and understood (see also Burrows 2011: ch 11). Similarly, Virgo's *The Principles of the Law of Restitution*, now in its third edition (Virgo 2015), contains a discrete chapter on "Exploitation" (Chapter 11), the burden of which is to essay the law's treatment of such phenomena as undue influence, abuse of fiduciary relationships of confidence, and unconscionable conduct.

It is, of course, possible that the exploitation concept deserves to figure more prominently than it currently does in contract law texts and curricula, but this must depend on what one understands "exploitation" to mean and on the role it is seen to serve toward optimizing students' comprehension of the relevant law. For example, if one apprehends the jural burden of the exploitation concept as primarily taxonomic, as Burrows, Finn and Todd, for example, do, then one would have to be operating under some conception of exploitation that allows one to say, as Burrows, Finn and Todd do, that the exculpatory doctrines of duress, undue influence and unconscionable bargain, severally and collectively, express and respond to an overarching legal precept of "non-exploitation" in relation to the procurement or receipt of transactional benefits. But it may transpire that proof of exploitation, properly defined, is unnecessary for rescinding a contract for either undue influence or duress (of which more later); if proof of exploitation *is* necessary for rescinding an "unconscionable bargain" (although the jurisdiction is not limited to "bargains"), then it is not always clear what *conception* of market-transaction exploitation is being applied in that connection and for that purpose. If used wrongly, the exploitation concept can surely only impede rather than enhance students' comprehension of contract vitiation.

Exploitation and the taxonomization of exculpatory categories in contract law

If we are to take seriously the claims of such writers as Burrows, Finn and Todd that a precept of anti-*exploitation* lies at the core of a number of legal and equitable exculpatory categories – especially unconscionable dealing, undue influence and duress – we are surely entitled to know under what particular *conception* of "exploitation" those writers are operating for that purpose. For upon analysis, one might well discover that "exploitation" is, in fact, being used quite contrary to its true criteria and dedicated conceptual meaning, necessitating either a modification of that meaning or else resorting to some alternative explanatory concept (or concepts) instead.

What does "exploitation" mean?

Virtually any legal, philosophical or ordinary dictionary will define "exploitation" along the lines of: "Taking unjust or unfair advantage of another for one's own advantage or benefit" (*Black's Law Dictionary* 1990: 579). Two important points follow from this definition. First, exploitation is a *normativized* concept: a notion of "unfairness" or "unjustness" is built into it. This, naturally, contributes to the contestability of the exploitation objection, since scope inevitably exists for a variety of conceptions of exploitation depending on competing theories of what people owe to one another by way of fairness of treatment in use. Second, although the idea of "advantage-taking" is at the heart of the exploitation concept, what exploiters unfairly or unjustly "take advantage of" in an act of interpersonal exploitation is an "advantage" of a strategic or relative kind – superior bargaining power, ability or opportunity – rather than an "advantage" of a substantive or material kind (here, the beneficial contract itself) (Goodin 1987: 168). In other words, properly notionalized, exploitation is merely a means to an end – a *method of gain* rather than a "gain" pure and simple (Goodin 1986: 194). This is confirmed, too, by doctrinal formulations in this area of the law, at least in the antipodes and parts of Canada (*Commercial Bank of Australia Ltd v Amadio* (1983) 151 CLR 447 (HCA) 462 (Mason J); *Downer v Pitcher* (2017) NLCA 13. What follows is that the essence of interpersonal exploitation – the source of our objection to that particular vice – must be sought in some characteristic of the *processes* of contract formation, rather than in the substantive demerits of the resultant contract itself: "Apparent unfairness of the bargain . . . is not the touchstone" of the equitable jurisdiction to set aside transactions for unconscionability (*Contractors Bonding Ltd v Snee* [1992] 2 NZLR 157 (NZCA) 174 (Richardson J)).

The "criteria" of an exploitation claim

Two broad proof elements comprise an exploitation claim in contract law: (1) "exploitable circumstances" – peculiar asymmetries in bargaining power, opportunity or ability inter se; and (2) "taking unfair advantage of the opportunities thereby arising" – the ensuing *act* of exploitation itself. The apparent simplicity of these criteria, however, belies the rather complex judgments required to be made under each criterion.

"Exploitable circumstances"

Only serious disparities in relative bargaining power, opportunity or ability qualify in law as "exploitable circumstances", not least because the very stability of economic transactions is ultimately at stake. What is significant about exploitable circumstances is that they translate into *interpersonal bargaining power* – an ability, on the part of the advantaged party, to direct, actively or passively, the contractual decision-making of the other, disadvantaged party (compare Zartman 1974: 396; De Crespigny 1968: 192) – which power the advantaged party might then "exploit" and hence "abuse". The *sources* of exploitable circumstances, hence interpersonal contracting power, are seemingly limitless: love, fear, family circumstances, pressing need, ignorance, error, permanent or temporary incapacity, economic circumstances, dependence, etc., might, severally or in combination, produce relevant interpersonal bargaining power.

Notable here is the substantial identity between what counts as an "exploitable circumstance" and the law's conception of "responsible", hence ultimately "binding", transactional consent. Exploitable parties are, for whatever reason, unable to act sufficiently autonomously when engaging in status-altering jural acts; hence, other things being equal, they should not be held "fully legally responsible" for their contractual assent that was signified under conditions of exploitation. This is either because such parties were not, at the time of so acting, possessed of the *normal capacities*, physical or mental, required for playing in games of strategy, advantage or power (such as free competitive bargaining), or else they lacked, at that relevant time, a *fair opportunity* to exercise their otherwise normal capacities (compare Hart's conditions of excuse in relation to the criminal law: Hart 1968: 152). Modern courts signify a level of inequality of bargaining opportunity, power or position such that the equilibrium between the parties has been distorted "to the point that the presumption of rational autonomy in self-interested contracting-making is displaced" (*Downer* [20]). An inability to act as a "rational autonomous decision-maker" (ibid [37]), of course, is precisely what renders a person vulnerable to merely instrumental utilization at the hands of another who *is* capable of acting as a rational autonomous decision-maker and recognizes the (strategic) opportunity for personal gain thereby arising.

The "act" of exploitation itself

Clearly, being "exploitable" is not synonymous with being "exploited". The one who perceives the strategic opportunity resulting from the serious vulnerability of another must actually *do something* with that opportunity; he or she must *exploit* the interpersonal power enjoyed in virtue of the other's known relative special disadvantage. Whether it takes an active or a passive form, then, exploitation is never an accidental, casual or obtuse process of human interaction. Exploiters must act in some sense *deliberately* in relation to the exploitable circumstances of their exploitees. Specifically, a charge of "exploitation" requires that the exploiter act purposefully or with reckless disregard for the weakness or vulnerability of his or her exploitee: he or she must either *intend* to take advantage of the exploitee's known weakness or vulnerability relative to him or her, or else *act in reckless disregard of* that probable condition (compare Hill 1994: 684).

But exploitation is not just the deliberate use of interpersonal power for gain, since there is an element of "wrongness", "unfairness" or "unjustness" that distinguishes exploitation from other, legitimate forms of utilization in market-exchange encounters. What, then, is the element of opprobrium resident in an "exploitative contract", especially considering that "pressing for advantage" is a natural feature of the bargaining game (Norton 1989)? Without some sort of consensus as to *why* exploitation is seen to dispense from legal contractual obligation, the hope of settling doctrinal criteria that are convincingly aligned with the rationale for intervention in the name of that particular concern diminishes significantly.

The "wrongness" of an exploitative contract

Common to theories of exploitation is an attempt, by the proponent of the particular theory, to explicate the wrongness, unfairness or unjustness that defines the act of interpersonal exploitation. Generally, the wrongness in exploitation can be expressed in either of two ways: (1) from the standpoint of the *processes* of the relationship or transaction in question (hence our objection will concern the manner in which one party behaved toward the other relative to the norms of interpersonal treatment that governed, or ought to have governed, the impugned interaction); and/or (2) from the standpoint of the processes *and the outcome* of the relationship or transaction in question. Concerning economic-exchange relationships in particular (like simple contracts), theories of the second type generally invite comparative assessment of the values exchanged inter se, and hence they assume stable applicable standards of fair division of the gains of trade (if such standards plausibly exist).

If one considers the regulation of interpersonal exploitation by courts in contract cases, a picture of consistency hardly emerges across the various jurisdictions of Anglo-Commonwealth legal systems. For example, if one takes the unconscionable dealing/bargain jurisdiction as the paradigm vehicle through which an anti-exploitation precept is administered in modern contract law, then certainly no uniformity appears as to where the relevant opprobrium lies. In England, for example, it is seen to lie at least partly in the *terms* of the bargain struck (*Alec Lobb Garages Ltd v Total Oil (Great Britain) Ltd* [1983] 1 WLR 87 (EWHC) 94–95 (Peter Millett QC); affirmed [1985] 1 WLR 173), although no reasoned explanation tends to be given as to why that should always be the case. In Australasia, in contrast, the jurisdiction is significantly more developed and is seen to regulate "procedural unconscionability" rather than "substantive unconscionability", with substantive unfairness serving merely a forensic rather than constitutive role (i.e., as "supporting the inference that a position of disadvantage existed", and "as tending to show that an unfair use was made of the occasion") (*Blomley v Ryan* (1956) 99 CLR 362 (HCA) 405 (Fullagar J)). The Canadian unconscionability doctrine for the most part echoes English law (see *Downer* at [25] – [29] and Bigwood 2005a), although some provinces are now shifting to a position resembling the antipodean version of the jurisdiction (*Downer* [34]). As the Newfoundland and Labrador Court of Appeal recently observed in *Downer*:

> Generally speaking, . . . restrictions on freedom of contract are process-related and do not extend into regulating the substance of a transaction that is a result of a process that is not tainted by fair process concerns. The

> evaluation of the merits of the transaction is generally for the parties, not the courts, to determine.
>
> (ibid [18] – [19])

Now, if we were to canvass competing perspectives on exploitation in legal contractual settings, we might consider exploitation to be wrong (hence eligible for curial superintendence) because it involves exploiters treating exploitees unfairly, specifically by failing to afford would-be exploitees the recognition and respect that is owed to all autonomous subjects and independent responsible agents. On this view, to which I am partial (compare Tormey 1973; Wilson 1978; Goodin 1986; Wood 1995), exploitation is wrong because exploiters "use" their human exploitees "merely instrumentally": they treat them as if they were mere tools or expendable resources to the exploiter's own ends, thereby preventing such exploitees from realizing their own operative goals in the relationship or encounter in question (Marietta 1972). The law's enmity toward exploitation in contract law is thus closely connected to its objection to conversion under tort law and theft under the criminal law: market-transaction exploitation involves an unauthorized interference with the inviolable (or at least specially protected) domain of another person's autonomy and proprietary integrity. Exploiters in contract formation selfishly violate the other party's general "right" ("legal immunity") not to have value transferred away from him or her – here under the colour of an objectively valid contract – without his or her fully responsible consent (or otherwise without lawful justification). In so doing, exploiters avail themselves of strategic opportunities that are denied to them under the rules and ethos of contract bargaining. By failing to observe the side-constraints that the law engrafts upon their contractual liberty when contracting with persons known to be peculiarly disadvantaged by reason of "exploitable circumstances" relative to them, exploiters ignore a basic demand articulated in the liberty principle, which is to respect the special status of all other human agents as "freely choosing, rationally valuing, specially efficacious moral personalit[ies]" (Fried 1978: 29).

Does a precept of "non-exploitation" explain the independent exculpatory categories of duress, undue influence and unconscionable dealing?

To summarize what I believe "exploitation" to involve in connection with the formation of a valid-but-defeasible contract, it involves one contracting party (D) taking advantage of his or her known strategic position of special advantage relative to the other contracting party (P), with the intention and for the purpose of, or in reckless disregard of the substantial likelihood of, influencing, actively or passively, P's decision to enter into a contract (or to agree to a particular contractual term or set of terms) with D (or with a third party at D's direction), regardless of D's (additional) motives for so influencing

P's behaviour, and regardless of the degree to which P "profits" as a result. The "unfairness" or "unjustness" in this practice lies in the purely instrumental utilization of P for D's own ends: that D has deliberately (intentionally, recklessly) chosen not to respond to the subjectively known possibility that P was unable to act fully legally autonomously relative to D in the proposed transaction inter se, which is to behave toward P in a manner that militates against the realization, by P, of P's own operative goals in the exchange relationship.

However, if exploitation really bears this conceptual meaning (or something approximating it), and in particular comprises the fault criteria that it does, then we have strong reason to question the taxonomical preferences of textbook writers, such as Burrows, Finn and Todd, who present the doctrines of duress, undue influence and unconscionable dealing as implementing an overarching precept against interpersonal exploitation. According to those writers, engaging in duress, undue influence or unconscionable dealing are just different ways of "exploiting" a person in the procurement of a bargain transaction.

However, neither duress nor undue influence depends on *proof of exploitation* (and certainly D's showing an *absence* of "exploitative intent" is no defence to either complaint). Duress, like misrepresentation, can be "innocent". That is to say, at least when we are speaking of "regular" duress, as opposed to the "lawful-act" variety (which *is* exploitation-dependent), the law of contractual duress draws no distinction between D's actual or proposed rights-violating conduct that is aimed at coercing P, and D's actual or proposed rights-violating conduct that unintentionally has a coercive effect on P (*North Ocean Shipping Co Ltd v Hyundai Construction Co Ltd* [1979] QB 705 being a case in point). And because an actual or proposed rights-violation is inevitably involved in regular duress situations, it should not matter that D honesty believed that she or he was entitled to make threat that she or he did, provided that the resulting pressure did in fact "compel the will" of P (as opposed, say, to providing the basis for the genuine compromise of a bona fide dispute as to rights on both sides). Lawful-act duress aside, "liability" for duress is basically strict.

As for undue influence, although it has said that that concept possesses "a connotation of impropriety" and involves a "misuse" of influence (*Royal Bank of Scotland plc v Etridge (No 2)* [2001] UKHL 44, [2002] 2 AC 773 (HL) [32] Lord Nicholls), this may simply comprehend an "abuse of trust" – a betrayal of confidence by reason of the influential party's preferring his or her own interests to those of the trusting party (compare *Etridge* at [9]) – which is wrongful quite independently of a strictly "exploitative" use of influence inter se. Still, even the Privy Council continues to resort to the locutions of "exploitation" in relation to undue influence, albeit without reflection or analysis (*Attorney-General for England and Wales v R* [2003] UKPC 22, [2004] 2 NZLR 577 [21]; *National Commercial Bank (Jamaica) Ltd v Hew* [2003] UKPC 51 [29]). But such a usage strikes me as incongruous with the history of the jurisdiction, and with the multiple ways in which undue influence has been found to have been exercised. As with duress and misrepresentation, undue influence (especially of the so-called Class 2, "relational" variety) can occur quite innocently and indeed may be well-motivated in fact (e.g., *Lloyds Bank Ltd v Bundy* [1975] QB 326 (CA) 342 (Sir Eric Sachs); *Cheese v Thomas* [1994] 1 All ER 35 (CA) 43 (Sir Donald Nicholls V-C)). Early cases spoke of the jurisdiction existing to regulate the "opportunity either by flattery or force, *by good usage unfairly meant*, or by bad usage imposed, to take . . . advantage" (*Hylton v Hylton* (1754) 2 Ves Sen 547, 548–49; 28 ER 349, 350 (emphasis supplied)), and of the subordinate party's mind being "misled by *undue kindness*, or forced by oppression" (*Hatch v Hatch* (1804) 9 Ves Jun 292, 297; 32 ER 615, 617 (Lord Eldon) (emphasis supplied)). That a factually innocent ascendant party might be treated as having exercised undue influence in virtue of the traditional "presumption" in the Class 2 cases was a concession to an overt public policy operant in those cases: the misattribution of liability was a risk worth tolerating given the wider interest that society was perceived to have in the maintenance of relations or tasks that are "fiduciary" in nature. (Although the "fiduciary" approach to Class 2 undue influence has fallen away in recent years, except perhaps in Canada (Maddaugh and McCamus 2004; Haughey 2012; Flannigan 2015), this has occurred without acknowledgment of, or rational grounds being supplied for, the demise.)

All major Anglo-Commonwealth jurisdictions seem to regard the unconscionable dealing/bargain jurisdiction as responding to *proof of exploitation* in the procurement or receipt of a contractual (or other) benefit, although, as mentioned, they do not all apparently share the same conception of market-transaction exploitation for this purpose. The antipodean (and possibly emergent Canadian) doctrine responds to a purely procedural conception of exploitation, while the less developed English version of the same requires proof of serious substantive unfairness as well (*Alec Lobb*: 95). So be it. But regardless of which conception of market-transaction exploitation happens to be adopted within the particular legal system, the fact that Commonwealth courts have routinely adopted attenuated knowledge criteria in relation to the superior-party misconduct that attracts the equitable jurisdiction – standards such as "ought to have known", "should have known", "being put on inquiry as a reasonable person", "constructive notice (or knowledge)", etc. – is simply incompatible with the mental criteria of a genuine exploitation claim. So, too, is the fact that judges have been prepared to relieve against unconscionable dealing while acquitting the defendant of "moral obliquity" (*Amadio*: 478 (Deane J)). Strictly speaking, an exploitation claim can be satisfied by nothing less than proof of *actual* knowledge (including wilful blindness), on the part of the superior party, of the weaker party's relative special disadvantage. Indeed, the High Court of Australia recognized as much in *Kakavas v Crown Melbourne Ltd* [2013] HCA 25, (2013) 298 ALR 35 at [152] – [161], but more recently a Canadian court was not persuaded by that decision on that point (*Downer* [48]), and even more recently still there is evidence in Australia that the High Court has begun to retreat from the potentially unjust stringencies placed upon the jurisdiction by its earlier decision in *Kakavas* (see *Thorne v Kennedy* [2017] HCA 49, (2017) 91 AJLJ 1260 at [38], [74]).

Duress, undue influence and unconscionable dealing: if not "exploitation", then what *does* explain their usual collocation?

For the above and other reasons (see Bigwood 2005a), I remain sceptical of the descriptive and justificatory adequacy of the exploitation concept in connection with the exculpatory doctrines of duress, undue influence and unconscionable dealing, as least as an *exclusive* reason for contract vitiation in the name of any or all of those doctrines. Exploitation there may well have been, which, of course, is a *sufficient* reason for reversing what appears to have been concluded between seriously unequal bargaining opponents, but none of the doctrines treat exploitation as a *necessary* condition for relief in all cases. When courts use "exploitation" in connection with contract vitiation, it is highly likely they are not always using it in its true, conceptually dedicated sense. Rather, they probably intend something more akin to "victimization", which, while sometimes assumed to be synonymous with "exploitation", is not. Obviously, to "exploit" someone is to make a "victim" of him or her – at least in the sense of treating him or her merely instrumentally and hence unjustly – but there are multiple other ways of "victimizing" people than exploiting them. For example, one can victimize another by failing, in some agency-responsible manner, to meet an applicable standard of interpersonal treatment in pre-contractual bargaining, regardless of whether that failure happens to be accompanied by an exploitative mind-state. The applicable standard might, for example, be one of "truth-telling" (e.g., misrepresentation), "rights-respecting" (e.g., duress), "trust-maintenance" (e.g., Class 2 undue influence), or "taking reasonable precautions toward avoidance of a foreseeable risk of ignorance, error or third-party imposition" (e.g., the principles in favour of non-commercial sureties in England (*Etridge* [87]), or the "special equity" in favour of "volunteer wives" in Australia: *Garcia v National Australia Bank Ltd* [1998] HCA 48, (1998) 194 CLR 395).

As with the exploitation concept, the broader notion of "victimization" is under-analysed by those who have seen fit to invoke it. In *Hart v O'Connor* [1985] AC 1000, Lord Brightman famously defined "victimization" synonymously with "equitable fraud", as signifying "an unconscientious use of the power arising out of the circumstances and conditions of the contracting parties", "which can consist of either the active extortion of a benefit or the passive acceptance of a benefit in unconscionable circumstances" (ibid 1024, quoting *Earl of Aylesford v Morris* (1873) [LR] 8 Ch App 484, 491 (Lord Selbourne LC)). On this understanding, "unfair exploitation of the weakness of the other party" clearly constitutes "victimization" (*Kakavas* [161]), but there is nothing in Lord Brightman's definition that restricts the law's conception of transaction-inducing victimization to acts of exploitation alone. There is certainly nothing *inherent* in the victimization concept, or that of "equitable fraud", that compels such an overly circumscribed stance. Indeed, in his mid-twentieth-century study on equitable fraud in English and Irish law, Sheridan wrote of the "infinite" manifestations of such fraud (Sheridan 1957: 2, citing Lord Hardwick in a letter to Lord Kames) and concluded that it "covers a scale of moral obliquity from the depths of depravity to the misplaced kindly intention" (ibid 214). Certainly, no *conceptual* reason exists why "victimization" ought to be confined to proven acts of exploitation, since interpersonal power can be used "unfairly" or "unconscientiously", if not deliberately, provided, of course, that some agency-responsible "blame" exists on D's part in relation to the impact of the power – vulnerability relationship upon P's relevant interests.

In my view, in each act of duress, undue influence or unconscionable dealing, the victim of the conduct that attracts the law's superintendence has been treated "merely instrumentally", and hence has been "victimized", because the party engaging in the conduct, D, has failed to ensure that the other party, P, has not been prevented, by D's own agency-responsible acts or omissions, from realizing his or her own operative goals in the transaction or encounter in question. This occurs because D has either failed to respect the background rights of P in securing a contractual benefit from P – which is essentially what happens in regular duress cases – or else failed to be influenced by relevant side-constraints that attended the parties' relationship or encounter by reason of D being sufficiently aware of P's vulnerability to merely instrumental utilization at the hands of D – which is what seems to characterize undue influence and unconscionable dealing cases. These side-constraints effectively translate into "protective responsibilities" that D must observe for the sake of preserving the transactional autonomy of P, and in the name of treating P "justly" or "fairly" when taking or receiving benefits from P. Typically, this involves a curial expectation that D would have at least recommended or ensured that competent advice was taken or received by P *ex ante* entry into the impugned transaction, and that pre-transactional "independence" was established in undue influence situations. Provided that these "responsibilities" were properly discharged by or on behalf of D, it cannot be said that P was prevented by D from acting legally autonomously in relation to the impugned transaction, such that D could then be said to have used P "merely instrumentally" and hence to have "victimized" P. The quality of the mind that happened to accompany D's agency-responsible failure to administer to P's autonomy interests before contracting with P may, of course, range from "active predation" at one end of the opprobrium scale, through to "mere neglect" (or "carelessness") at the other. Whether carelessness is a sufficient reason to deny someone the fruits of a contract with another who was known to be seriously unequal to the task of bargaining is, of course, a matter of policy for law-makers, given the perceived purpose(s) of the exculpatory doctrine(s) at hand. However, the notion that an unconscionable dealing might involve merely a *careless failure* by D to notice or appreciate P's relative special disadvantage before benefiting from P gestures more in the direction of a concept of "transactional neglect" than "exploitation" as the paradigm for interference with a bargain transaction on the ground of unconscionable dealing (Bigwood 2005b). Such a stance, however, is presently precluded, at least in Australia, by the High Court's express denial of a mere "negligence" standard for "unconscionable conduct" (*Kakavas* [161]).

My own approach to contract vitiation in the classroom

When it comes to packaging the "vitiating factors" of contract law for teaching purposes, particularly with a view to investing students with some sort of consistent and rational narrative about the law's patterns of interference with contracts apparently concluded, the modern teacher of contract law faces a considerable challenge. At least judging by the standard texts in the field, there is considerable divergence in outlook or opinion as to how the various vitiating factors should be organized and explained, whether individually or as a cluster. Moreover, the ability to provide a stable coherent account of the law in this area is becoming increasingly difficult to achieve, the more so when one takes a cross-jurisdictional perspective. The seeming lack of consensus around, and overarching vision for, these doctrines, and their joint or several purpose(s), seems to be worsening by the decade.

Personally, I have always taught the major exculpatory doctrines of contract law – especially misrepresentation, duress, undue influence and unconscionable dealing – in terms of the distinct *behavioural* phenomena that tend to attract each doctrine. However, even that approach is becoming increasing difficult to maintain as descriptively accurate, at least in the classrooms of Australian law schools. For one of the upshots of the High Court's recent decision in *Thorne v Kennedy* is that undue influence and unconscionable dealing are now disjunctively rationalized, despite continuing to be described as "closely related" (*Thorne* [39]). According to the majority in that case, the former is an internal exculpatory defence responding to the claimant's serious lack of "free agency" when entering into a transaction, whereas the latter is to be understood as a defendant-sided, wrongful-conduct-focused ground of relief (ibid [32], [34] – [35], [39] – [40], [59], [62] Kiefel CJ, Bell, Gageler, Keane and Edelman JJ; [86], [91], [93] Gordon J). I presently find myself unable to explain to my students why that is, or ought to be, a plausible version of the law in this field. Certainly, the relevant judges in *Thorne* do not supply a credible reason for the distinction to which I can refer my students; rather, prior dicta to similar effect in Australia (especially *Amadio*: 447 (Deane J) and 461 (Mason J)) was simply repeated and endorsed without reflection or analysis, which dicta, upon inspection, reveal themselves to be of rather dubious lineage (Mason J (ibid) cites no authority for the distinction, and the two Australian authorities that Deane J (ibid) cites are actually to the contrary at the pinpoints his Honour supplies). Moreover, senior dicta to opposite effect, both in Australia and abroad, were simply bypassed in

Thorne without mention (e.g., *Louth v Diprose* (1992) 175 CLR 621 (HCA) 627 (Brennan J); *Tanwar Enterprises Pty Ltd v Cauchi* [2003] HCA 57, (2003) 217 CLR 315 [23] Gleeson CJ, McHugh, Gummow, Hayne and Heydon JJ). In England, in contrast, undue influence is unambiguously rationalized as responding to an improper use of influence affecting the transactional consent of the relief-seeking party, and not simply in terms of a defect in transactional consent *simpliciter* (e.g., *Etridge* [32] Lord Nicholls).

Bracketing *Thorne*, I briefly explain below how I present the above-mentioned exculpatory doctrines of law and equity in my own classroom. Doubtless this approach will not command the agreement of all my fellow teachers of the subject, but it is an approach that at least allows for the continued treatment of vitiating factors as supporting *independent* doctrines, each being unified by an overarching curial precept against specific manifestations of "victimization" rather than "exploitation" more narrowly.

I begin, of course, with the classical "liberal" conception of contract: that we are each free as formal equals to engage in transfer and exchange, and to enlist others in the pursuit of our own economic projects or life plans (just as they are free to enlist us likewise). But equality does not always exist *inter partes*. For a variety of reasons, both constitutional and situational, people often find themselves seriously disequalized vis-à-vis others in social and transactional encounters. And although, according the liberal conception, no objection can be taken to the mere existence of (even very serious) inequality of bargaining power between actors per se (Nozick 1974: 224–227; Weinrib 1988; *Alec Lobb* (CA) 183 (Dillon LJ)), the law nevertheless does make it harder for power-holders to use their unofficial interpersonal power by ensuring that such power is only used consistently with the injunction against using free and equal moral agents "merely instrumentally" for personal gain. This may or may not entail that such agents are "exploited", since there are numerous ways of using another merely instrumentally – or of "victimizing" them – that does not involve exploitation. In general, I proceed to explain, the relevant exculpatory doctrines presuppose that there are "acceptable" and "unacceptable" ways of influencing another person's behaviour in an intended direction, hereby inducing *intentional* entry into a contract. And while this inevitably involves a lack of responsible consent on the part of the one subsequently seeking relief from the transaction – unacceptable ways of influencing another are always inconsistent with voluntary-hence-responsible action on the part of the other – a lack of responsible consent is not all that is involved, since the legitimate freedom of the power-holder to use his or her natural advantages in contract bargaining is also engaged whenever the law is deciding whether to strip a person of a benefit that has resulted from those advantages. There is, additionally, always a violation of some more specific applicable norm of interpersonal treatment on the part of the ascendant party that allows us to say that any consent produced in violation of that norm cannot be treated as "fully legally responsible", with the consequence that any resultant transaction is treated as voidable unless met with a defence on the ascendant party's side. In other words, doctrines such as misrepresentation, duress, undue influence and unconscionable dealing regulate the *means* by which voluntary or consensual transactions, such are contracts, have been concluded, and so I have long been partial to those accounts, such as Farnsworth's (1982: ch 4 pt C), that present the relevant doctrines in terms of "policing the agreement" or "abuse of the bargaining process". To be sure, each of the doctrines of misrepresentation, duress, undue influence and unconscionable dealing/bargain are attracted by pre-contractual conduct that somehow subjected the relief-seeking party to an *improper reason* for *intentional action*, namely, entry into the impugned transaction – a reason or motive from which, being inconsistent with responsible human action, the claimant ought to have been free.

Now, there are various ways in which one party (D) may "exercise power" over the other party (P) so as to alter P's behaviour – here to induce P's contractual assent – in a direction intended by D, where P would (or might) not have assented in the absence of D's exercise of power. For example, D might exercise power over P by actively altering P's decision-making environment in such a way that P is motivated to do as D desires. Both misrepresentation (innocent or culpable) and duress function in this way. With misrepresentation, D introduces a false factual statement into the parties' pre-contractual negotiations upon which, consistently with D's intention when making the statement, P factually relies. That the misrepresentation was contrary to the law's universal norm of truth-telling when it comes to pre-contractual statements of *fact* implies, *ex necessitate*, that D has motivated P to act by presenting her with an *unacceptable* reason for doing what D desired, regardless of the quality of mind that happened to accompany the false statement: D should have found out the truth before speaking a falsity. Moreover, given that P is generally under no responsibility to investigate factual statements made to him or her for the purpose of inducing entry into a contract (see, e.g., *Redgrave v Hurd* (1881) 20 Ch D 1 (CA) 14, 17 (Jessel MR), 22–23 (Baggallay LJ); *Smith v Land & House Property Corporation* (1884) 28 Ch D 7 (CA) 17 (Bowen LJ)), D's misleading conduct is inconsistent with "voluntary" (hence legally responsible) action on the part of P. Accordingly, any transaction so concluded ought, in the absence of an available defence, to be treated as voidable as against D.

Similarly, with duress, D manipulates P's decision to enter into a contract by exercising *coercive* power over P. D does this by proposing to make P *worse off* relative to P's pre-existing legal entitlements (whether sourced in tort law, contract law or elsewhere) unless P accedes to D's specific demand, thereby motivating P to do as D desires through *fear* of unwanted consequences: P would prefer to abandon one right (i.e., whatever it is that D has demanded) in order to protect another right (e.g., P's right to bodily, proprietary or economic integrity), which P perceives to be the lesser of the two evils comprising the choice conditions that D has created for P. Where D's application of pressure reduces P's menu of options to such a point that P has "no reasonable alternative" than submission to D's demand, and P does in fact submit for that reason,

D must be treated as having motivated P to act by presenting P with an *unacceptable* reason for doing what D desired, again regardless of the quality of mind (if any) that happened to accompany the application of the coercive pressure. If a court were to enforce an agreement made when D had violated or proposed to violate P's rights, this would simply entail that P's rights were not recognized or adequately protected *as rights*. Of course, the standard case of duress involves D threatening a consequence that is not D's to dispense, because it would be unlawful *per se*, that is, if the threat were to be implemented. But duress is not limited to such cases. D may exercise duress by conditionally proposing to exercise D's own *lawful* rights, liberties or powers in a manner unwelcome to P or to P's disadvantage, typically in a way calculated to "exploit" P's peculiar vulnerability to being pressed in the circumstances. Whether such cases are appropriate for the common-law duress doctrine or are better conceived of as "unconscionable dealing" or "undue influence" cases (for example) is a matter of current uncertainty, at least in Australia (see Bigwood 2008).

Turning to undue influence, that is somewhat harder to pin down. This was not always the case, but there has been such fragmentation around the Commonwealth as to what undue influence actually means or entails that it is becoming almost impossible to provide a coherent, universally agreed account of the law – at least one that allows for ready separation of undue influence from other exculpatory categories, especially duress and unconscionable dealing. Outside of Australia (where undue influence is now rationalized, somewhat unconvincingly, as a purely consent-oriented ground of relief), the jurisdiction continues to be conceived of as being rooted in the principle "that a transaction to which consent has been obtained *by unacceptable means* should not be allowed to stand" (*Attorney-General of England and Wales v R* [21] emphasis supplied). As to the *nature* of those unacceptable means, the law remains rather sketchy (although again, that has not always been the case). While some undue influence cases appear to regulate *coercion* (albeit by lawful means) (e.g., *Mutual Finance Ltd v John Wetton and Sons Ltd* [1937] 2 KB 389; *Robertson v Robertson* [1930] QWN, Case No 41 in [1930–31] Qd St R; *Langton v Langton* [1995] 2 FLR 890; *Bank of Scotland v Bennett* [1997] 1 FLR 801), the paradigm case of undue influence is not one of "duress" or "fear". In the typical undue influence situation, D is seen to work *through* or *with* P's "will" rather than against it (compare Fingarette 1985: 111; Chunn 1970). Unsurprisingly, then, undue influence is often described in terms of "unfair", "improper" or "unacceptable" *persuasion* rather than coercion (e.g., *Etridge* [6] – [7] Lord Nicholls; American Law Institute, *Restatement (Second) of Contracts* (1981) §177(1); American Law Institute, *Restatement of the Law Third, Restitution and Unjust Enrichment* (2011) 204). Generally, D exercises *persuasive* power over P by giving her arguments or reasons that appeal to P's (self-perceived) interests or principles, so that P *prefers* to do what D desires over P's status quo (or over some other alternative courses of action available to P). But when does "persuasion" amount to presenting another with an *unacceptable* reason for intentional action, such as entry into a contract? Before circa 1985 in England, and until *Thorne v Kennedy* was decided in Australia in late 2017, a significant body of undue influence law was tethered to basic fiduciary regulatory operations directed at avoiding unauthorized conflicts of interest or duty in relationships or arrangements that, generically or specifically, involve "trust and confidence" (Flannigan 2015; *Johnson v Buttress* (1936) 56 CLR 113 (HCA), especially the judgment of Dixon J at 134–135). Undue influence thus typically entailed the use (or mere *possible use*), whether active or passive, of influence that the law expected to be exercised solely in the interests of P, rather than in pursuance of an inconsistent personal interest of D within the scope of the influential relationship or encounter. Undue influence was unacceptable, therefore, because it basically involved a *conflictual* use (or possible such use) of influence, meaning that it was strictly speaking irrelevant *how* the influence happened to be exercised in the particular case (pressure, advice, argument, pleading, intercession, misrepresentation or whatever). The fact that the benefit transferred and received appeared inconsistent with the maintenance of the "trusting" relationship between the parties alone sufficed to call upon D to show free and informed consent, and to support rescission of the impugned transaction if D were unable to do so. The jurisdiction possessed a significant *prophylactic* element, expressed through the way in which the "presumption" of undue influence traditionally operated.

Of course, this view of undue influence seems to have withered on the vine in recent years, and for no apparent principled reason (Bigwood 2009). It is very difficult nowadays – or at least I find it so – to teach the subject to students in a way that maintains, convincingly, separation among the various exculpatory doctrines of common law and equity. Ignoring the (seemingly untenable) possibility that undue influence is *just* about the "impaired consent" of P and does not (additionally) involve a perceived *misuse* of influence by D, the fact is that the House of Lords in *Etridge* did not confine undue influence to "cases of abuses of trust and confidence", but extended it as well to "cases where a vulnerable person has been exploited" (*Etridge* [11] Lord Nicholls). This, unfortunately, renders it virtually impossible to distinguish the jurisdiction from "lawful-act duress" and "unconscionable dealing" – at least as those exculpatory categories would be understood in Australasia.

Turning to unconscionable dealing, the ascendant party (D) here typically "exercises power" over the other party (P) not by *creating* a problem with P's autonomy as such (like in misrepresentation or duress cases, for example), but rather by *working with* or *taking advantage of* a special disadvantage that D found, at least to some extent, "ready-made" in P, which disadvantage rendered P vulnerable to merely instrumental utilization at the hands of D. There may well have been active manipulation by D of P's special disadvantage, of course (e.g., *Louth v Diprose*), but the minimal sufficient condition and conceptual core of unconscionable dealing is simply that D as a rational agent chose not to respond to the subjectively known substantial possibility that P was, by virtue of his or her "special disadvantage", unable to act legally autonomously relative to D in a proposed transaction inter se. The paradigmatic case of unconscionable dealing simply involves D transacting with P without sufficient regard for P's autonomy interests in the transaction subsequently called into question (or, in England, without sufficient regard for the substantive fairness of the impugned transaction either). P is, in this sense, subjected to an improper reason for intentional action essentially through D's *omissive conduct* – through D's operative failure adequately to administer to P's special vulnerability before contracting with P (e.g., by ensuring the receipt of competent advice for P, or by fully disclosing or explaining the transactional risks to P, or by correcting known erroneous assumptions in relation to the proposed transaction, or, in England at least, by ensuring that P receives commensurate value in return for the consideration that moved from P in the exchange relationship). This, of course, sounds very much like *exploitation*, that is, if D's decision not to respond to P's known situation of special disadvantage was deliberate in the manner demanded by an exploitation claim. A mere *careless* failure to so respond, apparently, is not "unconscionable dealing", despite the fact that P is still effectively used "merely instrumentally" as a result of D's inadvertent, but nevertheless "agency-responsible", use of power.

It is possible, of course, that I have been doing my students a disservice all these years by trying to explain major exculpatory doctrines of common law and equity in the manner described above. However, if I were permitted to "reimagine" the pedagogy of vitiating factors in contract law, it would certainly involve an instructional environment where the exploitation concept was both better explained and less liberally employed, whether for taxonomical or justificatory purposes. In fact, to the extent that the exploitation concept is currently being used contrary to its true conceptual meaning, it can only hinder rather than assist our understanding of the law's response to contracts that, in some sense, are the product of "unfair advantage". What is needed, instead, in my view, is a more complete and sophisticated conceptual account of what it means for a party to be "victimized" in contract formation, "victimization" including but not being subsumed by the "exploitation" concern. We "victimize" others by failing to meet some relevant standard of conduct (or norm of interpersonal treatment) in securing their transactional consent; we do it by preventing them from realizing their own operative goals in the relationship or encounter in question; and we do this by subjecting them, through our own agency-responsible acts or omissions, to improper reasons for intentional action – reasons that do not sufficiently respect the agent's own right to autonomous participation in the transaction now under review.

References

Bigwood, R., 2005a. Antipodean Reflections on the Canadian Unconscionability Doctrine. *Can. B. Rev.*, 84, 171–216.

Bigwood, R., 2005b. Contracts by Unfair Advantage: From Exploitation to Transactional Neglect. *Oxford J. Legal Stud.*, 25, 65–96.

Bigwood, R., 2008. Throwing the Baby Out with the Bathwater–Four Questions on the Demise of Lawful-Act Duress in New South Wales. *U. Queensland L.J.*, 27, 41–84.
Bigwood, R., 2009. From Morgan to Etridge: Tracing the (dis)integration of Undue Influence in the United Kingdom. In: Neyers, J.W., Bronaugh, R. and Pitel, S.G., eds., *Exploring Contract Law*. Hart Publishing, Oxford, pp. 379–430.
Black's Law Dictionary., 1990. 6th ed. West Publishing Co, St Paul, MI.
Burrows, A., 1993. *The Law of Restitution*. Butterworths, London.
Burrows, A., 2011. *The Law of Restitution*. 3rd ed. Oxford University Press, Oxford.
Burrows, J.F., Todd, S.M. and Finn, J., 2016. *Law of Contract in New Zealand: A Successor to Cheshire & Fifoot's Law of Contract, New Zealand Edition*. 5th ed. LexisNexis, Australia.
Chunn, L., 1970. Duress and Undue Influence–A Comparative Analysis. *Baylor L. Rev.*, 22, 572–579.
De Crespigny, A., 1968. Power and its Forms. *Political Stud.*, 16, 192–205.
Farnsworth, E.A., 1982. *Contracts*. Little Brown & Co, Boston.
Fingarette, H., 1985. Victimization: A Legalist Analysis of Coercion, Deception, Undue Influence, and Excusable Prison Escape. *Wash. & Lee L. Rev.*, 42, 65–120.
Flannigan, R., 2015. Presumed Undue Influence: The False Partition from Fiduciary Accountability. *U. Queensland L.J.*, 34, 171–216.
Fried, C., 1978. *Right and Wrong*. Harvard University Press, Cambridge.
Goodin, R.E., 1986. *Protecting the Vulnerable: A Re-analysis of Our Social Responsibilities*. University of Chicago Press, Chicago.
Goodin, R.E., 1987. *Exploiting a Situation and Exploiting a Person*. In: Reeve, A., ed., *Modern Theories of Exploitation*. Sage, London.
Hart, H.L.A., 1968. *Punishment and Responsibility: Essays in the Philosophy of Law*. Clarendon Press, Oxford.
Haughey, M., 2012. The Fiduciary Explanation for Presumed Undue Influence. *Alta. L. Rev.*, 50, 129–156.
Hill, J.L., 1994. Exploitation. *Cornell L. Rev.*, 79, 631–699.
Maddaugh, P.D. and McCamus, J.D., 2004. *The Law of Restitution*. 2nd ed. Canada Law Book, Aurora, ON.
Marietta Jr, D.E., 1972. On Using People. *Ethics*, 82, 232–238.
Norton, E.H., 1989. Bargaining and the Ethic of Process. *NYUL Rev.*, 64, 493–578.
Nozick, R., 1974. *Anarchy, Utopia and the state*. Basic Books, New York.
Sheridan, L.A., 1957. *Fraud in Equity: A Study in English and Irish Law*. Pitman Publishing, London.
Tormey, J., 1973. Exploitation, Oppression and Self-Sacrifice. *Phil Forum.*, 5, 206–221.
Virgo, G., 2015. *The Principles of the Law of Restitution*. 3rd ed. Oxford University Press.
Weinrib, E.J., 1988. Right and Advantage in Private Law. *Cardozo L. Rev.*, 10, 1283–1310.
Wilson, J.R., 1978. In One Another's Power. *Ethics*, 88, 299–315.
Wood, A.W., 1995. Exploitation. *Soc. Phil. Pol.*, 12, 136–158.
Zartman, I.W., 1974. The Political Analysis of Negotiation: How Who Gets What and When. *World Politics*, 26, 385–399.

Chapter 6

Law in Action

Sally Wheeler

Introduction

Any consideration of how Law in Action studies in the field of contract might contribute to a pedagogy of contract has to begin with the groundbreaking work of Stewart Macaulay. In 1963 Macaulay produced two empirically informed papers about the role of contract in a business context (Macaulay 1963a, 1963b). These papers have become a foundational tool for modern contract scholarship. In research terms, one of these, 'Non-Contractual Relations in Business: A Preliminary Study' (Macaulay 1963a) is currently the 4th most highly cited paper in Sociology from the 1960s (Jacobs 2005) and some 30 years after its publication it was declared to be the 15th most cited law review article of all time (Shapiro 1996). Google Scholar records over 5000 citations for this paper.

However in the context of contract law teaching, certainly in the Commonwealth, if not the US where Macaulay co-authored a contract law casebook (Macaulay *et al* 2010), Law in Action scholarship has made little impression. Its more generous reception in the US might result from the deeper engagement with realist scholarship that occurred there. In the field of contract, the realists, whilst still focusing on appellate judgments as their source material, were asking questions not about the coherence of doctrinal categories in an abstract sense but about the correctness of judgments assessed against broad policy goals (for example assistance to business practice or consumer protection) through a close reading of the factual matrix ('situation sense' in Llewellyn's terms) of a decision – mainly party identity and type of contract (Friedman and Macaulay 1967; Macaulay 2005). The realists' ultimate success was the Uniform Commercial Code (UCC). Interestingly the policy goals and customs that the realists draw upon in these endeavors were not distilled from or validated against any empirical research into modern trade practices (Bernstein 2014). The coherence of doctrine was not an overriding concern. Thus the relative mainstreaming of Law in Action scholarship post this engagement might not have been as significant a challenge as it has been in the UK and elsewhere in the common law world.

An examination of the most recent editions of standard student texts available in the UK seems to indicate that if a law student knows anything of Macaulay's work, and the subsequent Law in Action scholarship of other authors following in his wake at the end of their contract course, it is a one line statement that businessmen might not rely on their contractual legal rights when resolving disputes. This statement stands entirely apart from doctrinal knowledge and most importantly from the tools of analysis (spotting and explaining conflicts, ambiguities and gaps in rules, and separating relevant facts from irrelevant facts, for example) that might have been taught within contract law. If we look at what might be termed 'accessible' student texts first, Stone's *Modern Law of Contract* has just one footnote to Law in Action scholarship in its chapter on breach and frustration (Stone and Devenney 2017: 441) and Andrews *Contract Law* (Andrews 2015) no reference at all. At the other end of the complexity spectrum of texts *Anson's Law of Contract* has one footnote reference to Macaulay in its introduction (Anson *et al* 2016: 3) while *Cheshire, Fifoot and Furmston's Law of Contract* accords a paragraph, also placed in its introduction, to explaining that Macaulay's work demonstrated 'that in substantial areas of business, contractual disputes were resolved by reference to norms which were significantly different from the theoretical legal position'. The text goes on to point out that this is not the case in 'other areas of business' where there is an insistence on legal rights' (Furmston *et al* 2012: 30). No suggestions are offered as to what these legal rights might be, or any guidance on why these differences exist or on how one might decide whether this is an area of business where strict legal rights prevail or not. None of these texts refer to anything Macaulay has written post 1963 despite his extensive subsequent work on consumer contracts and franchise arrangements.

The reluctance to engage with Law in Action scholarship comes, I think, from two interrelated but distinct concerns which I deal with in the first two sections of this chapter. The first is that any detailed engagement involves using contract doctrine as a straw concept. The position taken is that the contextual approach and the formalist approach are opposing forces which must be chosen between. Perhaps this is fueled by Macaulay's opening words – 'What use is Contract Law?' – in his seminal 1963a piece. However as I explain below this is not the relationship that Macaulay and the Law in Action School suggest that their work has to doctrine. They see the two as entirely complementary. The second concern is that Law in Action scholarship features empirical work carried out in a variety of different contractual settings and/or focusing on different contract terms thus meaning that nothing generalizable results. The quotation from *Cheshire, Fifoot and Furmston* above makes exactly this point when it contrasts 'substantial areas' (unspecified) of business with 'other areas of business', also unspecified.

However clumsily expressed it might be in traditional textbook accounts, there is some merit in this concern; Law in Action scholarship does not set out to offer a theory of exchange behavior in the way that relational contract theory does (Macneil 1973) for example. This is not to say that Law in Action scholarship operates with descriptive force only and has no theoretical basis. Macaulay's theoretical foundation for his 1963 work came from the anthropological work of Malinowski (Halliday and Schmidt 2009: 23). Law in Action scholarship is composed of a series of often small-scale but beautifully drawn and detailed empirical pictures of different aspects of contract relations drawn from business and consumer transactions in particular industries that are often situated in particular locations thus introducing an element of localized geographically situated relations. This results in a fragmented picture of contract with sometimes that appear to be conflicting findings depending on the industry studied.

Perhaps the most famous of these conflicts sets the work of Lisa Bernstein on the Uniform Commercial Code (UCC) (1996, 1999, 2014) against that of other Law in Action scholars (Bernstein 2014: 244, cf Macaulay 2000; Woodward 2001). Bernstein's position is that it is impossible, as the UCC purports to do, to give legal effect to customary business norms in a general sense. Her reasoning as to why this is impossible is based on empirical and historical inquiry and is multifaceted. The part of her reasoning that concerns this chapter is that it is impossible to find widespread agreement on trade usage of terms and concepts across different industries and contexts. According to Bernstein, even in close-knit business communities agreed ideas around 'commercial standards' and 'usages of trade' do not exist. Whilst geographical proximity might enhance the likelihood of their presence, they will be much more general in scope than the UCC imagines. Specific norms and understandings are likely to develop within particular relationships, rather than coming in from the external environment as general understandings of business practice, and will therefore have little meaning outside that relationship. Many businesses have no desire for general trade usage to be used to interpret their agreements (Gilson *et al* 2013). This would appear to be little different from the assertion of the Law in Action School that the absence of generalizability in their accounts of particular settings and interactions is a strength rather than a detraction.

Lying behind the criticism of Law in Action as ungeneralizable is an assumption that even in its abstractions doctrinal contract law presents a picture of uniform and coherent rules. It does not. Every part of it has contradictions and exceptions. The most that can be attempted with any degree of certainty is a rough classification of contracts types, contract terms and the parties to a contract with general principles extrapolated from that classification; for example consumers in a contractual situation are viewed differently from commercial parties (Lyons and Mehta 1997). There is no reason to suppose that Law in Action findings should be any more uniform than the explanations given by courts of decisions to imply terms into what one of the contracting parties suggests is an incomplete contract (Collins 2014) or of explanations offered for the declining numbers of judicial adjudication on contract disputes (Macaulay 2004).

However, focusing on these differences only serves to support what Law in Action scholars themselves say about their work; it is not intended to be generalizable to all areas of contract law and to all contracts. Macaulay could not make this clearer in his 1963a account. He refers to 'complete answers' to the questions of who uses contract, when they use it and how they use it as only being available if one were to study every type of transaction between individuals and organizations. Section 1 below explains in more detail Macaulay's concerns about representativeness both in the design of his 1963 study and its findings. Law in Action scholarship can be synthesized to produce a range of social or behavioral norms around contracting behavior that should provoke students to ask wider and deeper questions of the contract materials they are presented with. They might think about the intentions and needs of the parties at different stages of their transaction and whether they have dealt with each other before and whether they intend to do so again in the future. Of relevance will be their answers to how and why the parties planned their contract relationship in the way they did. They might consider, in the light of these questions, the appropriateness of applying particular doctrinal concepts to particular situations and in general think about how the idea of competitive exchange behavior is really framed in capitalist societies (Macaulay and Whitford 2015: 799, 802).

In the first section of this chapter I examine in detail Macaulay's foundational 1963 article (Macaulay 1963a). The intention is to explain how Macaulay's original observations (still) fit into the world of contract dominated by formalist thinking and enrich it without contradicting or denigrating its worldview. Examining the framework that Macaulay creates for his findings and the norms or shared expectations of behavior that he uncovers, provides us with a lens for examining other Law in Action scholarship. It was not Macaulay's intention to do this. His 1963a work does not make this claim nor does his subsequent work. However his 1963a piece has attained iconoclastic status in the world of Law in Action; it was the first in the field of contract studies, it is beautifully written and accessible whilst being also subtly subversive and disruptive. In the second section of this chapter I look at the observations and social norms that subsequent Law in Action scholarship in contract has generated and identify how they might enrich the teaching of contract law. In the third and final section of the chapter I look at some empirical, perhaps better described as attitudinal, studies in contract that focus on ideas of theoretical significance – for example the notion of efficient breach and the role of obligation in a moral sense which might develop how ideas of promise within contract are presented to students.

Section 1: the foundational ideas in contract's world of Law in Action

Macaulay began his 1963 empirical work with a definition of contract that most lawyers would recognize as being broadly within the legal canon; contract is a mechanism not for necessarily achieving an efficient allocation of resources in the terms that an economist would model but as the device that facilitates, and encapsulates the terms of, the exchange as the parties plan it. To facilitate exchange, a contract must do two things: it must try to capture an element of rational planning by offering a risk-based solution for future contingencies, and it must include legal sanctions to either induce performance or compensate for non-performance (Macaulay 1963a: 7). Macaulay's study was situated in the machinery manufacturing industry of Wisconsin. It covered a broad sweep of industries, but there were concentrations in the farm machinery area, in paper processing and in commercial construction machinery such as air conditioning and ventilation. By the end of his project, long before academic lawyers were concerned with the suitability of chosen research methods and the mechanics of data collection, Macaulay had assembled a very impressive sample for any qualitative study; he had contact with 68 lawyers and business executives from 43 manufacturing firms and six law firms.

The size of the sample that Macaulay drew upon for this is large by contemporary standards where saturation point is deemed by researchers to have been reached much earlier. Examples of empirical work in Law in Action contract scholarship that have involved much smaller samples are Teichman's fascinating study of currency preferences in the Israeli property market where 18 interviews were conducted (Teichman 2010) and Gulati and Scott's rich and detailed study of the *pari passu* provision in cross-border financial contracts (Gulati and Scott 2012). In some qualitative studies the specifics of sample size and research participant cohort identity are not deemed necessary to mention (see for example Ben-Shahar and White's study of the contractual relationships between car part suppliers and car assembly manufacturers, Ben-Shahar and White 2005). Concerns about the scale and quality of the data Macaulay obtained for his 1963 study still concerned him some 45 years later (Halliday and Schmidt 2009: 18). His continuing angst on this point may reflect a concern that his work was in danger of being taken as both too representative of a pervasive non-use of contract which he was not and never has suggested (cf Gilmore 1995: 1) and not representative enough in that it did not cover every industry and every contractual situation and therefore did not offer an adequate description of business practice. It is also the case, as Macaulay himself attests to (Halliday and Schmidt 2009: 24), that he was not versed in social science methodology in the way that a scholar of his standing conducting Law in Action research today would be. Hence the search for replication post finding a 'precedent' is likely to have trumped the search for saturation both when he conducted his interviews and reflected upon them later. As section 3 indicates technology has created the ability to construct much larger qualitative data sets.

The manufacturing firms in Macaulay's sample were some of the largest in the US at the time – General Electric and Harley Davidson, for example. That these actors should have a manufacturing or production facility in the American Midwest takes us back to an era pre-globalization. The business world is a much bigger place and far more technically complex than it was in 1963. The relationships that Macaulay found and reported upon are rather unlikely to be found there now. Many business relationships take place across national boundaries, and computer-generated automatic re-ordering procedures have replaced many personal dealings. However, just as doctrinal contract evolves new practices to deal with changing behaviors – an example would be the emergence in common law of pre-legislative intervention judicial rules of construction such as *contra proferentem* and fundamental breach for exclusion clauses – it is possible for new forms of business relationship to emerge in the contractual space to replace both industries and practices that have been changed by technology and the availability of lower cost labor and lower environmental standards elsewhere. Some 30 years after Macaulay's study Esser was able to find that there was still manufacturing activity occurring in Wisconsin in the three principle sectors that Macaulay had generated his data from: paper processing, farm machinery and engineered construction materials. What he found in terms of contractual relationships was that the demands of flexible production (as opposed to what he termed 'job shop' production) characterized by the supply of specialized products produced at short notice from constantly retooled manufacturing process resulted in the creation of long-term exclusive supply contracts called 'partnerships'. These partnerships abandon any notion of the adversarial in their construction and execution. They are founded on cooperation and feature information sharing between contractual partners on costs and pricing (Esser 1996).

As Macaulay recognized, his findings in this study were culturally contingent on the setting he was studying (Macaulay 1991: 188). However, much of doctrinal contract law is culturally and/or contextually contingent in a variety of ways. If we take contract law as a conceptual system Feinman offers a reading of it that tracks its development through a series of phases that reflect the prevailing cultural norms of the time. In simple terms, according to Feinman, in the eighteenth century liability in contract was not triggered by agreement and promissory liability but by conferral of benefit or detrimental reliance. This reflected the dominance of established social orders and social ties. In the nineteenth century these orders were being challenged by values of self-help and individual advancement through endeavor and thus we see the rise of consent and imposition of liability through contract, only where rights had been created by the parties' agreement (Feinman 1983). The accommodation of contextual factors within contract doctrines can be illustrated by the division of express terms into conditions, warranties and innominate terms. Innominate terms create the space to examine the context of the contract and the breach that is alleged to give rise to the right to terminate. For the contract law student the cultural settings of Law in Action scholarship and the contexts it reveals become the world behind contract law's broad general principles; only some understanding of culture and context enables critical appraisal of the results of litigated disputes (Macaulay 2000).

Macaulay's findings were that his sample of manufacturers attempted to plan exchanges completely. Written contracts took the form of standardized documents which were only very rarely used subsequently to adjust or enforce exchanges; adjustment or enforcement took place informally with legal sanctions being resorted to only after careful consideration of the possible undesirable consequences of such a course of action. Using law to achieve a remedy risked turning a cooperative relationship into an adversarial one where performance would occur only according to the terms of the contract strictly construed. Using law was not about appealing to the court as arbiter for a 'just' solution to a problem or for a vindication of a position taken. It was a maneuvre taken for tactical reasons when other options had been exhausted and the risks to relationships had been assessed. The presence of 'non-contractual relations' allowed disputes to be avoided as the importance of maintaining these relations acted as an enforcement mechanism. What these findings tell an undergraduate law student is that the planning of exchanges in a free market society is not anchored into social life simply by the possibility of resort to state supported sanctions. Social norms or non-contractual relations are required.

These non-contractual relations were based around ideas of good faith in business, such as industry-wide customs, past dealings and personal relations between actors in different organizations, and ideas of trust, reciprocity and reputation, both personal and professional. The focus was on ensuring that business continued between the parties to the exchange. In particular two behavioral norms were identified as being more important than the rational planning of an exchange: being seen as having and supporting a good product; and not 'welching' on a deal. Formal instruments of contract were of more assistance in explaining detailed product specifications and requirements within the firm than in securing inter-firm exchanges. By 1985, based upon his own further work and the work of others, Macaulay had added power, dependence and exploitation as further relationship dynamics. These were introduced as recognition that parties in a business relationship did not necessarily remain in it through active choice. They may have few alternative trading partners, they may have expended too much in material terms in the course of the relationship to remove themselves from it, or they may be too economically weak to secure a superior alternative partner (Macaulay 1985).

Macaulay is not offering an alternative theory of contract in opposition to doctrinal contract law or suggesting that doctrine should be abandoned. He rejects both of these propositions (Macaulay 2003). Instead his points were ones of scale and significance. Both of these are central to contract pedagogy. Doctrinal contract law matters, he tells us, but not in the way that we think it matters. Contract law along with most legal scholarship makes assumptions about the way the world is structured; *inter alia* laws (in the broadest sense of that word) have a natural coherence and consequently a system, the rules embodied in the system reflect normative positions in society, and courts are central to the working of the legal system (Galanter 1975). Only Law in Action scholarship can tell us whether the assumptions made are valid. What it has consistently told us is that the problems doctrinal contract law seeks to solve are empirically insignificant. For Macaulay formal contract focuses on a small subset of contract disputes adjudicated upon by courts where drafting, legislative intervention or technological change would deal with adverse or unforeseen consequences in a time frame of less than two decades (Macaulay 2004, 2006).

Macaulay saw himself as explaining, informed by empirical research, that formal contract law was not as conclusive of contractual relationships as academic lawyers thought it was. It forms only part of the relationship between most contracting parties. Only for a small segment of contracts – one-off events between parties who had no intention of dealing with each other again (what Macneil would later describe as discrete contracts; Macneil 1973) – was contract law painting an accurate picture (Macaulay 1977; Gordon 1985: 569). The question of why some transactions are more formal than others in terms of the contract entered into is not one that Macaulay seeks to answer. The norms that are revealed by Macaulay are ones which tell us about the character of the individuals involved and the relationships between them. They tell us very little about the nature of the transactions these individuals are undertaking or about the wider social norms that underpin the society in which their interactions take place. Observations of this nature are the province of relational contract, and this difference of conceptual scaling between the two approaches is one of the key things that separate them as philosophical approaches.

Section 2: following Macaulay

Beale and Dugdale in their study of engineering firms in the UK expressly link their findings to Macaulay's 1963a findings. They see themselves as asking more detailed questions about contract formation and the use of contractual remedies in disputes around payment, delay and defects. They find that there is an appreciation of risk built into decisions about whether to use contract as a planning device; contracts seen as high risk in terms of loss if something goes wrong receive a higher degree of attention in the planning stage than those that are seen to be low risk. The counterbalance to planning is the need to maintain flexibility (seen as essential to facilitating businesses exchanges) and the cost of detailed planning. The reputation of proposed contract partners was taken into account in deciding to do business with them, and there was, as Macaulay found, a resort to a range of self-help mechanisms should things go wrong. Only if a relationship was at the end and litigation was relatively inexpensive would there be a use of legal sanctions through a court; debt recovery and payment disputes were two examples of this (Beale and Dugdale 1975).

The key difference between the Beale and Dugdale study and Macaulay's study is their starting places. Macaulay sets out to discover how exchanges are planned, what facilitates them and what does not. Beale and Dugdale begin their inquiry with lawyerly conceptions of contract formation and the contract remedial structure. They are, thus, always reasoning back from preordained categories and setting their observations against them. Social and economic life is being filtered through the prism of law (Cotterrell 1984: 37). This militates against this type of empirical study being able to offer any suggestions for constructing alternative categories to the ones that lawyers use to describe exchanges. Beale and Dugdale's closing statement to their article is to the effect that despite their findings (and presumably those of Macaulay) they believe contract law will continue to be taught in terms of doctrine because of its huge value as an exercise in common law reasoning. The doctrinal structures of contract law may well lend themselves to facilitating an exegesis of common law reasoning, but it is disingenuous to think that they are presented in this way. They are presented to students as the structure that parties use when they conduct exchanges, as the knowledge that is required to plan and execute transactions. The reality is that they are a small part of a much bigger and more complicated picture.

Arrighetti *et al* (1997) in their cross-country study (UK, Italy and Germany) of kitchen unit manufacturers and mining machinery manufacturers report significant jurisdictional differences in terms of the type of risks covered in contracts and the level of detail contained in contracts. The most highly specified contracts were found in Germany. This finding is supported by empirical work done on software development contracts (Dietz 2012). The least specified contracts were found in Italy with the UK forming a middle ground. As the authors explain there are significant differences between the UK's common law contract doctrine and the civil law contract doctrine of Italy and Germany. These differences place the UK as a relative outlier when compared with the broad similarities of civil law systems. However, these differences do not translate in the way we might expect them to in relation to contract design. This suggests that there are other cultural and social norms which underpin contract design. The differences in underpinning legal structure notwithstanding, Arrighetti *et al* found considerable trust in contract doctrine and parties agreed contracts were providing a foundation for shared expectations of acceptable behavior within the contracting relationship across all three jurisdictions. Their study provides greater specificity to Macaulay's findings; written contract terms were important in the event of dispute where going to court for a resolution was a last resort option. They did not find that there was increased willingness to use the courts for dispute resolution; on the contrary the presence of a detailed written contract indicated a reluctance to use that forum. Informal agreements and loose understandings were regularly used to build on these formal agreements.

Bernstein's work on particular commodity markets (grain, diamonds and cotton) and on original equipment manufacturers (OEMs) in the American Midwest allows us to expand the field of knowledge that we have about the place of contract in exchange relationships between commercial actors. I use the term 'actors' because whilst some of the parties whose behavior Bernstein studies are incorporated businesses, others are individual traders or partnerships. In the first three studies Bernstein is examining extra-legal contractual arrangements made between actors in the shadow not just of the availability of legally enforceable contracts but also their own well-established and formalized industry-based dispute resolution mechanisms. The relationships formed between commercial actors in these four studies show that a conscious choice is made to leave large parts of the business relationship to be governed by extra-legal commitments and sanctions. In economic terms the actors do not prefer extra-legal agreements because the transaction costs of negotiating and then drafting legally enforceable agreements are too high. Extra-legal arrangements also have transaction costs, the principle one of which is acquiring sufficient information to determine the trustworthiness of the other party (Bernstein 1992: 132, 133). Thus their rejection of confining their arrangements to just those that are contained in legally enforceable agreements must be founded in social norms. OEMs use very detailed Master Supply Agreements, but the actors do not see them as contracts that will establish a platform for claiming expectation damages in the event of non-performance. Rather they are a narrative account of how the parties intend to do business without resort to formal legal process (Bernstein 2015: 577f).

Information goes to the route of establishing what is pushed into the formal contracting regime and what remains at the extra-legal level. Any aspect of the relationship that depends on observable information remains at the extra-legal level; only if information is both observable and verifiable to a third party does it move to the legally defined relationship between the parties (Bernstein 1996: 1719). Trustworthiness, derived from reputation, is also key to deciding at what level within the relationship commitments and sanctions sit; the legal relationship includes provisions that will provide the best result if the contracting partner turns out to be untrustworthy and extra-legal commitments are made that will become self-enforcing agreements if the contracting partner is trustworthy (Bernstein 2015). Reputation is largely forged through behavior reinforced by community ties, geographical proximity and repeated dealing, all of which are present in the commodity markets that Bernstein examines. However, the absence of these factors will not necessarily indicate that a reputation bond between the parties cannot be forged (Charny 1990) as technology and the informational activities of bodies such as trade associations can replicate the familiarity produced in these spheres. In the cotton industry the best reputation to have as a contracting party is as a flexible business partner who can deal positively and quickly with unexpected circumstances, keeps their word, is open to renegotiation if necessary, pays debts on time and does not 'lay down on the contract' (Bernstein 2001: 1749). Any departure by a contracting party from the word as their bond approach creates unwelcome uncertainty in the relationship. Contracting parties are working towards performance of their agreement rather than a breach and pay scenario, even being prepared to take a loss on a transaction or split the difference in circumstances where they feel sure that their contracting partner would do the same in future transactions (Bernstein 1996: 1798; Bernstein 2001: 1756). The availability of expectation damages as the ultimate reward for using the formal legal process is not sufficient to move the parties outside this cooperation matrix.

The activities described above that build reputation are labeled by Bernstein as 'relationship preserving norms' (RPNs). These norms she splits into two groups; 'performance norms' and 'dispute resolution norms'. Performance norms capture the extra-legal relationship between the parties which they have agreed to remain in as long as they continue to trust each other and wish to enter into repeat transactions. Dispute resolution norms are the processes that commercial actors follow to resolve disputes when notwithstanding the current hiatus in their trading relationship they wish to deal with the other party again. RPNs will often be very different from the ones that are contained in the legally enforceable contractual agreement between the parties because the terms there will reflect, according to Bernstein, the norms that the parties would want a neutral third party adjudicator of their dispute to apply. RPNs may also reflect obligations that parties are prepared to undertake in a flourishing relationship but do not wish to promise to do in a relationship that has floundered. If the parties reach the stage of third party adjudication then they have gone past the point at which RPNs are relevant; their relationship needs radical attention and the relevant norms are 'end-game norms' (EGNs) (Bernstein 1996: 1796, 1797). The use of ENGs occurs in two instances: first, fairly obviously, where the events that have occurred mean that the parties will not deal with each other again and second, a more tactical usage to make it clear to the party allegedly in breach of the agreement that, whilst the long-term relationship between them was not in danger, the other contracting party saw the use of ENGs as a credible threat to secure cooperation. Many of Macaulay's findings (Macaulay 1963a) can be seen through the prism of RPNs and EGNs. For example, the equipment purchasers he interviewed expected to be able to cancel orders and pay the sellers only their out-of-pocket expenses, contracting parties regularly negotiated their way around events that the terms of the legally binding contract would classify as breach (both RPNs), and only when the demands of one of the contracting parties were deemed to be unreasonable were the terms of the formal contract invoked (an EGN) (Bernstein 1996: 1800).

Bernstein and Macaulay give us rather different answers to the question of why contractual disputes are not litigated or at least Bernstein's answer is more complicated and multi-layered. For Macaulay it is about avoiding using an EGN in a situation where an RPN is more appropriate. For Bernstein all of the contracting practices she examines take place in markets where there is a stage between the deployment of EGNs and the intervention of legal processes: voluntary industry-based arbitration. This system of private ordering is preferred as a dispute resolution to formal legal processes in the three commodity markets she studies. There are several reasons for this preference that all center around a dislike of open textured standards and a preference for the formalism of the private ordering approach that commercial actors know from both their experience and from the relevant rules of each industry body that will be applied (Mitchell 2013). As there is little ground conceded to discretion or to an interpretative approach there is certainty and predictability for the parties in the event of a dispute. The process is streamlined and cost effective because parties know exactly what information will be required by the arbitration system rather than needing to produce information, if that information is even available, from which an award of expectation damages can be calculated (Masten and Snyder 1993). The absence of expectation damages from the arbitration's sanction system means that much of the business model of the contracting party can remain secret (Bernstein 2001: 1740–1744, 1757).

We can extrapolate from Bernstein's observations about the positive way in which commercial actors embrace industry-based arbitration rather than formal legal processes that there is more discomfort with legal processes for them than simply the selection of an EGN when an RPN would be better. This discomfort seems to stem not just from the damages award point above but also to a more general disquiet about the status of *certainty of interpretation* of contract terms in their context. Bernstein's commercial actors wanted flexibility from each other to make their relationships work (RPNs) but required certainty from the judicial process. They were thinking about formal legal processes taking place within the framework of the UCC (see in particular UCC 1–103, 1–303, 2–202 and 2–204). The UK equivalent to this might be the approach of the courts to assessing the context of an agreement. Courts increasingly see this as part of their role. However, their struggles to accommodate concepts such as good faith and their interpretative strategies of context and terms in cases like *Interfoto Picture Library v Stiletto Visual Programmes Ltd* [1989] QB 433 and *Shell UK v Lostock Garages Ltd* [1976] 1 WLR 1187 do not inspire confidence that the predictable outcome (one that is strictly doctrine based) commercial actors want will be achieved (Mitchell 2007: 54–57; Collins 2014).

What we can take from Bernstein's work on the grain, diamond and cotton markets and her work on contract networks together with that of Arrighetiti *et al* for teaching purposes is that students need to think about contracting problems from the perspective of the contracting parties as they structure their relationships and execute their obligations rather than identifying the relevant piece of doctrine that might address a difficulty that one of the parties has encountered and working backwards from that. They need to understand agreements between commercial actors as being spread across levels; the formal legally binding agreement sits at a level above the day to day agreement that sees the parties act flexibly towards each other being prepared to sacrifice their profit margin if that allows their relationship to be preserved. Parties operating in a commercial context consider legal action only when a relationship-ending event occurs, not when a 'mere breach of contract occurs' (Bernstein 2015: 570). Bernstein's work introduces students to network dynamics which can be seen as adding a conceptual layer to Macaulay's account of the informal relationships between contracting parties. The idea of networks takes them beyond seeing transactions as dealings between individuals and encourages them to think instead of a web of connections between firms in which social capital is built based upon prior transactions. This allows firms in the network to price transactions with other network members based on their reputation across the network. Loss of reputation with one network member has the potential to ripple out into reputational loss across the whole network (Bernstein 2015: 599).

Problem questions that push students to think about RPNs before they consider EGNs enable them to go a long way beyond seeing contract as a vehicle for the honing of common law reasoning skills. Law in Action-based accounts of contracting practice introduce students to the complexities of commercial life; the documents supporting transactions stand in a hierarchical relationship with each other and contracts for supply might include detailed requirements around labor employment conditions, environmental provenance of components and the footprint of production conditions, and the drafting of repair and maintenance handbooks (Bernstein 2015: 568). Drafting exercises that encourage students to think through and map out the importance of document structure and document relationships together with ideas of market structure and buyers' and sellers' past, present and future relationships add transferable skills such as commercial awareness and negotiation possibilities to doctrinal knowledge and analysis.

Section 3: beyond business relationships

In this section I move from thinking about the role of contract in business-to-business relationships and considering why it might be used in a rather different way for planning exchanges from that understood by the doctrinal model of contract. Here the focus is on the behavior of less sophisticated actors in a contract situation. The Law in Action studies examined consider the contents of contracts from a consumer perspective and consumer perspectives about what they understand contract to be as a phenomena. By this I mean whether consumers actually read contractual terms and understand them as defining and/or restricting their rights and whether contract as a structure is seen as a legal artifact or as a moral obligation. These are issues that relate to fundamental assumptions that the doctrinal model of contract makes about both the philosophy of contract and how and why interventions from both the courts and the legislature to control the use of particular terms and restrictions of liability are seen as necessary.

Increasingly goods and services are offered to consumers on the basis of a standard form contract or a contract of adhesion (Ben-Shahar 2007). In some instances these contracts are so adhesive that buyers only see the terms after they have concluded their purchase (Radin 2014). Contracting in this way is considered to be efficient for both parties in terms of lowering transaction costs around drafting and negotiation between buyer and seller; the creation of bespoke contractual arrangements or individually dickered terms creates additional costs which may seem unnecessary for mass produced goods and services. However, the absence of individual negotiation might encourage sellers to offer contractual terms that disadvantage the buyer. Protection for consumers from unfair and unclear terms contained with these contracts is achieved by legislation such as the Consumer Rights Act 2015, itself an amalgamation of legislative intervention dating back to 1977. Prior to that protection was provided by the courts through the use of interpretative and construction devices. The system of standard form contracting sits uneasily with the ideal of freedom of contract in exchange that the doctrinal model lauds such that Eigen describes such contracting as 'zombie contracts'; they take the shape of contract, they are assumed to be contract, but they 'live by consuming contract's soul' (Leib and Eigen 2017).

Radin for example suggests, from the perspective of the consumer, that what she terms 'massively distributed boilerplate' contract terms cannot stand with at least one of the key principles of contract; that the parties to a contract can be said to have reached a *consensus ad idem*. In particular it is not possible to conclude that each consumer who has 'clicked' to purchase goods or services whilst shopping online has read and consented to the unalterable terms that have been presented to them (Radin 2017: 12, 16, 17). Consent in this context is a largely illusory concept. Radin, it should be noted, is formulating her position from within US contract law which has only the tool of unconscionability to deal with unfair and unclear terms in consumer contracts, unlike the UK system which has a comprehensive legislative structure derived in part from EU directives (Radin 2014: 216). From the opposite perspective held by those who see regulatory intervention to police terms as an erosion of freedom of contract there is an argument that protection for all consumers occurs through the role of the *informed minority* of consumers. This is a group of consumers that reads and understands the terms of the standard form contract and is sufficiently sophisticated to reject poor quality terms. This group of buyers is supposed to be numerically significant enough to persuade sellers not to offer poor quality terms (Schwartz and Wilde 1979). Sellers will not discriminate between informed and uninformed consumers and so will offer enhanced terms to all purchasers. The risk of losing the informed group as purchasers outweighs the benefit of offering poor terms to the uninformed group (Baird 2006).

A series of Law in Action studies addresses both these positions. They try to answer the question of whether consumers do read standard form contracts and if they do whether they do so in sufficient numbers to provide an informed group the existence of which would lead to the softening of pro-seller terms. They also examine whether standard form contracts are routinely offered as pro-seller agreements. Bakos and his colleagues examined the click stream data of 48,000 visitors to the websites of 90 software retailers over a period of month. Software retailing was chosen as the research site because non-price terms around use restrictions for example were thought to be of interest to purchasers and locating these goods on the internet and comparing their terms of sale is relatively straightforward. If consumers read terms or if an informed minority that reads terms exists, both of those things are likely to be confirmed by studying the browsing habits of software buyers (Bakos *et al* 2014). The results of this quantitative study were that only one or two buyers in 1000 spent longer than one second on the end user license agreement (EULA) page. This means that consumers in general do not access or read contract terms and that an informed minority sufficient to persuade sellers to offer more pro-buyer terms does not exist.

This study is the first observational rather than self-reporting study done of how consumers behave when faced with detailed contract terms in an apparently non-negotiable standard form contract situation. The obvious question that follows on from the revelations that the overwhelming majority of consumer purchasers do not so much as glance at, never mind read, contract terms and that it is likely there is no informed minority of consumers is does this mean that sellers of goods and services in the consumer market offer standard form contracts with terms that are heavily biased in their favor. A study conducted by Marotta-Wurgler supplies the answer to this question and so fills in another piece of the empirical picture about the reality of contracting outside the business space (Marotta-Wurgler 2007). She examined the terms contained in 647 EULA she obtained from the sellers of software. She identified 23 common terms across the EULAs and used a bias indexing methodology to score the terms against the standard provided in UCC Art 2. Any term that was enhanced for the buyer above the set standard received a score of 1, any term that favored the seller over the standard received a score of -1 and terms that mirrored the Art 2 standard received a score of zero. She was therefore able to determine the distance towards favoring buyer or seller that any of the EULAs had moved from the default Art 2 standard. She found that EULAs were more pro-seller than pro-buyer with an average of five terms worse than the Art 2 default position would be. There was also some considerable variation in EULAs around what Marotta-Wurgler identified as core terms for inclusion. This indicates that standard form contracts are not uniform or almost uniform. The most pro-buyer contracts are harder to locate on the seller's website, requiring a higher number of clicks to access them. The conclusion that we can draw is that software package sellers were not hiding one-sided pro-seller contracts behind relative inaccessibility.

Marotta-Wurgler's study is based in US law and obviously, like Radin's observation above, the UK position of black list and grey list terms contained within the Consumer Rights Act 2015 gives a very different control structure. However, what Marotta-Wurgler is offering is not a normative critique of the UCC Art 2 position but an empirically grounded series of observations about the drafting preferences of sellers in the consumer market. We know that even in the absence of an informed minority of consumers, standard form contracts are neither uniform in shape nor resolutely pro-seller. Students might like to think about whether sellers see a potential future reputational risk in drafting aggressively biased contract terms that are subsequently exposed. Consumers for their part may be more sophisticated than we might think and see not reading terms as entirely rational behavior as they know or expect their position to be protected by legislation. Their consent to the terms is malleable, as they enter contracts not expecting the limitations of seller liability and the restrictions imposed on them to be upheld (Eigen 2008).

The methodology that Marotta-Wurgler used is replicable by students; close reading and a bias index could be used to examine mobile phone contracts or insurance contracts, for example. Students would be able to map terms across different providers and perhaps identify how and to what extent the Consumer Rights Act 2015 has penetrated 'stored boilerplate' (Radin 2017: 9; Gulati and Scott 2012). An examination of this sort would make it clear that the doctrinal picture of contract, as Macaulay pointed out, applies to very few scenarios. Students will come to a clear understanding that contracts, rather than being freely negotiated arrangements that allocate risk in accordance with the parties' preferences, in fact involve the imposition of terms by the superior (in terms of market experience and economic power) party. It is a matter of debate whether consumers realize this power imbalance and feel unable to affect change, or think that alternative sellers will offer similar terms or consider that they will be protected from unfair or unclear terms in any event (Wilkinson-Ryan 2014). What is clear is that doctrinal ideas of contract formation and the notice and incorporation of terms simply do not play the role that is ascribed to them in this situation. Consumers do not experience contract law in the way that the underlying assumptions of contract doctrine think they do.

Several Law in Action studies have continued the theme of how contract is experienced outside the world of business by exploring whether contract and particularly breach of contract, contrary to the doctrinal model, is seen by the general population as having a moral component stemming from the idea of promise and breach of promise. Wilkinson-Ryan and Baron elicited responses from 500 people, broadly demographically representative of the US adult population, to a series of questions around two scenarios. One scenario involved breaching a contract to refurbish a kitchen to avoid making a loss because the price of materials had increased dramatically and unexpectedly. The second scenario also involved breaching a contract for kitchen refurbishment but, rather than to avoid a loss, breach occurred for gain because the contractor found another more profitable source of work. In this instance of efficient breach there was no suggestion that the buyer would not be fully compensated. Invited to choose from a rising scale the level of damages they would award in each case, the respondent group chose to award higher damages in the efficient breach scenario. The group also, by a significant majority, wanted the contract to be fulfilled by performance and thought that there should be a legal obligation to do so. The respondent group sees a contractual promise as a promise to perform and not a promise to perform or alternatively do something as valuable as performance in monetary terms, i.e. pay expectation damages. Breaking a promise to achieve a gain but nevertheless providing compensation is seen as being more blameworthy than breaking a promise to avoid a loss (Wilkinson-Ryan and Baron 2009).

Missing from this study are some of the social norms that Macaulay and Bernstein would identify as relevant: reputation, previous dealings and a desire or not for a continuing business relationship. We have no idea whether the respondents would behave differently if they found themselves in a situation where RPNs were part of their consideration. It seems that EGNs were the factors under consideration. The idea that contract is a promise that creates a moral obligation to perform is explored further by Eigen (Eigen 2012). Eigen's study involved 1400 participants being asked to fill in a survey on the internet about work and employment. They were informed that they had entered a contractual relationship with the research team by agreeing to complete the survey for which they would receive a free but low value and commercially available DVD. The survey was deliberately designed to be cumbersome and lengthy such that participants would stop filling it before they reached the end. When this happened they received one of four randomly assigned messages that made an appeal to them to continue on to completion. The messages framed the appeal in a legal, moral, social or instrumental way. The moral appeal sounded in the language of promise and the importance of keeping one's word was most successful in inducing the respondents to answer further questions. Just like Wilkinson-Ryan and Baron's study, this lacks any of the contexts that might be present in a real contractual scenario. However, even its artificiality cannot detract from the feeling that for many what is binding about a contract is the moral force of promise rather than ideas of exchange and the possibility of relying on legal sanctions to secure performance or monetary compensation. This gives students an important insight into the continuing relevance of the position taken by Fried (Fried 2015) and reveals the exchange as bargain principle to be a position rather than the position.

Conclusion

Advocates for the Law in Action approach to contract present the absence of general principles that can be extracted from its studies as a key strength. This absence reflects the difference between the 'real deal' and the 'paper deal' and the messy reality of the lived experience of exchange (Macaulay 2003). The clear, bright lines and fundamental assumptions held up by the doctrinal structure of formal contract law are put into a perspective that makes clear that they describe accurately only a very small number of exchanges. Examining the contract scenarios that are the subject of Law in Action studies allows students to understand that different actors use contract in different ways. The reality of a contractual relationship between business parties is that it expands beyond the part of the transaction that formal legal processes will adjudicate on to capture a range of social norms. Some of these norms are specific to the trading history that exists between particular parties, while others are ones that exist across a broader network. Exchange interactions between consumers and businesses are rarely individualized, and the social norms that underpin those transactions are much less well mapped. On the side of businesses they may include some idea of reputation management and on the side of consumers ideas of the morality of keeping promises and general disinterest in the actual terms on which exchange is being affected.

References

Andrews, N., 2015. *Contract Law.* 2nd ed. Cambridge University Press, Cambridge.

Anson, W.R., Beatson, J., Burrows, A.S. and Cartwright, J., 2016. *Anson's Law of Contract.* 30th ed. Oxford University Press, Oxford.

Arrighetti, A., Bachmann, R. and Deakin, S., 1997. Contract Law, Social Norms and Inter-Firm Cooperation. *Cambridge J. L. Econ.*, 21, 171–195.

Baird, D., 2006. The Boilerplate Puzzle. *Mich. L. R.*, 104, 933–952.

Bakos, Y., Marotta-Wugler, F. and Trossen, D., 2014. Does Anyone Read the Fine Print? Consumer Attention to Standard-Form Contracts. *J. Legal Stud.*, 43, 1–36.

Beale, H. and Dugdale, T., 1975. Contracts Between Businessmen: Planning and the Use of Contractual Remedies'. *Brit. J. Law Soc.*, 2, 45–60.

Ben-Shahar, O., 2007. *Boilerplate: The Foundation of Market Contracts.* Cambridge University Press, New York.

Ben-Shahar, O. and White, J., 2005. Boilerplate and Economic Power in Auto Manufacturing Contracts. *Mich. L. R.*, 104, 953–981.

Bernstein, L., 1992. Opting Out of the Legal System: Extralegal Contractual Relations in the Diamond Industry. *J. Legal Stud.*, 21, 115–157.

Bernstein, L., 1996. Merchant Law in a Merchant Court: Rethinking the Code's Search for Immanent Business Norms. *U. Pa. L. Rev.*, 144, 1765–1821.

Bernstein, L., 1999. The Questionable Empirical Basis of Article 2's Incorporation Strategy: A Preliminary Study. *U. Ch. L. Rev.*, 66, 710–780.

Bernstein, L., 2001. Private Commercial Law in the Cotton Industry: Creating Cooperation Through Rules, Norms, and Institutions. *Mich. L. R.*, 99, 1724–1790.

Bernstein, L., 2014. Merchant Law in a Modern Economy. In Klass, G., Letsas, G. and Saprai, P., eds., *Philosophical Foundations of Contract Law.* Oxford University Press, Oxford, pp. 238–271.

Bernstein, L., 2015. Beyond Relational Contracts: Social Capital and Network Governance in Procurement Contracts. *J. Legal Anal.*, 7, 561–621.

Charny, D., 1990. Nonlegal Sanctions in Commercial Relationships. *Harv. L. Rev.*, 104, 373–467.

Collins, H., 2014. Implied Terms: The Foundation in Good Faith and Fair Dealing. *CLP*, 67, 297–331.

Cotterrell, R., 1984. *The Sociology of Law.* 1st ed. Butterworths, London.

Dietz, T., 2012. Contract Law, Relational Contracts and Reputational Networks in International Trade: An Empirical Investigation into Cross-Border Contracts in the Software Industry. *L. 7 Soc. Inq.*, 37, 25–57.

Eigen, Z., 2008. The Devil is in the Details: The Interrelationship Among Citizenship, Rule of Law and Form-Adhesive Contracts. *Conn. L. Rev.*, 41, 381–430.

Eigen, Z., 2012. When and Why Individuals Obey Contracts: Experimental Evidence of Consent, Compliance, Promise and Performance. *J. Legal Stud.*, 41, 67–94.

Esser, J., 1996. Institutionalising Industry: The Changing Forms of Contract. *L. Soc. Inq.*, 21, 593–630.

Feinman, J., 1983. Critical Approaches to Contract Law. *UCLA L. Rev.*, 30, 829–860.

Fried, C., 2015. Contract as Promise: A Theory of Contractual Obligation. Oxford University Press, New York.

Friedman, L.M. and Macaulay, S., 1967. Contract Law and Contract Teaching: Past, Present, and Future. *Wis. L. Rev.*, 805–821.

Furmston, M.P., Cheshire, G.C. and Fifoot, C.H.S., 2012. *Cheshire, Fifoot and Furmston's Law of Contract*. 16th ed. Oxford University Press, Oxford.

Galanter, M., 1975. Why the "Haves" Come Out Ahead: Speculations on the Limits of Legal Change. *Law & Soc'y Rev.*, 9, 95–160.

Gilmore, G., 1995. *The Death of Contract*. Ohio State University Press, Columbus.

Gilson, R., Sabel, C. and Scott, R., 2013. Contract and Innovation: The Limited Role of Generalist Courts in the Evolution of Novel Contractual Forms. *N.Y.U.L. Rev.*, 88, 170–215.

Gordon, R., 1985. Macaulay, Macneil and the Discovery of Solidarity and Power in Contract. *Wis. L. Rev.*, 565–579.

Gulati, M. and Scott, R., 2012. *The Three and a Half Minute Transaction*. University of Chicago Press, Chicago.

Halliday, S and Schmidt, P., 2009. *Conducting Law and Society Research*. Cambridge University Press, Cambridge.

Jacobs, J., 2005. ASR's Greatest Hits. *Am. Soc. Rev.*, 70, 1.

Leib, E. and Eigen, Z., 2017. Consumer Form Contracting in the Age of Mechanical Reproduction: The Unread and the Undead. *Illinois L. R.*, 65, 65–109.

Lyons, B. and Mehta, J., 1997. Private-Sector Business Contracts: The Text Between the Lines. In Deakin, S. and Michie, J., eds., *Contracts, Cooperation and Competition*. Oxford University Press, Oxford, pp. 43–66.

Macaulay, S., 1963a. Non-Contractual Relations in Business: A Preliminary Study. *Am. Soc. Rev.*, 28, 55–67.

Macaulay, S., 1963b. The Use and Non-Use of Contracts in the Manufacturing Industry. *Practical Lawyer*, 9, 13–40.

Macaulay, S., 1977. Elegant Models, Empirical Pictures and the Complexities of Contract. *Law Soc. Rev.*, 11, 507–528.

Macaulay, S., 1985. An Empirical View of Contract. *Wis. L. Rev.*, 465–482.

Macaulay, S., 1991. Long-Term Continuing Relations: The American Experience Regulating Dealerships and Franchises. In Joerges, C., ed., *Franchising and the Law: Theoretical and Comparative Approaches in Europe and the United States*. Nomos Verlagsgesellschaft mbH & Co. KG, Baden-Baden, Germany, pp. 179–237.

Macaulay, S., 2000. Relational Contracts Floating on a Sea of Custom: Thoughts About the Ideas of Ian Macneil and Lisa Bernstein. *N.W. U. L. REV.*, 94, 775–804.

Macaulay, S., 2003. The Real Deal and the Paper Deal: Empirical Pictures of Relationships, Complexity and the Urge for Transparent Simple Rules. *Mod. L. Rev.*, 66, 44–79.

Macaulay, S., 2004. Freedom from Contract: Solutions in Search of a Problem. *Wis. L. Rev.*, 777–820.

Macaulay, S., 2005. The New versus the Old Legal Realism: "Things Ain't What they Used to be". *Wis. L. Rev.*, 365–403.

Macaulay, S., 2006. Contracts, New Legal Realism, and Improving the Navigation of *The Yellow Submarine*. *Tul. L. Rev.*, 80, 1161–1196.

Macaulay, S., Braucher, J., Kidwell, J. and Whitford, W., 2010. *Contracts: Law in Action*. 3rd ed. LexisNexis, Australia.

Macaulay, S. and Whitford, W., 2015. The Development of *Contracts: Law in Action*. *Temp. L. Rev.*, 87, 793–806.

Macneil, I., 1973. The Many Futures of Contract. *S. Cal. L. Rev.*, 47, 691–816.

Masten, S. and Snyder, E., 1993. United States Versus United Shoe Machinery Corporation: On the Merits. *J L & Econ.*, 36, 33–70.

Mitchell, C., 2007. *Interpretation of Contracts*. Routledge Cavendish, London.

Mitchell, C., 2013. *Contract Law and Contract Practice*. Hart, Oxford.

Marotta-Wurgler, F., 2007. What's in a Standard Form Contract? An Empirical Analysis of Software License Agreements. *J. Empirical Legal Stud.*, 4, 677–713.

Radin, M., 2014. An Analytical Framework for Legal Evaluation of Boilerplate. In Klass, G., Letsas, G. and Saprai, P., eds., *Philosophical Foundations of Contract Law*. Oxford University Press, Oxford, pp. 215–237.

Radin, M., 2017. The Deformation of Contract in the Information Society. *Oxford J. Legal Stud.*, 37, 505–533.

Schwartz, A. and Wilde, L., 1979. Intervening in Markets on the Basis of Imperfect Information: A Legal and Economic Analysis. *U. Pa. L. Rev.*, 127, 630–682.

Shapiro, F., 1996. The Most-Cited Law Review Articles Revisited. *Chi. Kent L. Rev.*, 71, 751–780.

Stone, R. and Devenney, J., 2017. *The Modern Law of Contract*. 12th ed. Routledge, Abingdon.

Teichman, D., 2010. Old Habits are Hard to Change: A Case Study of Israeli Real Estate Contracts. *Law & Soc'y Rev.*, 44, 299–330.

Wilkinson-Ryan, T., 2014. A Psychological Account of Fine Print. *Iowa L. Rev.*, 99, 1745–1784.

Wilkinson-Ryan, T. and Baron, J., 2009. Moral Judgment and Moral Heuristics in Breach of Contract. *Journal of Empirical Legal Stud.*, 6, 405–423.

Woodward, W., 2001. Neoformalism in a Real World of Forms. *Wis. L. Rev.*, 971–1005.

Chapter 7

Students as consumers

Using student experiences to teach consumer contract law

Richard Hyde

Introduction

Whilst in the UK contract law may once have been seen as a unitary subject, with every contract governed by the same legal framework, this is no longer the case. The laws that governs business to business and business to consumer contracts are different, due to the intervention of both domestic (e.g. the Unfair Contract Terms Act 1977 as enacted provided greater protection for consumers compared to the protection afforded to business) and European law (see e.g. the Unfair Terms Directive, the Consumer Rights Directive and the Unfair Commercial Practices Directive). Different terms are implied, express terms are controlled more stringently, consumers may have the right to withdraw, and consumers are entitled to different remedies in the event of breach. In many ways, the consumer contract is a separate legal form. However, a consumer contract is something that every one of the students who has sat in our lecture theatres has been a party to. Therefore, it is something that can be used to enable students to understand contract law by considering their own interactions. Whilst the examples in this chapter are drawn from the authors teaching of UK and EU consumer contract law, the pedagogical lessons are wider.

This chapter considers pedagogic techniques that may be used in the consumer contract law sphere. First, it argues that students' own experiences as consumers can be harnessed and enhanced. By situating these experiences within the landscape of consumer contract law, students can understand their own behaviour in the context of consumer law and contract law, leading to awareness of the broad application of those laws. This chapter suggests that virtual learning environments can be harnessed to provide opportunities for situated learning. By using e-tivities students can engage with both their own experiences of consumer and contract law and with the experiences of others (Salmon 2002). E-tivities have the further advantage of being cheap, scalable and reusable (Salmon 2002: 3). As asynchronous learning tools they allow students to engage in their own time, supplementing synchronous taught sessions. Through this engagement students can better understand consumer contract law and contract law in general. Second, it considers the ways that "consumer protection" can be used as a lens through which classic contract law cases can be examined in order to better understand the protections afforded to consumers. Situating students in the position of the consumer in past contract law cases encourages reflection on the behaviour of the claimants framed within the law governing their situation and the developments in the law since the classic case was decided.

Teaching consumer contract law

In my teaching practice consumer contract law is covered in both the core Contract Law course, a first-year compulsory subject taken by over 300 students, and in the optional Consumer Law course, a final year option taken by around 80 students.

Consumer contract law is primarily covered in the latter course, with dedicated lecture slots covering the implied terms under the Consumer Rights Act 2015 regarding goods, services and digital content; the unfair terms provisions of the Consumer Rights Act (and the Unfair Terms Directive); and the civil liability provisions of the Consumer Protection from Unfair Trading Regulations 2008 (Part 4A). Remedies, including both general contractual remedies (such as termination for breach, damages and specific performance), which remain important in consumer contract cases, and the bespoke remedies in the Consumer Rights Act and the Consumer Protection from Unfair Trading Regulations 2008, are also considered. Other consumer contract issues, such as the right of cancellation in distance or online contracts, are covered throughout the course. One tutorial focuses on the substantive law surrounding consumer contracts; the consideration of the other issues raised pervades other tutorials, particularly when issues of consumer redress are discussed.

In the contract law course, doctrines of contract law relevant to consumer contracts and cases involving consumers are frequently discussed. This is particularly the case in topics such as offer and acceptance, consideration, implication of terms, misrepresentation and remedies. Unfair terms teaching focuses on the amended Unfair Contract Terms Act 1977 but considers the meaning of a consumer contract and the different types of contract covered by the UCTA and the Consumer Rights Act. Whilst the UK is closer to a consumer contract code than it has been in the past, the common law of contract provides an important background for consumer contract issues, from determining whether a contract exists to determining whether a contract has come to an end.

Contract law, taught as a compulsory module, often appears to students to be divorced from the reality of their contractual experiences. Very few students will have experienced the types of incidents that underpin many of the contract cases that they study, such as entering into a charterparty, or a complex commercial agreement of the type that appears in many of the remedies cases. However, unlike many of the other subjects they study, students will have lived experience of the formation of a contract (for example with the University or a student finance provider, in shops, in restaurants) and, in many cases, will have experienced a breach of contract, for example by purchasing something which has been delivered late or not at all. This experience can be usefully harnessed in teaching. When I ask my consumer law students about their experiences of breach, almost all of them have purchased goods which have failed to conform to the description, were not fit for purpose or were not of satisfactory quality. I can explore with them what they did and utilise this lived experience to illustrate the range of responses to breach and the remedies that are available.

However, using students shared experiences in face-to-face sessions can be somewhat ad hoc, dependent on the consumer issues experienced by the students in the class. Therefore, it is necessary to develop a mechanism to harness the experience of students as consumers and utilise them in a more systematic and structured manner. To do this, I have turned to situated learning, as outlined in the next section.

Situated learning and consumer contract law

Situated learning seeks to enable students to learn through "participation in the sociocultural practices of a community" (Lave and Wenger 1991: 29). Situated learning involves more than "learning by doing" (Lave and Wenger 1991: 29). It involves learning as an "integral and inseparable" part of practice, and practice as an important part of learning (Lave and Wenger 1991: 29). By using situated learning techniques as part of my consumer law teaching, the students engage with the academic learning of consumer law through their practice as consumers, and they come to appreciate how consumer contract law is constructed and performed by their activities in procuring goods and services, and dealing with issues that arise within these contractual relationships.

The classic example of situated learning is an apprenticeship, where an apprentice is taught how to engage in a trade or profession through their participation in that trade. Apprenticeship in this context should not be viewed narrowly (Lave and Wenger 1991: chapter 3). The traditional apprenticeships of, for example, carpenters or plumbers share clear similarities with training pathways for doctors, solicitors or accountants. However, the apprenticeship concept should not be limited to learning specifically for employment. All learning through experience involves a period of 'apprenticeship.' Therefore, the model can be usefully adapted to learning in the consumer contract law space.

All citizens undergo an 'apprenticeship' in being a consumer, learning how to act in the marketplace. During early life, children undergo a socialisation process that results in them becoming consumers (Ekstrom 2010: 43–46). As they become fully fledged consumers they gain "mastery of knowledge and skill" that enables full participation in the sociocultural practices of the consumer marketplace (Lave and Wenger 1991: 29). This process is likely to be ongoing during students undergraduate studies, as students engage with, for example, consumer credit contracts for the first time (Warwick and Mansfield 2000;

House of Commons 2017) and become more independent as consumers, away from the influence (and market knowledge) of their parents or guardians. Part of this apprenticeship is developing an awareness of consumer rights, and contractual rights in particular. Consumers learn about these rights by acting in the marketplace. This apprenticeship can be harnessed and strengthened through situated learning during a consumer or contract law course. By engaging students with their own situation as consumers, their ability to handle consumer law problems that affect them or others is increased.

To ensure that the situated learning through which individuals become consumers supports student learning in consumer contract law it is necessary to ensure that the experience is tied to exposition of the relevant legal principles. To rely on situated experiences may be enough to ensure that consumers begin to practice their consumer behaviour in the light of the norms that govern relations between consumers and traders, but for students of consumer law it is necessary to engage fully with the 'why' question – 'why can I do this' or 'why can I not do this.' Further, to achieve a higher level learning outcome, including critical analysis of the existing legal regime and suggestions for changes to law and policy, it is necessary to encourage engagement not just with the students' own experiences but also with the experiences of others. Therefore, the situated learning must offer the opportunity to explore varied experiences of consumer behaviour, and to analyse and critique them. To achieve this, the potential of e-tivities can be harnessed.

Enabling situated learning through blended learning e-tivities

In this model e-tivities are small, discrete activities that a student undertakes within a virtual learning environment ('VLE'). Through a suite of e-tivities a participant familiarises themselves with the e-tivity process; socialises as a participant in the module and as a consumer; exchanges knowledge about their consumer contract experiences; constructs knowledge and skills about the consumer contracts that they are involved in; and (alongside and following the e-tivity, and indeed the module) applies and develops these skills as a consumer (Salmon 2002: 11). Each e-tivity involves an invitation, that is a single message sent by an e-moderator to all participants in the activity which contains (1) all the instructions necessary for the participating students to complete the activity (explaining the purpose of the activity; the task they must undertake; the response that they should make to others; and the outcome to be achieved) and (2) a 'spark,' which stimulates or starts the interactive activity (Salmon 2002: 116). The spark may be the legal content covered in the e-tivity (for example it could be a statute or a judgment), but need not be, particularly where the e-tivity is used alongside the face-to-face teaching. As will be seen below, the author prefers to use photographs or videos to spark an activity. E-tivities can enable a more personalised and participative learning experience, which works well when the goal of the teaching is to utilise a student's experience to encourage participation in consumer society. E-tivities are therefore well suited to situated learning, as participants create their "own internal representations of knowledge, linking it directly to personal experience" (Salmon 2002: 29). Of course, e-tivities are not a necessary component of situated learning; such learning is possible through many different teaching mechanisms: synchronous or asynchronous, face-to-face or distance.

As will be discussed in this chapter, e-tivities are used as part of a blended learning strategy and are not substitutes for teaching sessions (the role of such sessions is discussed below). The face-to-face portion of the course is briefly described above. Of course, e-tivities can function well as a method of encouraging interaction in online learning or as part of a Massive Open Online Course ('MOOC') (Lee and Rofe 2016), and the five-stage model can be adopted to any form of teaching. To operate an e-tivity, a VLE is required to enable the asynchronous interaction between all participants in a module. Using a VLE which is familiar to students is the best technological platform for facilitating an e-tivity. The author has used both Blackboard and Moodle, but similar functionalities exist in other VLE products. As Salmon notes, quick and easy access to the online platform is important to enable full participation in the e-tivity, and familiarity with the software facilitates this (Salmon 2002: 12). A discussion board, a forum or perhaps a wiki is the most appropriate. However, as students may not be familiar with the exact functionalities of the VLE that are to be used, they may require some familiarisation with these functions. Therefore the first invitation should explain the process of, for example, posting on a discussion board. Other technological models can be adopted if a VLE is not available or does not have appropriate functionality. For example, a twitter hashtag may be used to allow students to post about consumer law experiences. However, the risk of using such technology is that the e-tivity is less controlled and is more open to the public, who could read student experiences or even get involved themselves. Whilst this may have benefits from a public engagement perspective, it should be balanced against the risk that contributions may be less controllable and students less willing to contribute.

Whichever technology is chosen, it must be possible for students to post their experiences for all other students to see and for students to respond to those posts. Moderation must be possible, both to ensure that the responses are relevant and appropriate, and to ensure that the responses to students' posts are engaging with the shared experiences in an appropriate manner. Moderation should allow posts to be edited or removed if necessary. However, the author has not found this necessary. A VLE may allow a number of conditions to be imposed on the use of these mechanisms. For example, it may be possible to require that students post before they can see the other posts on the forum, or it may be possible to limit the number of threads that a student can start on any forum. These mechanisms are not essential and may inhibit the freedom to engage in discussion, meaning that they should be used with care.

Other than the technological issues, the most important thing in ensuring successful participation, and therefore successful situated learning, is equipping the participants with the social and emotional willingness to engage in the e-tivity. Students are sometimes unwilling to contribute their experiences, during the discussion, perhaps due to a reticence to share personal experiences with fellow students. It is necessary to explain why the participants will benefit from the activity. This should be done both in the VLE and during face-to-face taught sessions, explaining to participants "why they are learning [and] why in this way" (Salmon 2002: 16). Care should be taken if engaging in summative assessment of participation in these e-tivities, particularly before an online community has been built, as summative assessment may have the effect of inhibiting free participation.

Further, when using e-tivities some effort should be devoted to building an online community which is a safe space for students to share their experiences, and equipping students with the soft skills that enable them to do so. Building trust between the participants is essential (Salmon 2002: 20). In the blended learning approach, such trust can be built both online and offline, but it is essential that it is not assumed that offline interaction is enough to ensure online trust and socialisation. Therefore, to achieve the situated learning that is the goal of this chapter, it is necessary to use e-tivities to create an environment where students are familiarised with the process of an e-tivity and socialised into the e-tivity community.

Technological possibilities to encourage socialisation must be considered, and it should be considered whether particular technologies can lead to better participation. It has been occasionally suggested that sharing may be encouraged, if the technology allows, through enabling anonymous posting. Possibilities for anonymity depend on the VLE. Some do not enable anonymous posting; in others anonymous posting must be enabled. However, anonymity has challenges. It prevents monitoring of participation (at least insofar as the anonymity extends to anonymity from the academic moderators). Further, it removes an important connection between the "practices of the community" and the individual (Lave and Wenger 1991), because the person claiming to have undergone the experience is not identifiable, and the students may be less situated if this linkage is not present.

Familiarisation and socialisation

To familiarise the participants with the process and to socialise them so that they are willing to share (and particularly to share mistakes) it is important to initially use very simple e-tivities (Jones and Peachey 2005). The first invitation sparks discussion by embedding a photograph of my last purchase at the supermarket before asking students to do two things. First, introduce themselves via a post on a dedicated discussion board and tell other participants about the last contract that they made, identifying the parties and the subject matter of the contract. Second, to respond to one other comment on the thread, asking a question about the making of the contract. The invitation does not instruct students to respond to questions about their contract but encourages them to interact. Participants' posts will generally identify a contract to buy household goods, but students sometimes identify other contracts that they have entered – perhaps for a gym membership, for a mobile phone or for accommodation. Interactive questions usually revolve around the method of payment or the length of time; sometimes more detailed questions arise about the identity of the parties (a contract between a student and "McDonalds" led to an interesting discussion about the contracting parties in this case, as a franchisee is likely to be the party with whom the student contracted). This activity ensures that the students are familiar with the technology, and with the activity of sharing experiences and responding to the experience of others, and builds trust that each student will work together in exploring consumer experiences through the e-tivities.

Whilst it may be best practice to undertake further e-tivities aimed at familiarisation and socialisation, it is the author's experience that when using e-tivities alongside face-to-face teaching there is often insufficient time to undertake more than one activity with this goal. However, if the moderator does not feel that participants are sufficiently socialised by this activity, then a further e-tivity can be undertaken. A possible model is to spark discussion by using a photograph of a mobile phone or a gym, and ask participants to (1) post about one of their long-term contractual commitments (Netflix or Amazon Prime subscriptions are frequently identified), identifying the length of the contract; and (2) respond to the post of another participant, asking a question about the contract. Questions about rights to terminate tend to dominate. Similar e-tivities can be constructed around consumer credit (ask the students to identify one consumer credit agreement that they have entered into in a defined period of time), or the participant's registration agreement with the University (using that agreement as the spark). Even if further activities are not devoted to familiarisation and socialisation, these goals should be encouraged in the further e-tivities.

Knowledge exchange

Following this initial familiarisation and socialisation, participants are hopefully equipped to progress to knowledge exchange. An example of an e-tivity focusing on knowledge exchange is as follows. The invitation sparks the discussion by linking to a video of the Monty Python "Dead Parrot" sketch on YouTube (the "Car Salesman" sketch from *How to Irritate People* might also be used). The parrot was not of satisfactory quality (as the parrot had been purchased "not half an hour ago" the customer should have been entitled to exercise his short-term right to reject), no matter how vigorously the shopkeeper (played by Michael Palin) sought to argue otherwise. The invitation then asks students to post on a dedicated discussion board about the last time that they returned goods to a retailer. It then asks them to set out (1) why they were entitled to return the goods; (2) how they returned the goods; and (3) what happened when they returned the goods – did they get their money back; did they receive an exchange; did the business refuse? Participants should then respond to another student's post, raising a question about the experience.

Throughout the discussion, and particularly at the end of the exercise, the moderator should collect the experiences and comment upon them, linking the comments to the legal entitlements of the consumers. The experiences can generally be categorised into those of participants who exercised their cancellation rights (either contractual or under the Consumer Rights Directive); of participants who exercised their short-term right to reject; and of participants who exercised their right to repair or replacement. In some cases, participants are not clear about which right they exercised; this can be probed by the moderator in comments made to participants or by other participants in their responses to contributions. Building awareness of the rights that can be used, and which are used, is an important part of the situated learning of the participant, as such awareness enables the participants to move towards "mastery of knowledge and skill" of the consumer marketplace (Lave and Wenger 1991: 29). Once the participants' experiences are posted, the moderator may wish to make comments on the common legal issues exposed by the posts, drawing on the experiences shared by the participants. During the exercise, the moderator might wish to direct the conversation in particularly productive directions or to ensure that underexplored areas are discussed. For example, it is often the case that the time for repairs is not discussed by participants who exercised their right to repair; in such a case a moderator might wish to ask questions to bring about a conversation regarding what amounts to a reasonable time.

Knowledge construction

After the knowledge exchange e-tivities are completed, and participants can "find and exchange information productively and successfully" (Salmon 2002: 28), it is necessary to move on to knowledge construction. This requires students to "engage in critical, creative and practical thinking about problems and issues" (Salmon 2002: 29). An e-tivity that encourages knowledge exchange invitation (1) asks students to find a piece of popular culture (a song; a passage from a book; a clip from film or TV; a vlog; etc.) raising consumer issues and post it on the forum; and (2) respond to a different student's post by advising on the consumer law issues raised by the shared content. A second e-tivity can return to the experiences shared during the knowledge exchange exercise, and asks each participant (1) to respond to their shared experience and (2) to respond to an experience shared by another participant, advising on how they may have handled the issues differently, based on the awareness of consumer contract law nurtured during the course and the moderator's comments in response to the knowledge exchange activity. These activities can be sparked by the sharing of experiences by the moderator or by sharing of links to appropriate lectures or statutory provisions (usually the Consumer Rights Act 2015).

Applying knowledge and skills

The final stage of the e-tivities segment of the situated learning process is for the participants to utilise their knowledge of consumer contract law and their skills in handling the consumer marketplace. An e-tivity used at this stage could be to ask the participants to report on their next consumer contract issue and to reflect on how they handled this issue differently compared to the start of the course. This activity is best sparked by asking the participants to look at their past posts, at the familiarisation and socialisation, knowledge exchange and knowledge construction stages. Another activity could involve asking participants to reflect on their current contractual relationships, to consider their contractual and statutory rights under these contracts, and to report the results of their reflection to the group. This exercise may result in the participants making decisions about their contractual situations; in some cases, it led to switching providers; in other cases, it led to the return of goods. The moderator can play an important role during these exchanges by gathering experiences, summarising those experiences and asking participants to reflect on the experiences that have been shared. As well as applying knowledge, participants continue to develop in the consumer marketplace, building on the foundations created during the face-to-face portions of the class and the earlier e-tivities.

Issues with e-tivities

E-tivities can be messy. The students produce "short, sometimes ungrammatical and disorganised, responses to the invitation. Sequencing is difficult to follow" (Salmon 2002: 26). The asynchronous nature of the activity means that some participants have "finished" an e-tivity before others have started. This can be confusing for some participants and can put them off engaging as they feel that others have said everything that they could say. To overcome these challenges, e-tivities require time and engagement by the moderator to cultivate the discussion, perhaps providing additional prompts to the participant in order to "direct the conversation in the right direction or summarising the progress of the e-tivity throughout the process" (Salmon 2002: 27). The moderator must also ensure that each contribution is valued. This is particularly vital at the knowledge and skill construction stage, with the moderator needing to both ensure that the critical and practical knowledge is deployed appropriately and that the participants are aware that there are multiple possible ways that a participant could utilise the law to achieve their goals, commenting on the quality of arguments and the strength of their support from the relevant legal sources. Further, the moderator should suggest "fresh strands of thought, introduce new themes and suggest alternative approaches" (Salmon 2002: 31).

Blending e-tivities with face-to-face learning is therefore a time and resource intensive exercise, and is not something to be undertaken lightly. In order to enable moderation it is best to put aside a fixed period of time in which to carry it out rather than to seek to do this on an ad hoc basis. By having a set time in which the complex job of "weaving" the different strands of conversation can be carried out, the author has found the task of moderation less overwhelming than it first appears. Of course, some time should be set aside each day to ensure that the e-tivity is progressing satisfactorily, but treating the more intensive moderation as a time-bound task enables a balance between moderator- and participant-driven experience.

Blending e-tivities with face-to-face learning requires the timetable for e-tivity release and completion to be linked with the face-to-face learning. Whilst the familiarisation and socialisation activities can take place at any time during the module (and in some cases may begin to build a community before classes start), the knowledge-based activities may need to correspond to the lectures and tutorials scheduled for the module, as the e-tivities discussed above are often premised on the existence of some knowledge about consumer contract law. Further, as the goal of the e-tivities is to enable the development of consumer law consciousness in the participants, the e-tivity timetable must work towards this goal, ensuring that participants are able to carry out assigned consumer activities and report them back via the VLE in the timescale allotted. Therefore, the time period for which e-tivities are open must be sufficient to allow completion in an asynchronous manner, but must not be too extensive, because a long period may be disruptive to the blended nature of the learning. It is possible to operate multiple e-tivities simultaneously, but this must be carefully considered to avoid overburdening participants, which may lead to more limited engagement (completion of the set task and no more) and therefore a less successful situated learning experience. Whilst a fully online e-tivity-based course can run at its own pace, with the stages extended until the moderator is satisfied that the participants have reached the appropriate level of socialisation or interaction, this is more difficult in a blended setting, where the achievement of learning outcomes may be dependent on the interaction of the various delivery mechanisms and on assessment taking place at a set time. These timing issues must be carefully managed in order that the goals of the blended learning can be achieved.

Despite these issues the e-tivity model does enable students to engage in situated learning of consumer contract law. However, to achieve the goals of situated learning through the consumer contract law course, the author has found that it is useful to engage in situated learning in face-to-face taught session. However, in order to distinguish these exercises from the e-tivities discussed in this section, the face-to-face activities focus on classic cases and ask students to consider the application of the consumer contract law considered in lectures, tutorials and e-tivities to these factual situations.

Situating students in classic contract cases

As well as harnessing students' experiences to build consumer law knowledge, students can be 'situated' in past contract cases. By placing themselves in the position of the consumer in these cases, students are able to appreciate the 'consumer' nature of these cases, to better understand the different issues and interests that lead to the decision, and to grasp the difference between the law that applied when the case was decided and the law that they have experienced through their own participation in the consumer marketplace. These exercises tend to take place after the knowledge construction e-tivities have begun, so utilise and informally evaluate the student's progress in their situational apprenticeship.

As an in-class spark, students are introduced to situations which mirror the facts of classic cases, and they are asked to consider the steps that they would take in the particular situations. The students' suggestions are then compared to the experiences of the consumers in those cases, leading to a critical engagement with the consumer experience and the development in contract law of the separate, more protective, consumer contract protections that the students explore through their situated learning e-tivities. This critical engagement is intended to raise questions about the proper position of consumers within the contract law space and the developments in the law to protect consumers.

An example is as follows. A spark is prepared to place the student in a factual situation: the student is shown an advertisement for a product which claims to prevent the common cold and told that they have been using the remedy as instructed. After a number of weeks, they come down with a cold. Students should recognise these facts as approximating to *Carlill v Carbolic Smokeball Company* ([1893] 1 QB 256), but without the express term that promised compensation when the smokeball failed to work (The "express promise to pay 100l in certain events" according to Lindley LJ), and are asked to consider the (contractual) steps that they would take using their knowledge of the legal regime arising from the module and the situated learning process outlined above. A student might suggest that the remedies under the Consumer Rights Act 2015 would be appropriate (a student often suggests that the remedy is not in conformity with description); another student would be asked to contribute and analyse how such remedies would operate in this case (the short-term right to reject) would not be appropriate as the time-limit may have been surpassed and the product would have been (at least partially) consumed; replacement would not bring the goods into conformity with the contractual description (the issue is not with the particular goods sold, but with all goods of the description); a price reduction might be appropriate (Consumer Rights Act 2015 s 24); a third student would be asked to consider the possibility of remedies under the Consumer Protection from Unfair Trading Regulations 2008, examining whether the advertisement amounted to a misleading action; and a fourth student would consider which remedies would be available. A class discussion comparing the situated participant with Mrs Carlill is used to illustrate the development of the law protecting consumers over the 20th century.

A similar activity would place the students in the position of the trader. Whilst the goal of the situated learning is to increase student awareness of their consumer rights, an awareness of the limits of these rights through an activity based on the perspective of the trader is useful. Students would be asked to consider the traders risks, perhaps by advising on a marketing campaign for a product before it is placed on the market. This type of exercise is useful for considering contract terms and the controls that are placed on them. Classic cases involving exclusion clauses can be used to provide the factual spark for the discussion, examining whether the clauses would now be void as a result of the Consumer Rights Act, and considering ways that the trader could protect their interests without falling foul of the restrictions placed on such clauses.

Conclusion

This chapter has sought to outline a method for enabling situated learning of consumer contract law using blended learning, and particularly e-tivities. Participants gain an understanding of their consumer law rights in the context of their own practice as a consumer, as well as academically. The activities help the students complete their apprenticeship and become fully competent users of their consumer contract law protections. By combining the online activities with face-to-face teaching using past cases as consumer law examples, the student is encouraged to become critically engaged with the development of the law, and to consider how the rights and obligations of consumers and traders should be balanced, assisting with their development as a critically reflective consumer lawyer and helping them to include academic and practical perspectives in their work. Whilst the chapter has considered consumer contract law in the context of a specific consumer law module, the techniques considered here can be adopted to a contract law module (although sparks may have to be adopted to ensure participants engage with the e-tivities), or can be used for a broader online course that aims at introducing consumer rights to a broader audience including non-lawyers.

Undertaking this type of teaching is rewarding for both students and academics. It reveals new perspectives on consumer law and consumer behaviour, even for academics who specialise in the area. It isn't always easy, and mistakes, usually in the design of an e-tivity that just doesn't work, are inevitable. But such mistakes are a valuable tool in developing this blending learning approach and should not be a deterrent to undertaking it. Ultimately, the approach outlined in the chapter is both fun and academically valuable, and is therefore a very useful technique in the toolbox of teaching contract law.

References

Ekström, K.M., 2010. Consumer Socialization in Families. In: *Understanding Children as Consumers*. Sage, London, pp. 42–60.

House of Commons, 2017. *The Higher Education Market*, HMSO, London.

Jones, N. and Peachey, P., 2005. The Development of Socialization in an On-line Learning Environment. *J. Interact. Online Learn.*, 3, 1–20.

Lave, J. and Wenger, E., 1991. *Situated learning: Legitimate Peripheral Participation*. Cambridge University Press, Cambridge.

Lee, Y. and Rofe, J.S., 2016. Paragogy and Flipped Assessment: Experience of Designing and Running a MOOC on Research Methods. *Open Learn.: J. Open, Distance and e-Learn.*, 31, 116–129.

Salmon, G., 2002. *E-tivities: The Key to Active Online Learning*. Routledge, London.

Warwick, J. and Mansfield, P., 2000. Credit Card Consumers: College Students' Knowledge and Attitude. *J. Consumer Market.*, 17, 617–626.

Chapter 8

Teaching the law of contract in a world of new transactional technologies

Roger Brownsword

Introduction

Many years ago, a colleague liked to tease me by saying that we teachers of the law of contract spent too much time asking our students to think about improbable scenarios such as what the legal position might be should a snail consume a letter of acceptance in a pillar box. Nowadays, the same point might be made even more tellingly by asking why we spend so much time teaching the finer points of the postal rule when people increasingly communicate their offers and acceptances by means other than letters. If once I would have been dismissive in my response to the suggestion that the law of contract is of diminishing relevance to the regulation of transactions, I would now take that proposition much more seriously – and it would be the emergence of a raft of new transactional technologies together with the increasing automation of transactions that would give me pause. Never mind about snails and letters of acceptance, what do we make of the law of contract when offers are being initiated and accepted by machines, with the deal being done in less than a fraction of a second (compare Schammo 2008)?

Accordingly, in this chapter, I want to offer some short reflections, not on how we teach the law of contract given the many new technological options for presenting our lectures and seminars, but on how we relate the law of contract to the technology-driven changes that are taking place in the transactional landscape. There are, I suggest, three key questions to be included in the curriculum. First, how does the law of contract fit in to the wider regulatory environment for transactions? Second, as new transactional technologies become available and are taken up, should we try, like "coherentists", to fit these developments into the existing body of doctrine or should we think about such matters in a more "regulatory-instrumental" way? Third, what should we make of the possibility of regulatory restrictions or requirements being, so to speak, "designed into" the emerging technological platforms or infrastructures for contracts? In other words, what should we make of the "technological management" of transactions?

Before expanding on these questions and sketching some answers, let me concede that, for some law teachers, this discussion (which responds to questions concerning the relevance of the law of contract) might itself seem irrelevant. This depends upon how we answer the prior question of what we take to be the purpose of our teaching the law of contract. If we take the purpose to be the inculcation of a set of professional skills that centre on writing legal opinions, or advocating a particular view of the law, or judging in relation to that body of doctrine that we call the law of contract, then what I have to say will not be relevant. However, if we take the purpose to be broader, so that the law of contract is situated in its economic and social context, then my discussion – albeit a discussion that highlights the regulatory and technological features of the context – should at least seem relevant.

The law of contract and the regulatory environment for transactions

Our first question asks how the law of contract fits into what I am calling "the regulatory environment for transactions". However, this is not one of the concepts that are explained in standard texts on the law of contract. Accordingly, in this part of the chapter, I start by outlining the general idea of the regulatory environment for transactions as a way of framing our teaching of the law of contract and then I sketch three particular conceptions or specifications of the idea.

The general idea of the regulatory environment for transactions

When, as an undergraduate in the mid-1960s, I was introduced to the law of contract, it was in the context of an embryonic modern consumer marketplace fuelled by consumer credit. In that context, the law of contract, with its commitment to freedom and sanctity of contract, found itself in something of a crisis. Evidently, the law licensed the use of standard form terms and conditions (which consumers did not read, would not understand, and played no part in negotiating) and, in particular, it licensed suppliers (of cars, fridges, televisions, and the like) to rely on standard term exemption clauses that put the risks of fitness, quality, and safety on the purchaser. In that context, it was said, quite rightly, that some changes to the law needed to be made, and, in due course, legislative changes were made. It was not said – or, at any rate, I do not recall anyone saying it – that the regulatory environment for transactions (or for consumer transactions) was not fit for purpose.

These days, I would expect the conversation to be rather different. Today, if the law licensed a dealer to leave a "car" outside the purchaser's premises when the vehicle was a shell, incapable of self-propulsion, and with various parts of the engine broken and burnt (compare the facts in *Karsales (Harrow) Ltd v Wallis* [1956] 2 All ER 866), and if this were anything like a common occurrence, then it surely would not be long before someone would suggest that the regulatory environment, like the car, was broken. After all, in the wake of one crisis, catastrophe, or scandal after another, we find some part of the blame being apportioned to a regulatory environment that proved to be unfit for purpose. Nowadays, if we detect a crisis in the consumer marketplace, we will know that an effective response to the problem is likely to involve more than a tweak to the law of contract (or even a bespoke piece of legislation such as the Consumer Rights Act 2015). To get the regulatory environment right, it might also be necessary to make reforms in competition law, credit law, and criminal law as well as changes in the technical standards for consumer goods and services. It might also be necessary to make changes to the regulatory agencies and, crucially, to take steps to change the business culture of those who supply goods and services in the consumer market.

To pick up the autobiographical thread, soon after I started teaching the law of contract, I became aware of the seminal work of Stewart Macaulay and Ian Macneil (Macaulay 1963; Macneil 1980). At this stage, "law in context" was barely off the drawing board, and it was not obvious how these commentaries might be fitted into my lecture narrative that started with offer and acceptance and ended with remedies. Even if there had been slots for "context" in that narrative, there would have been a temptation for students to interpret whatever contextual content was supplied as marginal to the main doctrinal story. So, how do insights about the practice of business contractors or about the web of social relations in and around transactions become an integral and equal part of the story?

Clearly, so long as the main story that we tell as teachers of the law of contract is the traditional doctrinal story, there is a problem. Rather than starting with some segment of the law of contract, I suggest that the story needs to start with the idea that the field of interest is transactions (whether deep in the business world or in the consumer marketplace or in the emerging peer-to-peer shared economy) and that the particular focus is on the regulatory environment for transactions. By the "regulatory environment", I mean a signalling environment that guides and directs the conduct of human agents (for extended analysis, including discussion of the tensions within and between regulatory environments, see Brownsword 2015) – for present purposes, specifically by guiding and directing people who are involved in transacting. The signals represent the ground rules, and the law of contract is one such set of signals. However, we should not assume that the signals given by the law of contract necessarily are dominant in any particular transactional setting. There is a lot of noise in and around transactions, and, in some environments, such as those studied by Macaulay, the signals given by the law of contract might be very weak indeed. Similarly, we know that in our everyday experience as consumers, whether offline or online, the legal signals are often much less prominent than the suppliers' particular custom and practice, their concern for their trading reputation, and the side-arrangements that have been made for guarantees and warranties. We find ourselves, as Macneil points out, in a web of social relations.

So, the first lesson in contract law does not start within the law of contract itself (whether with offer and acceptance or with remedies) but with transactions and the regulatory environments in which transactors operate. The law of contract sends signals to transactors, but it is just one element in the regulatory environment. If we start here, the question then is how wide we should go in drawing the boundaries of this environment. It is to this question that I now turn.

Three conceptions of the regulatory environment for transactions

One of the challenges for any contextual approach to teaching law is to determine the scope of the context. As the context broadens, the particular doctrinal component that is ostensibly at the core of the course becomes less and less significant. If we are to start teaching the law of contract by placing it in the larger context of the regulatory environment for transactions, we have to meet this challenge. In what follows, I sketch three possible conceptions, or specifications, of this contextual idea, starting narrow and becoming broader.

A narrow (legal) specification

We might restrict the regulatory environment for transactions to the law of contract together with whatever other bodies of law provide signals to transactors. For example, while the law of contract provides some regulatory control for fraud and coercion, it might be argued that the primary regulatory burden is carried by the criminal law. Fraudsters, it is fair to say, are not likely to be much discouraged by concerns that their fraud, if detected, will give their co-transactors grounds for relief. Indeed, when eBay looked to the law to reinforce its reputational system, it was to the agencies of the criminal law, not to the law of contract, that it turned (Goldsmith and Wu 2006). Similarly, the regulatory environment for platform services in the shared economy – currently being tested in more than one respect (as, for example, in Case C-434/15 (May 11, 2017), where Uber is treated as providing transport rather than information society services) – will draw on legal resources that go beyond the law of contract.

One thing that the law of contract goes out of its way *not* to regulate is the price. A peppercorn rent is fine but so, too, is a price that is excessive (unless it is treated as unconscionable). The price is for the parties to agree. However, when suppliers know so much about their customers that they can engage in dynamic pricing (changing the price from one customer to another and even changing the price minute by minute in relation to the same customer) how is the abuse of this power to be regulated? The law of contract is not equipped for this task, and, according to Ariel Ezrachi and Maurice Stucke, neither is competition law (Ezrachi and Stucke 2016: chs 1–12 on collusive and discriminatory pricing). If this is correct, it might be the case that we should conclude that the regulatory environment is not fit for purpose and that it needs some attention. In any event, the key point is that, if there is a problem about dynamic pricing, we need to tackle it by engaging with the full sweep of the law that constitutes (on the narrow specification) the regulatory environment for transactions.

A broader (normative) specification

If we are prepared to step beyond the positive law, to recognise not just the de jure but also the de facto regulatory environment for transactions, then we can locate the law of contract in a signalling environment that includes just the kind of norms that Macaulay and Macneil identify in their work. From this perspective, we see that transactions, like interactions, take place in an ocean of normativity and that the legal norms are just one island. Here, the work of Macaulay and Macneil is part of a much larger literature that draws attention to the self-regulatory practices of groups and communities, representing so to speak the "living law" for members of those groups and communities (seminally, see: Ehrlich 2001; modern examples, see: Ellickson 1991; Raustiala and Sprigman 2012; Lobel 2013).

The juxtaposition of the official "top down" law with the unofficial "bottom up" law of self-regulating groups and communities raises a host of interesting issues. Where top down law is largely viewed as being an option for transactors (as is the case with much of the law of contract), the fact that the option is not taken up is not likely to be viewed as problematic. However, where top down regulators want transactors to adopt the official rules or, say, a state-backed payment mode or transactional technology, then resistance in some parts of the business community will lead to some turbulence in the regulatory environment. Moreover, those who sponsor new transactional technologies might find that what look like benefits on paper simply do not translate well into actual business practice (Levy 2017).

As I have already intimated, though, with this broader frame of reference and a new agenda of issues arising, the significance of the law of contract might be diminished. From this perspective, it is not just other lawyers who might wonder why we spend so much time arguing about difficult applications of the law of contract; it is a puzzle for lay people too. No doubt, there are pedagogic aims relative to which it makes perfect sense to focus so much attention on snails, letters of acceptance, and smokeballs, but, once we frame our teaching in terms of the regulatory environment for transactions conceived in this more ambitious way, the burden of explanation lies with those of us who teach the law of contract in a largely doctrinal way.

A radical (normative and non-normative) specification

The two answers proffered so far have it in common that they take the regulatory environment to be constituted by norms; the signals are normative; they direct regulatees as to what is permissible, what is required, and what is prohibited. For transactors who want to know what they ought to do in negotiating or performing a deal, or what they might reasonably expect in the event of a dispute, the regulatory environment gives some answers. We might, however, conceive of the regulatory environment for transactions in a way that reaches beyond norms to features of the technological infrastructure or platforms on which parties deal. If we do this, we allow that some elements of the regulatory environment are not normative in the sense that we think is the case with the rules of law, ethics, codes of practice, standards, and so on.

In what sense then might the signals given by particular technological features be non-normative? What the features in question signal is that a certain act in a transactional setting is or is not possible; the signals to transactors relate not to what they ought or ought not to do but to what they can and cannot do. For example, at an automated car park of the kind that English contract lawyers first debated in *Thornton v Shoe Lane Parking Ltd* [1971] 2 QB 163, the lights at the entrance to the car park might have signalled to motorists whether or not they were permitted to enter, but the architecture of the car park and the presence of the barrier at the entrance were non-normative signals of what was physically possible. Similarly, in modern online environments, unless users click to agree to the terms and conditions for accessing a web site, in many cases it will not be possible to access the site. The technology is set up in a way that regulates the options that are actually available to users. It is not merely a matter of being normatively required to agree to certain terms and conditions, the technology ensures that without the required "agreement" it is simply not possible to proceed (Lessig 1999).

One of the virtues of this radical specification is that it facilitates a more sophisticated analysis of the relationship between law and liberty, taking into consideration both the normative and the practical optionality of doing some act x. We can then ask whether according to some given set of laws or rules there is a "normative liberty" to do x (whether doing x is permitted, is treated as optional) as well as whether there is a "practical liberty" to do x in the sense that, irrespective of the rules, doing x is a real possibility, a real option (Brownsword 2017b: 41).

If, in future, we can expect the making, the performance, and the enforcement of transactions to be increasingly automated (employing a suite of emerging technologies that will support "smart" contracting), and if the design of these technologies is such as to limit the practical options (the practical liberties) available to the parties (even to remove humans from the transactional loop), then the regulatory work is not being undertaken by the rules of the law of contract, indeed not by rules of any kind. In this future world of transactions, the regulatory environment is radically different and we might want to teach students about the law of contract in a way that highlights inter alia the relationship between normative and practical liberty by explicitly framing the law in this increasingly technological context.

Emerging technologies: should we think like "Coherentists" or "Regulatory-Instrumentalists"?

Regardless of how we answer the first question (in fact, even if we reject the idea of placing the law of contract in a larger regulatory context), the emergence of new technologies can provoke questions about how the law, or how regulators, should respond. In this part of the chapter, I will draw a contrast between two modes of response: a "coherentist" mode, which is typical of common law and judicial responses; and a "regulatory-instrumentalist" mode, which is more typical of legislative responses. I will then sketch the significance of this distinction in the face of new transactional technologies.

The distinction between coherentism and regulatory-instrumentalism

According to Edward Rubin, we live in the age of modern administrative states where the law is used "as a means of implementing the policies that [each particular state] adopts. The rules that are declared, and the statutes that enact them, have no necessary relationship with one another; they are all individual and separate acts of will" (Rubin 2017: 311). In other words (Rubin 2017: 311), regulations enacted by administrative agencies that the legislature or elected chief executive has authorised are related to the authorising statute, but have no necessary connection with each other or to regulations promulgated under a different exercise of legislative or executive authority.

In the modern administrative state, the "standard for judging the value of law is not whether it is coherent but rather whether it is effective, that is, effective in establishing and implementing the policy goals of the modern state" (Rubin 2017: 328; compare the regulatory-instrumentalist approach: Brownsword 2009: 87). By contrast, the distinctive feature of "coherentism" is the idea that law forms "a coherent system, a set of rules that are connected by some sort of logical relationship to each other" (Rubin 2017: 312), or "a system of rules that fit together in a consistent logically elaborated pattern" (Rubin 2017: 313). For coherentists, such doctrinal integrity is desirable in and of itself.

For my purposes, we can draw on Rubin to construct two ideal-typical approaches to the reform or renewal of the law of contract. One ideal-type, "regulatory-instrumentalism", views the rules of contract law as a means to implement whatever policy goals have been adopted by the state; the adequacy and utility of contract law is to be assessed by its effectiveness in delivering these goals. The other ideal-type is "coherentism", according to which the adequacy of the law of contract is to be assessed by reference to the doctrinal consistency and integrity of its rules. Where regulatory-instrumentalism informs a proposal for reform, the argument will be that some part of the law of contract "does not work" relative to desired policy goals – for example that the law does not sufficiently encourage the growth of online markets or support small businesses. By contrast, where coherentism informs a proposal for reform, the argument will be that there is a lack of clarity in the law or that there are internal inconsistencies or tensions within the law that need to be resolved.

Such a concern with formal coherence runs through much of the law of contract (particularly where common law and equitable doctrines are juxtaposed) as well as through critical commentaries on the state of the law. To take just one example, in *Stena Line v Merchant Navy Ratings Pension Fund Trustees Limited* [2011] EWCA Civ 543 at [36], Arden LJ made a significant intervention in the development of the modern jurisprudence on implied terms when she emphasised the contribution to the coherence of the law made by Lord Hoffmann's speech in *AG of Belize v Belize Telecom Ltd* [2009] UKPC 10 (see Hooley 2014):

In *Belize*, the Privy Council analysed the case law on the implication of terms and decided that the implication of terms is, in essence, an exercise in interpretation. This development promotes the internal coherence of the law by emphasising the role played by the principles of interpretation not only in the context of the interpretation of documents *simpliciter* but also in the field of the implication of terms. Those principles are the unifying factor. The internal coherence of the law is important because it enables the courts to identify the aims and values that underpin the law and to pursue those values and aims so as to achieve consistency in the structure of the law.

However, in a trio of recent Supreme Court decisions – *Marks and Spencer plc v BNP Paribas Services Trust Company (Jersey) Limited* [2015] UKSC 72 (on implied terms); and, *Arnold v Britton* [2015] UKSC 36 and *Wood v Capita Insurance Services Ltd* [2017] UKSC 24 (on interpretation) – we find a reaction against expansive implication and interpretation of terms, particularly in carefully drafted commercial contracts. This leaves coherentists with many questions (for a sophisticated coherentist reading of *Arnold v Britton*, see Tan 2016). For some, the question is how to square contextualist with non-contextualist approaches; for others, the question is why the contextualist approach (to the extent that it has primacy) should be limited to interpretation and implication – for example why not also determine the reasonableness of terms in a contextualist way?

By contrast, we can detect a regulatory-instrumentalist approach underlying such legislative interventions as the Arbitration Act 1979, which is conspicuously designed to serve larger economic purposes, and, even in the courts, where we might expect there to be less confidence in shaping the economy or taking on larger policy questions (see, e.g., Lady Hale in *Radmacher v Granatino* [2010] UKSC 42 at [134]), we can detect an implicit instrumentalism in the importance attached to English commercial contract law continuing to be competitive as the choice of law in international trading communities (see, e.g., Lord Bingham's remarks in *Golden Strait Corporation v Nippon Yusen Kubishka Kaisha: The Golden Victory* [2007] UKHL 12, at [1]; and, Lord Hodge noting, in *Wood v Capita*, [2017] UKSC 24, at [15], that "[o]ne of the attractions of English law as a legal system of choice in commercial matters is its stability and continuity, particularly in contractual interpretation". Significantly, Lord Hodge also maintained, at [13], that "[t]extualism and contextualism are not conflicting paradigms in a battle for exclusive occupation of the field of contractual interpretation".). Nevertheless, the characteristic default of common lawyers is to coherentism (compare Rosenberg 1997).

The significance of the distinction relative to new transactional technologies

Although coherentism centres on the internal consistency of doctrine, it has an extended manifestation in a tendency to apply existing legal frameworks to new technological innovations that bear on transactions, or to try to accommodate novel forms of contracting within the existing categories. We need only recall Lord Wilberforce's much-cited catalogue of the heroic efforts made by the courts – confronted by modern forms of transport, various kinds of automation, and novel business practices – to force "the facts to fit uneasily into the marked slots of offer, acceptance and consideration" or whatever other traditional categories of the law of contract might be applicable (*New Zealand Shipping Co Ltd v A.M. Satterthwaite and Co Ltd: The Eurymedon* [1975] AC 154 at 167).

With the advent of twenty-first century transactional technologies, this is a significant characteristic. So, for example, coherentists will want to classify e-mails as either instantaneous or non-instantaneous forms of communication (or transmission) (Murray 2000: 17; Mik 2009 concluding that such classificatory attempts should be abandoned); will want to apply the standard formation template to online shopping sites; will want to draw on traditional notions of agency in order to engage electronic agents and smart machines (compare Weitzenboeck 2001); will want to classify individual "prosumers" and "hobbyists" who buy and sell on new platforms (such as platforms that support trade in 3D printed goods) as either business sellers or consumers (compare Twigg-Flesner 2016); will try to apply ideas of "duress" and "undue influence" to the control that online suppliers have over their profiled consumer customers; and, highly importantly, they will persist in treating online shopping sites as functionally, contextually, and normatively equivalent to offline shopping environments (Brownsword 2017d). As the infrastructure for transactions becomes ever more technological, the tension between this strand of common law coherentism and regulatory-instrumentalism becomes all the more apparent.

To take the case of the supposed equivalence between offline and online transactional settings, there is now a queue of commentators lining up to challenge that assumption, insisting that the differences rather than the similarities need to be accentuated. The point, as Ryan Calo (2014: 1002) emphasises, is that purchasers in online environments are technologically "mediated consumers", approaching "the marketplace through technology designed by someone else". Thanks to this technology, prices can be changed minute by minute and customer by customer; and the particular vulnerabilities of consumers can be identified and exploited. Even if there is nothing new in shopping environments being designed to influence purchasing decisions, in online environments this art is taken to a whole new level of technological sophistication (Mik 2016). If, in these new transactional settings, online suppliers are opportunistically loading their standard forms to the detriment of consumers in a way that does not happen in offline contracting, this immediately raises questions not only about the equivalence of offline and online contracts but also about whether online suppliers are taking unfair advantage of the online environments in which they can now sell to consumers (Hillman and Rachlinski 2002; Mann and Siebneicher 2008). The crucial question, however, is whether we should try to correct any unfairness by means of a coherentist doctrinal tweak or adjustment or by a bespoke regulatory intervention that seeks out a more acceptable balance of interests in the online consumer marketplace.

In contrast with any lingering coherentism, we might note the conspicuously regulatory-instrumentalist approach of the European Commission in its push towards a single, and now digital, market. For example, as the Commission has put it (European Commission 2015: 7):

> The pace of commercial and technological change due to digitalisation is very fast, not only in the EU, but worldwide. The EU needs to act now to ensure that business standards and consumer rights will be set according to common EU rules respecting a high-level of consumer protection and providing for a modern business friendly environment. It is of utmost necessity to create the framework allowing the benefits of digitalisation to materialise, so that EU businesses can become more competitive and consumers can have trust in high-level EU consumer protection standards. By acting now, the EU will set the policy trend and the standards according to which this important part of digitalisation will happen.

Prompted by such an approach, what we need to be asking is whether, by forcing the new technological facts to fit into the doctrinal slots that we have in the law of contract, we are asking the right questions. Even if we can find a slot that seems to fit, perhaps we should be focusing instead on the nature of the transactional risk or problem and thinking more purposively about how to fix it. However, once we start thinking in such risk regulatory terms, and about where new technologies offer new instruments for assessing and managing risk, we have taken a significant step towards a radically different approach to the regulation of transactions.

Transactions and technological management

If we accept the radical understanding of the regulatory environment, we might not only note that some of the regulatory burden is now borne by technological design but also ask whether it is desirable to shift the burden from rules (such as those of the law of contract) in this way. In this part of the chapter, I will start by elaborating on the concept of technological management (whether of transactions or any other human activity) before considering how this regulatory approach might be applied to transactions and what we might then make of this.

The concept of technological management

Broadly speaking, technological management – typically involving the design of products or places, or the automation of processes – seeks to exclude (i) the possibility of certain actions which, in the absence of this strategy, might be subject only to rule regulation or (ii) human agents who otherwise would be implicated in the regulated activities. In this way, the regulatory focus is not on the paper permissions but on the real practical options available to regulatees.

The paradigmatic form of technological management can be presented in the following terms:

- Let us suppose that a regulator, R, has a view about whether regulatees should be required to, permitted to, or prohibited from doing x (the underlying normative view)
- R's view could be expressed in the form of a rule that requires, permits, or prohibits the doing of x (the underlying rule)
- but R uses (or directs others to use) technological management rather than a rule
- and R's intention in doing so is to translate the underlying normative view into a practical design that ensures that regulatees do or do not do x (according to the underlying rule)
- the ensuing outcome being that regulatees find themselves in environments where the immediate signals relate to what can and cannot be done, to possibilities and impossibilities, rather than to the underlying normative pattern of what ought or ought not to be done.

That said, when regulators first turn to technological assistance, it might be in support of the rules rather than as a replacement for the rules. For example, fair trading agencies might use smart machines to scan online terms and conditions highlighting unusual or potentially unfair provisions (compare Micklitz *et al* 2017). Or, we might find that regulators require or encourage retailers to instal surveillance and identification technologies, or technologies that sound an alarm should a person carry goods that have not been paid for through the exit gates, all this signalling that it is not in one's interest to engage in shoplifting, drive away without paying, or the like. Such an assistive role for these technologies does not yet displace the rules (of the criminal law or of contract law). These are still "soft" applications of these technological tools. However, the applications can become harder, to the point that we have full-scale technological management (compare O'Malley 2013: 280). When this is the case, the technologies will be operating at both the entrance and the exit points of retail outlets to ensure that those who have poor profiles for ability to pay or honesty do not enter and that those who have not paid are not able to exit (for example instead of sensors triggering alarms, they trigger the immediate closing of exit doors – or, of course, the exit doors might be set for "closed" and open only when a customer has been cleared for exit).

How would technological management be applied to transactions?

Quite plausibly, Kieron O'Hara and Nigel Shadbolt (2008: 193) imagine a future when, thanks to "RFID tags and smart payment cards, together with a reader able to link the information together and some biometric security, [customers can] merrily wheel [their] trolley[s] out of the supermarket without either queuing or being arrested". However, as we have already suggested, technological management might be employed to identify and exclude bad risk customers before they even enter the supermarket. Moreover, we can imagine a future where humans are simply taken out of the loop so far as the routine consumption of goods and services is concerned – in other words, a future where smart machines do all the transactional work.

Imagining such a future, Richard Ford foresaw that consumers would sign over their paychecks to "cyberbutlers" who would hold it in trust for each consumer's benefit. Then, guided by the particular consumer's profile, the cyberbutler would place appropriate orders so that, each day, the consumer would "come home to a selection of healthy and nutritious groceries from webvan.com or a Paul Smith shirt from boo.com or the latest Chemical Brothers CD from cdnow.com" (Ford 2000: 1578). If, in place of paychecks and cyberbutlers, we now imagine virtual money, personal digital assistants, and the Internet of Things, as well as suppliers who were not dot.com failures, Ford's sense of the future is far from science fiction – indeed, it is a future that is on the near horizon in some parts of the world.

Once such supply systems are up and running, humans (whether as suppliers or as consumers) largely drop out of the picture; technological management takes over. Now, the technology not only manages the "ordering" and the supply of goods and services to the consumer's needs, it also manages whatever risks or problems might arise. For example, if the scheme of technological management is designed to be consumer-friendly, it will not be possible for the supplier to be credited with the payment unless the goods or services are supplied in accordance with the order and with specified standards. Conversely, if the design is supplier-friendly, the technology will ensure that consumers pay for the ordered goods and services before they are supplied. At the root of this arrangement, there might be a transaction, very much like a traditional contract (and to which the traditional law of contract might apply) that commits the parties to a certain protocol of technological management; or, it might be that there are background rules that prescribe the design features for systems of this kind. In this latter case, there are rules about the features of transactional technologies, but these are rules that are directed at designers and manufacturers, not at transactors. It is a new world, but, before long, it might be the world in which our students find themselves as consumers, and, if this is so, students might reasonably ask how precisely the law of contract connects to this world.

What should we make of technological management?

Suppose that digital products are supplied under contracts that require users to act in accordance with the intellectual property rights of the suppliers. Now, suppose that, instead of relying on the protection of the contractual terms and conditions, the suppliers simply code in their intellectual property rights – given the coding, it is not possible for the product to be used other than in a way that complies with the relevant rights. Thus far, we might not have serious concerns about the switch from contract to code. However, if the contract or the code were to give the supplier more protection than intellectual property law recognises, this would be a problem. While a legal challenge might be mounted against the contract, the coding of products – which might not be transparent and which would be restrictive of practical liberty – might be more worrying. In both cases, though, we should insist that the actions of the suppliers should be compatible with the rule of law (see further Brownsword 2016b).

Suppose there is already a rule that prohibits x (such as wheeling supermarket trolleys off site and abandoning them) but, because the rule is ineffective, regulators resort to technological management to eliminate the possibility of x (using GPS to redesign the trolleys so that they are immobilised once they reach their permitted limits). Even if the rule that prohibits x is superseded by technological management and "retired", it is not entirely redundant because it expresses the regulators' normative view (namely, that regulatees ought not to do x), and this allows for one way of testing whether a particular use of technological management satisfies the rule of law. Quite simply, if the *rule* to which the technological management is linked satisfies the rule of law, then (assuming that the technological measures are congruent with the rule, and unless there are additional requirements for the use of technological management) the particular use of technological management also satisfies the rule of law (compare Asscher 2006).

In a case where there is not already a rule that prohibits x but where the regulator clearly believes that regulatees ought not to do x, then the use of technological management by the regulator to make it impossible to do x can be tested for rule of law compliance in a similar way. Here, the linkage is between the use of technological management and the rule that regulators would have put in place if they had adopted a rule that prohibits x. If such a rule would not have satisfied the rule of law, then the measures of technological management will also fail to do so. Conversely, if such a rule would have satisfied the rule of law, then technological management will also be compliant.

If we demand that measures of technological management are congruent or co-extensive with rules that would be compliant with the rule of law, many concerns should be assuaged. However, it will be a matter for debate in each community as to whether there should be additional requirements for the use of such regulatory measures – for example requirements about transparency, reversibility, bringing humans back into the loop, and human override and oversight (Weimer *et al* 2017). There is also the question of whether, even if technological management is free of vice, there is some virtue in leaving it open to contractors to self-regulate in the customary normative way (Brownsword 2017a).

While it remains to be seen which particular technological infrastructures for transactions will be developed and how precisely technological management might insinuate itself into the regulation of transactions, it is already clear that emerging technologies are doubly disruptive: first, they disrupt existing legal frameworks and concepts, alerting us to the need for new rules; and, second, they disrupt the assumption that the regulatory framework is to be constituted exclusively by rules – rather, technological assistance or management might be an option. Anyone who wants to wrap context around the teaching of the law of contract (or, for that matter, criminal law or torts) needs to be aware that technology has had and is continuing to have these disruptive effects. (For a systematic review of these disruptive effects in relation to criminal law, tort law, and contract law, see Brownsword forthcoming: chs 8–12.)

Conclusion

In this chapter, I have made three suggestions with regard to the teaching of the law of contract – or, at any rate, three suggestions that should be considered by those teachers who see one of their purposes as being to set the law of contract in context.

My first suggestion is that our introduction to the law of contract should start with the idea of the regulatory environment for transactions. I have sketched three ways in which we might specify this regulatory environment. In each specification, the law of contract is a part of that environment, but, with each specification, the law of contract has to be set alongside an expanding range of other rules and norms until, in the most radical specification, it also has to be set alongside the regulatory effects of new technological infrastructures for transactions.

Second, I have suggested that, regardless of how one might specify the regulatory environment for transactions, we should alert students to the choice between a coherentist and a regulatory-instrumentalist approach to the renewal of the law. Moreover, where new transactional technologies provoke debates about the fitness of the law, I have suggested that we should not mechanically default to a coherentist response but, rather, consider whether such a mode of response is appropriate (Brownsword, 2017c).

Third, anticipating a radically different milieu for transactions – captured by Ford's cyberbutler or by the image of business being conducted by a "conversation" between smart machines – coupled with a regulatory willingness to use technological management rather than rules, I have suggested that we need to ponder the place of contract law in such a world as well as being clear about the conditions that should govern whether the employment of technological measures for regulatory purposes is acceptable.

Finally, it remains only to say that, so taught, the law of contract would remain a building block for a general understanding of law. In the twenty-first century, technology will not stop at mediating transactions; it will be ubiquitous. The sooner that students are introduced to its disruptive effects, the sooner they will grasp the role and relevance of law at such a transformative time (Brownsword 2016a: 112).

References

Asscher, L., 2006. "Code" as Law: Using Fuller to Assess Code Rules. In: *Coding Regulation: Essays on the Normative Role of Information Technology*. Asser Press, The Hague, pp. 61–90.

Brownsword, R., 2009. Regulating Transactions: Good Faith and Fair Dealing. In: *Modernising and Harmonising Consumer Contract Law*. Sellier, Munich, pp. 87–113.

Brownsword, R., 2015. In the Year 2061: From Law to Technological Management. *L. Innov. Technol.*, 7, 1–51.

Brownsword, R., 2016a. Field, Frame and Focus: Methodological Issues in the New Legal World. In: van Gestel, R., Micklitz, H.W. and Rubin, E.L., eds., *Rethinking Legal Scholarship: A Transatlantic Dialogue*. Cambridge University Press, Cambridge, pp. 112–172.

Brownsword, R., 2016b. Technological Management and the Rule of Law. *L. Innov. Technol.*, 8, 100–140.

Brownsword, R., 2017a. 'Post-Technique': The New Social Contract Today. In: Campbell, D. Mulcahy, L. and Wheeler, S., eds., *Changing Concepts of Contract: Essays in Honour of Ian Macneil*. Palgrave Macmillan, Basingstoke, pp. 14–37.

Brownsword, R., 2017b. Law, Liberty, and Technology. In: Brownsword, R., Scotford, E. and Yeung, K., eds., *The Oxford Handbook of Law, Regulation and Technology*. Oxford University Press, Oxford, pp. 41–68.

Brownsword, R., 2017c. After Brexit: Regulatory-Instrumentalism, Coherentism, and the English Law of Contract. *J. Cont. L.*, 34, 139–164.

Brownsword, R., 2017d. The E-Commerce Directive, Consumer Transactions, and the Digital Single Market: Questions of Regulatory Fitness, Regulatory Disconnection and Rule

Redirection. In: Grundmann, S. ed., *European Contract Law in the Digital Age*. Intersentia, Cambridge, pp. 165–204.

Brownsword, R., forthcoming. *Law, Technology, and Society: Re-imagining the Regulatory Environment*. Routledge, Abingdon.

Calo, R., 2014. Digital Market Manipulation. *Geo. Wash. L. Rev.*, 82, 995–1051.

Ehrlich, E. and Ziegert, K.A., 2001. *Fundamental Principles of the Sociology of Law*. Transaction Publishers, New Brunswick.

Ellickson, R.C., 1991. *Order Without Law: How Neighbors Settle Disputes*. Harvard University Press, Cambridge.

European Commission, Communication from the Commission to the European Parliament, the Council and the European Economic and Social Committee, *Digital contracts for Europe – Unleashing the potential of e-commerce* COM(2015) 633 final (Brussels, 9.12.2015).

Ezrachi, A. and Stucke, M.E., 2016. *Virtual Competition*. Harvard University Press, Cambridge.

Ford, R.T., 2000. Save the Robots: Cyber Profiling and Your So-Called Life. *Stan. L. Rev.*, 52, 1573–1584.

Goldsmith, J. and Wu, T., 2006. *Who Controls the Internet?: Illusions of a Borderless World*. Oxford University Press, Oxford.

Hillman, R.A. and Rachlinski, J.J., 2002. Standard-Form Contracting in the Electronic Age. *NYUL Rev.*, 77, 429–495.

Hooley, R., 2014. Implied Terms After Belize Telecom. *Cambridge L.J.*, 73, 315–349.

Lessig, L., 1999. *Code and Other Laws of Cyberspace*. Basic Books, New York.

Levy, K.E., 2017. Book-Smart, Not Street-Smart: Blockchain-Based Smart Contracts and the Social Workings of Law. *Engaging Sci., Technol. Soc.*, 3, 1–15.

Lobel, O., 2013. *Talent Wants to Be Free: Why We Should Learn to Love Leaks, Raids, and Free Riding*. Yale University Press, New Haven.

Macaulay, S., 1963. Non-Contractual Relations in Business: A Preliminary Study. *Am. Soc. Rev.*, 28, 55–67.

Macneil, I. R., 1980. *The New Social Contract*. Yale University Press, New Haven.

Mann, R.J. and Siebneicher, T., 2008. Just One Click: The Reality of Internet Retail Contracting. *Colum. L. Rev.*, 108, 984–1012.

Micklitz, H.W., Pałka, P. and Panagis, Y., 2017. The Empire Strikes Back: Digital Control of Unfair Terms of Online Services. *J. Cons. Pol.*, 40, 367–388.

Mik, E., 2016. The Erosion of Autonomy in Online Consumer Transactions. *L. Innov. Technol.*, 8, 1–38.

Mik, E.K., 2009. The Effectiveness of Acceptances Communicated by Electronic Means, or – Does the Postal Acceptance Rule Apply to Email? *J. Cont. L.*, 26, 68–96.

Murray, A.D., 2000. Entering Into Contracts Electronically: The Real www. In: Edwards, L. and Waelde, C., eds., *Law and the Internet: A Foundation for Electronic Commerce*. Hart Publishing, Oxford, pp. 17–36.

O'Hara, K. and Shadbolt, N., 2008. *The Spy in the Coffee Machine: The End of Privacy as We Know It*. Oneworld Publications, London.

O'Malley, P., 2013. The Politics of Mass Preventive Justice. In: Ashworth, A., Zedner, L. and Tomlin, P., eds., *Prevention and the Limits of the Criminal Law*. Oxford University Press, Oxford, pp. 273–296.

Raustiala, K. and Sprigman, C., 2012. *The Knockoff Economy: How Imitation Sparks Innovation*. Oxford University Press, Oxford.

Rosenberg, D., 1997. The Path Not Taken. *Harv. L. Rev.*, 110, 1044–1048.

Rubin, E.L., 2017. From Coherence to Effectiveness. In: van Gestel, R., Micklitz, H.W. and Rubin, E.L., eds., *Rethinking Legal Scholarship: A Transatlantic Dialogue*. Cambridge University Press, Cambridge.

Schammo, P., 2008. Regulating Transatlantic Stock Exchanges. *Int'l & Comp. L. Q.*, 57, 827–862.

Tan, Z.X., 2016. Beyond the Real and the Paper Deal: The Quest for Contextual Coherence in Contractual Interpretation. *Mod. L. Rev.*, 79, 623–654.

Twigg-Flesner, C., 2016. Conformity of 3D prints – Can Current Sales Law Cope? In: Schulze, R. and Staudenmayer, D., eds., *Digital Revolution: Challenges for Contract Law in Practice*. Nomos Verlagsgesellschaft mbH & Co. KG, Baden-Baden, Germany, 35–65.

Weimer, M. et al., 2017, The Rule of Law in the Technological Age Challenges and Opportunities for the EU Collected Papers (July 20, 2017). Amsterdam Law School Research Paper No. 2017-35. Available at SSRN: https://ssrn.com/abstract=3005914 or http://dx.doi.org/10.2139/ssrn.3005914

Weitzenboeck, E.M., 2001. Electronic Agents and the Formation of Contracts. *Int. J. L. Inform. Technol.*, 9, 204–234.

Chapter 9

Contract theory

Brian H. Bix

Introduction

Teachers of contract law vary significantly on whether they believe that theory should be taught as part of a contract law course, and, if so, how it should be taught. This chapter will offer an overview of different justifications for, and different approaches to, teaching contract theory. Also discussed will be the way that, sometimes, contract law professors teach (a kind of) theory, even when they do not intend to do so.

One thing that should be clarified first is what is meant in the present discussion by "contract theory." The term will be understood broadly, as applying both to "theories of contract law" – theories (e.g., will theories (Gordley 1991: 161–213), promissory theories (Fried 2015), reliance theories (Atiyah 1986: 10–56), etc.) that focus primarily on understanding the nature of the particular doctrinal area of law – and also to theories with broader scope with potential interpretive or prescriptive application to contract law in general or to specific doctrines within contract law. Thus, law and economics or related welfarist or consequentialist theories may be theories generally about what law is or should be, but they have also been applied to particular contract law rules (e.g., Posner 2014: 95–158). Also included are theories the scope of which is broader than just contract law but narrower than all of law: e.g., civil recourse theories that, in some versions, apply to all of private law (Zipursky 2003; Oman 2011).

Sometimes contract theory is taught in a class of its own, a seminar that offers an overview of the most influential contemporary theorists, or perhaps a discussion based on a current draft of one contract theorist's work-in-progress. However, this is rare. Much more common is for theory to be taught – if taught at all – as an interstitial supplement to a course whose primary focus is doctrinal law (or doctrinal law combined with policy analysis).

Why teach theory?

There is resistance among some teachers, and among many students, to giving significant amounts of time in a contract law course to discussing theory. The concern is that time given to theory is time taken away from learning the doctrine needed for legal practice (and for the examinations that must be passed to become practicing lawyers). And often the first question asked when a theoretical topic is introduced is, "Will this be on the exam?" (as anything that is not tested can be safely ignored).

One response is that teaching theory has practical benefits, both direct and indirect. The argument for a direct practical benefit is that being able to speak of the larger purpose of contract law (or parts of contract law, or, in the other direction, of law in general) gives one a basis for arguing for one outcome over another in cases where the law is unsettled (Moore 2000). For example, if one thinks that contract law is, or should be, all about efficiency, then where there is no clear answer as to what the law is on some issue, the judge should choose the outcome that would be most efficient (either the most efficient outcome for the particular dispute before the court, or the rule that would have the most efficient overall effects taking into account future contract negotiations and disputes).

A different sort of objection might come from those who are skeptical about theories of contract law, either questioning whether much can be said about contract law across time and different jurisdictions, or claiming that contract law cannot be reduced to one primary value, and instead instantiates a plurality of values (Bix 2017). If the project of contract theory is faulty, then perhaps there is nothing of value to teach. However, even those who raise doubts about the possibility or value of "a theory of contract law" are willing to speak of the functions or justifications of *particular* contract law doctrines. (Well, most doctrines, in any event. Many find the common law doctrine of consideration perplexing at best (e.g., Fried 2015: 28–39) and might think that the best one can offer by way of "theory" is a historical/causal explanation of how we ended up with the doctrine we now have (Simpson 1975: 316–488).)

We assume that the various doctrinal rules and principles of formation, defenses to enforcement, interpretation and remedies each serve a purpose, reflecting general reasons, even if the application of the doctrines to difficult facts in some hard cases might lead to anomalous results. However "anti-theoretical" or "a-theoretical" some law professors (and lawyers and judges) claim to be, few think that the courts should not even strive for coherence in their application of the law. Our justifications for extending (or not extending) a doctrine in a new case – the explanations of the doctrinal rules and principles that we apply in daily legal practice – are, in an important sense, theory on a small scale.

At another level, theory is valuable because it trains us to think of "the bigger picture": the role of law within society, the role of the lawyer, how we should respond when law diverges from morality, etc. Additionally, many forms of legal theory are directly about the connection (or lack thereof) between contract doctrine and contract practice. American legal realism, law and society (also known as socio-legal studies and law in context), critical legal studies, and law and economics, just to name four approaches, all focus, in different ways, on this issue. If, as many theoretical approaches claim, "law in books" diverges sharply from "law in action" (Pound 1910), this would clearly seem a fact that soon-to-be lawyers should know, and students of contract law should learn how and why this occurs in that area (Macaulay 1985).

It should be noted that some commentators have argued that there are certain critical, cynical, or nihilistic forms of theory which it is inappropriate to teach in a professional school, the mission of which is to train and encourage the practice of law (Carrington 1984). I think that this view is unjustified. There might be a reasonable limit – one would not want a law faculty where *every* teacher questioned the legitimacy of the practice of law – but certainly having a variety of views available to students across a faculty or within a single course seems warranted by the project of university education. One does not construct a justification of contract law in particular, or law in general, by ignoring the most critical views. As Mill argued (2003: chap. 2), even an assumedly false challenge to an assumedly true doctrine is valuable, as it helps adherents to learn how to defend and justify the doctrines they hold.

The better view, it seems to me, is that if legal training is appropriately part of a university education (and we are not to go back to a time when those wanting to become lawyers apprenticed with practicing lawyers, much as those wanting to become a blacksmith apprenticed with practicing blacksmiths), then law and legal practice should be covered in depth. Legal practice should be learned in a way that connects it to history, economics, morality and justice, and practical reasoning. In other words, legal rules should be supplemented by theory.

Indirect education

A fair amount of the theory taught about contract law is taught *indirectly*, and often unintentionally. It is "showing, not telling," as they say in the creative writing courses. This is theoretical content we did not plan to teach, and we are generally unaware that we are teaching it. What we mean to teach and what the students learn from us are not always the same things. It is like the "slippage" noted in the cultural study of law, between what lawmakers intend to do with legislation, and the effects that the legislation ultimately has (Mezey 2001: 58–60). For example, the "Socratic method" that is still pervasive in American legal education, especially in first-year courses like contract law, often involves a persistent questioning of students. Whenever the student offers a justification for an outcome, the teacher raises a modification of the facts to bring in a situation where the justification would still apply but our intuition of its correctness is no longer present. In general, the Socratic method involves raising counters to *whatever* answer students offer regarding outcomes or reasons. The constructive lesson is teaching students the panoply of available arguments and counter-arguments. For some teachers, the less constructive value of the Socratic method was in its ability to humiliate and intimidate students, or perhaps its usefulness in filling a 60-minute class when one only has 10 minutes of material. However, the unintentional lesson may include that there are (often) no right answers to legal questions and that the arguments on both sides of (at least the harder) legal disputes are equally legitimate (Kennedy 2004: 17–29).

There is another way in which it comes about that theory about contract law can be taught, and is taught, indirectly. In this case, the indirect teaching comes from the structure of the textbook. This point requires some historical background. Christopher Columbus Langdell, Dean of the Harvard Law School from 1870 to 1895, famously believed that the way to teach contract law was to present the students with the right collection of cases, and nothing else. Students could thereby learn the basic principles of contract law, just as a botanist might learn the basic principles of that science by looking at a large number of plants (Grey 1983; see also Kimball 2007). So many of the early textbooks for law school classes were *Cases on Contracts* or *Cases on Torts* or the like. All students needed to learn basic principles were well-selected, well-written appellate court cases. And even if one did not believe that doctrinal areas of law had essential or jurisdiction-transcending central principles, one could justify the exclusive focus on cases by the belief that it was a law student's job to learn the "black-letter law" – the doctrinal rules – and that studying cases (with the help of the Socratic method) was the best way to do that.

The American legal realists (and in Europe, the Free Law Movement) undermined the idea that legal materials were sufficient on their own to determine the answer for the legal disputes that came before the court – at least for the harder cases. The resulting conclusion was that frequently it would take more than the legal materials (cases, statutes, etc.) to determine the outcome (e.g., Bix 2015: 195–206). So instead of having textbooks called *Cases on Contracts*, we have textbooks called *Cases and Materials on Contracts*. Along with cases, there are discussions of what the realists called "policy" – reasons based on consequences for having one rule or standard rather than another. And in modern parlance, arguments of "policy" are often more precisely seen as arguments based on morality, political theory, history, economics, behavioral psychology, etc. And contract theory was also sometimes included in the "materials" added to cases in the textbooks.

Another kind of indirect education – this time through the structure of the textbooks – also reflects the influence of American legal realism. The conventional way to teach contract law and to write contract law textbooks is to proceed, as it were, chronologically: formation, interpretation and performance, remedies. However, some books – including, famously, Lon Fuller's original textbook (Gerber 2003) and more recently the Dawson textbook (Dawson *et al* 2013) – begin with remedies. The justification for this goes back to Oliver Wendell Holmes's argument that talk of rights and duties in law only invites confusion with morality, and some demystification (my word, not his) is needed. As regards contract law ("Nowhere is the confusion between legal and moral ideas more manifest than in the law of contract." (Holmes 1897: 462)), Holmes (1897: 462) wrote: "The duty to keep a contract at common law means a prediction that you must pay damages if you do not keep it, – and nothing else." It is potentially misleading to tell clients (or law students) about "contractual rights" without emphasizing what those rights mean in practical terms – and how often they might mean very little indeed. What most clients want to know is what they can do (treat a contract as over and deal with third parties?) and what they can get (an order of specific performance?; if only damages, how much and how soon?) in response to an apparent breach of the agreement by the other party. And, of course, the same concern comes from the other side of the situation, from the potential breacher of the contract: if I were to fail to perform, or if my performance was defective in some way, what could the other party get from me in court? Theorists who thought such "bottom line" issues to be the most important ones, or at least ones that should always be kept in mind, argued that contract law courses should begin with remedies.

Finally, there is a third way that one can teach theory indirectly through the textbook – and again it connects with views of the American legal realists. This is an idea, associated primarily with Karl Llewellyn (1960), that it is potentially misleading to speak of contract law in general, and that it is wiser and more practical to focus on specific transaction types. In many legal systems, the contractual rules and principles applicable, e.g., to the sale of real property will be quite different from those applicable to employment, which in turn will be different from those applicable to franchise agreements, landlord-tenant agreements, consumer transactions, etc. Some contract law casebooks (e.g., Macaulay *et al* 2016–2017) reflect this view, by emphasizing the rules for different transaction types as much as they emphasize general principles of contract law.

Reimagining: more and less

For most contract law courses and textbooks, theory is a marginal or interstitial matter. There may be a section at the beginning of a book, and classes at the start of the course, where some general comments are offered about the nature of contract law and its place in society. Often, there are notes after individual appellate cases in a casebook form of textbook (the most common type of teaching book in American law school courses), where there will be scattered brief discussions about, e.g., the critical legal studies perspective on unconscionability, or the law and economics critique of the rule against penalty clauses. For many contract law teachers and courses, this is as much theoretical matter as can be fitted in, and it is, for most teachers and students, enough. For other teachers, and a few students, however, contract law (or law in general) cannot be understood without a more pervasive attention to more abstract or more foundational truths.

When one speaks with contract law teachers generally about how the course could be taught better, the answers usually come in a series of "more" wishes: more comprehensive coverage of doctrine, more coverage of international aspects of contract law (the CISG, the UNIDROIT principles, etc.), more time on problem-solving and negotiation exercises (Thomson 2015: 13–14), and last, and, for many teachers, least, more time on theory. The problem is that these wish lists of "more" come up against the reality of "less." In many US law schools, contract law once was a full-year course, but now it is in most places a single-semester course. And while the course was once at many schools six semester hours (three class hours each week, over two semesters), it is now in most places three or four semester hours. Contract law teachers are all trying to fit more material into less time, which usually results in either rushed and superficial teaching or, more commonly, giving up some of our ambitions for course coverage. And one of the first things to be sacrificed, unfortunately, is any substantial attention to theory.

Conclusion

As this chapter has tried to show, there are many reasons for teaching contract law theory and also many different ways to do so. On one hand, the chapter has emphasized the practical advantages to students of being taught theory – theory at different levels – for these are the sorts of arguments necessary for persuasion in new or unsettled cases. Beyond that, learning theory has been advocated for the value of knowledge (of law, and areas of law) and self-knowledge (relating to the role of law and lawyers within society). The chapter has also focused on the way that theoretical views are often taught – not always knowingly – through the way that the textbook is structured or the way that that the legal materials are presented. I am not sure that we even have a choice in the matter as teachers. If we do not discuss policy, critical theory, or economic analysis, we are implicitly teaching that these matters are not relevant, or at least that they are far less important than the things we are teaching. And finally, the hard reality was recognized that theory is competing with many other valuable parts of contract law teaching for space in a seemingly ever-shrinking course.

References

Atiyah, P., 1986. *Essays on Contract*. Clarendon Press, Oxford.

Bix, B.H., 2015. *Jurisprudence: Theory and Context*. 7th ed., Sweet & Maxwell, London.

Bix, B.H., 2017. The Promise and Problems of Universal, General Theories of Contract Law. *Ratio Juris*, 30, 391–402.

Carrington, P.D., 1984. Of Law and the River. *J. Legal Educ.*, 34, 222–228.

Dawson, J.P., Harvey, W.B., Henderson, S.D. and Baird, D.G., 2013. *Contracts: Cases and Comment*. 10th ed., Foundation Press.

Fried, C., 2015. Contract as Promise: A Theory of Contractual Obligation. Oxford University Press, New York.

Gerber, S.D., 2003. Corbin and Fuller's Cases on Contracts (1942): The Casebook That Never Was. *Fordham L. Rev.*, 72, 595–658.

Gordley, J., 1991. *The Philosophical Origins of Modern Contract Doctrine*. Oxford University Press, Oxford.

Grey, T.C., 1983. Langdell's Orthodoxy. *U. Pitt. L. Rev.*, 45, 1–54.
Holmes, O.W., 1897. The Path of the Law. *Harv. L. Rev.*, 10, 457–478.
Kennedy, D., 2004. *Legal Education and the Reproduction of Hierarchy: A Polemic Against the System*. New York University Press, New York.
Kimball, B.A., 2007. Langdell on Contracts and Legal Reasoning: Correcting the Holmesian Caricature. *L. Hist. Rev.*, 25, 345–399.
Llewellyn, K.N., 1960. *The Common Law Tradition: Deciding Appeals*. Little, Brown, Boston.
Macaulay, S., 1985. An Empirical View of Contract. *Wis. L. Rev.*, 465–482.
Macaulay, S., Whitford, W., Hendley, K., and Lipson, J., 2016–2017. *Contracts: Law in Action*, two vols. Carolina Academic Press, Durham.
Mezey, N., 2001. Law as Culture. *Yale J. L. Human.*, 13, 35–67.
Mill, J.S., 2003. *On Liberty*. Penguin Books, New York.
Moore, M., 2000. Theories of Areas of Law. *San Diego L. Rev.*, 37, 731–741.
Oman, N.B., 2011. Consent to Retaliation: A Civil Recourse Theory of Contractual Liability. *Iowa L. Rev.*, 96, 529–579.
Posner, R.A., 2014. *Economic Analysis of Law*. 9th ed. Wolters Kluwer Law & Business, New York.
Pound, R., 1910. Law in Books and Law in Action. *Am. L. Rev.*, 44, 12–36.
Simpson, A.W.B., 1975. *A History of the Common Law of Contract: The Rise of the Action of Assumpsit*. Oxford University Press, Oxford.
Thomson, D.I., 2015. Defining Experiential Legal Education. *J. Exp. Learn.*, 1, 1–27.
Zipursky, B., 2003. Civil Recourse, Not Corrective Justice. *Geo. L. J.*, 91, 695–756.

Chapter 10

Teaching contracts from the perspective of relational contract theory

Paul J. Gudel

Introduction

Let me begin with a brief bit of autobiography. In my first year of law school I was fortunate enough to take Contracts from Ian R. Macneil. Later, after I became a law professor myself, I prepared the third edition of Macneil's casebook, which is now Macneil and Gudel, *Contracts: Exchange Transactions and Relations* (hereinafter Macneil and Gudel). I have been teaching Contracts, using this casebook in one of its editions, for over twenty-five years. As a result, I have thought a great deal about what it means to teach Contracts from the standpoint of relational contract theory. In this chapter, I would like to describe what I think are main differences between teaching Contracts from a relational standpoint and what I will refer to as a more "traditional" standpoint. Necessarily, many of these differences are reflected in differences between the Macneil and Gudel casebook and more traditional casebooks. Also necessarily, this chapter will largely take the form of an explanation of what I myself do in my first year Contracts class. I have enjoyed writing this chapter, but I could only wish that Ian Macneil were here to write it himself. But if he were here, he would have insisted to the editors of this anthology to have me write it anyway. Ian Macneil was a dyed in the wool Scot but he was also a *mensch*.

Relational contract theory

I will begin with a brief characterization of what is meant by a "relational standpoint." Macneil's first major contribution to contract theory was the distinction between discrete and relational contracts (Macneil and Gudel 2001: 24–25). These contracts represent the two ends of a continuum. At one end of the spectrum we have "the epitome of discrete contract transactions": at noon two strangers come into town from opposite directions, one walking and one riding a horse. The walker offers to buy the horse, and after brief dickering a deal is struck in which delivery of the horse is to be made at sundown upon the handing over of $10. The two strangers expect to have nothing to do with each other between now and sundown; they expect never to see each other thereafter. At the other end of the spectrum are on-going relations such as employment, franchising, union/management collective bargaining agreements and marriage.

The difference between discrete and relational contracts can be characterized in a number of ways. Discrete contracts are of short duration, have generally only two parties, are limited to simple, monetizable economic exchange and have a very limited degree of personal involvement so that performance is usually transferable to others by both parties. Relational contracts are of long duration; are often multi-polar (i.e. consisting of more than two parties); contain an exchange of complex, personal, non-economic satisfactions; and manifest a whole-person involvement which is non-transferable. But the most important distinction between discrete and relational contracts is that in discrete contracts the goal of the parties is to make the entire content of the contract (all the rights and duties of both parties) fully *presentiated* (i.e. made present and transparent to each other) at the time the contract is formed. That is, the purely discrete contract is *fully planned* at its outset. In relational contracts, on the contrary, "the participants never intend or expect to see the whole future of the relationship as presentiated at any single time, but view the relation as an ongoing integration of behavior to grow and vary with events into a largely unforeseeable future" (Macneil and Gudel 2001: 14–15). That is, a relational contract establishes a *structure* within which the party's rights and responsibilities are worked out and adjusted to each other over time. Relational contracts cannot be understood simply as an "unpacking" of an initial contractual intent and contractual planning. "The relationships are not governed by contractual intention, but reflect a variety of influences, including social norms and the norms of conduct that develop within the relationship" (Macneil and Gudel 2001: 15).

It is important to stress that discrete and relational contracts represent two "ideal types." Especially in a highly developed society such as ours, with a tremendous amount of invested capital and a high degree of specialization of labor, there is no such thing as a truly discrete contract. *All* contracts are deeply embedded within on-going contractual relationships. It is hard to think of any that are not overlaid heavily with significant relational elements. A sale of 100 shares of GM stock between two strangers who do not even know each other's name? It is part of a massively relational pattern affecting every aspect: brokers, members of the stock exchange, the stock exchange, the SEC, etc. On the other hand, within heavily relational contracts, there do occur interludes which the parties treat "as if" they were discrete (e.g. the negotiations for a new contract which periodically punctuate collective bargaining relationships) (Macneil 2000: 895–897).

Macneil's relational contract theory has, as a description of the world, gained wide acceptance. Robert Scott, a leading practitioner of law and economics, has said, "We are all relationalists now. In that sense Macneil and Macaulay have swept the field. All contracts are relational, complex and subjective" (Scott 2000: 852). The disagreements (both academic and judicial) that remain concern what is the proper response of the legal system to this highly relational world.

Eric Posner has propounded a useful set of possible legal reactions to our relational world. The first was advocated by Macneil himself, "that courts should enforce relational contracts by determining what the norms of the relationship are and enforcing those norms" (Posner 2000: 749). A second approach, adopted for example by Goetz and Scott (1981; Scott 2000), is that courts should enforce relational contracts by filling the (inevitable) gaps in the contract with whatever terms would maximize the value of the contract. (This approach usually relies heavily on the "hypothetical ex ante bargain.") Third and finally, Alan Schwartz has argued that courts should enforce all contracts, including relational ones, in a purely literal way, as written, on the ground that this approach lessens the possibility of judicial error and gives the parties the greatest incentive to renegotiate the contract themselves if circumstances change (Schwartz 1992).

The Macneil and Gudel casebook naturally focuses on Posner's first approach. Macneil has said that he has offered a prescription respecting relational contract law, which is "that relational contract law should generally track the relational behavior and norms found in the relations to which it applies" (Macneil 2000: 900). Macneil argues that classical (e.g. the 1st Restatement) and neoclassical contract law (e.g. the 2nd Restatement) tend to emphasize two norms: implementation of planning and effectuation of consent. There are numerous other norms necessary to understanding the world of contract; these include at least: reciprocity, contractual solidarity or trust, propriety of means, creation and restraint of power, role integrity and harmonization with the social matrix. Without the presence of all these norms, exchange relations cannot exist, in the sense that if any of the norms begins to deteriorate or erode within a contractual relationship, that relation will begin to break down (Macneil and Gudel 2001: 20). In Macneil and Gudel we have, however, as noted below, tried to include materials which present an alternative approach, so as not to force our views on the students regarding what is *the* most important issue in contract law today.

Scope of the course

Macneil and Gudel begins with the following words:

> This book is designed to be used in a law school course on Contracts. You will notice, however, that the book is not entitled, "Contract Law" – and most likely, neither is the course in which you are using it. Both are entitled, "Contracts." This is no accident. The title of the course probably reflects the fact that generations of law teachers have equated Contracts with Contract Litigation, the subject of their courses. The same title in this book, however, reflects a different notion: contract law, and particularly

> contract litigation, is but a small part of contracts. You cannot begin to understand the law of contracts unless you also come to an understanding of contracts – what they are, how they work, why people enter into them and what people use them for. Only by understanding contracts as a social and economic institution can you begin to grasp the role of the law, and of the lawyer, in that vast network of human activity which is contracting.

When students first think about "a contract," they tend to think of a relatively discrete transaction. They conceive even the relational contracts they have recently entered into themselves (most often, apartment or lease agreements) as discrete: possession for a definite term of a definable piece of property for an identified sum of money. The first thing I do in my Contracts class is to begin to make students aware of the relational nature of the world. I ask the students to think about the contractual relation they have just entered into with California Western School of Law, a beautiful example of a highly relational contract. What do they expect to get from the law school? Only a degree? An education? A good education? Do they know what that is? A career? And what are they expected to give in return? It is a lot more than tuition! Do they know what the school's legitimate expectations of a law student are? And the contract doesn't last for just three years; they will discover that it is a lifetime relationship which will evolve in unforeseen ways.

In teaching Contracts (and this is true of any Contracts course, whether taught from a relational perspective or not), it is important to overcome the tendency of the case method to make the role of the lawyer seem like litigation only. The case method has many advantages, but its main drawback is that the constant presentation of judicial decisions gives the impression that what lawyers mostly do is litigate over the remains of dead contractual relationships. Therefore, we have made an effort to work into the beginning of the book, in Chapter 1, a great deal of text material on the role of the lawyer in contract planning. This includes a rather lengthy commercial contract. We raise numerous questions about the role of the lawyer in planning and drafting the contract. One of the problems with most contracts casebooks is that students don't get to see, and reflect on, enough complete real contracts, but only the little bits referred to in the decisions. A great emphasis on contract planning pervades the structure of both the casebook and the course.

The casebook is divided into only two parts, so that the transition from the first to the second is quite significant. The first part is entitled "Introduction to the Nature of Contracts" and the second part is entitled "Planning Contractual Relations." As those titles suggest, Macneil and Gudel is *not* organized doctrinally; this is a significant difference from all other contracts casebooks save Macauley *et al* (1995), which imitates the first two editions of Macneil's casebook. The chapters are not each devoted to particular legal doctrines or clusters of doctrines. Rather, in Part I, the chapters are organized as a series of answers to the question: "What is the role of the law in effectuating and promoting exchange?" In Part II, the chapters are organized as treatments of specific contract planning problems.

Part I begins with an introductory chapter which introduces the nature of economic exchange, the role of the lawyer in contract planning and the basic distinctions we are going to use in the course. These are, first, of course, that between discrete and relational contracts and, second, between performance planning and risk planning. *Performance* planning is planning for what the parties have to do if both parties are to get their expected benefits from the contract. *Risk* planning is planning for what does not have to be carried out if the contract has to come to a successful conclusion; indeed, it is planning for things the parties generally hope will not have to be carried out in response to events the parties hope will not happen (the music hall burns down, the Panama Canal closes). After this introductory chapter, Chapters 2–4 of Part I are organized as progressively broader answers to one question: how does the law reinforce the system of exchange which is contract? Part II is then devoted to a range of specific problems in contract planning.

This emphasis on functional problems in contract *planning* separates Macneil and Gudel from other casebooks, but it might seem to be only accidentally related to the relational theory perspective. Couldn't a law and economics contracts casebook also be organized around problems in contract planning rather than contract law doctrines? This is true to an extent; the focus on planning is meant to give a more practical emphasis to the training of transactional lawyers, and to counteract the tendency, noted above, of the case method of teaching to give students the impression that legal practice is litigation. It is also true, however, that a focus on planning is inherent to a relational perspective. From the relational perspective, precisely because planning can *never* be complete and contracts are *always* open-ended, contract planning is a more complex and fraught activity than most contracts books present it. Part II of Macneil and Gudel is organized around numerous common planning provisions (e.g. conditions of satisfactions, agreements to agree, limitations on liability, etc.). In each case, Macneil and Gudel is concerned to present both the usefulness of the provision *and* the potential legal issues that can be raised by its use. All provisions have their inherent temptations, in that they leave open different possibilities for one or the other party to behave opportunistically. These issues and temptations arise precisely because they are planning techniques used in situations where the development of the contractual relationships makes *full* planning impossible. The emphasis on planning in Macneil and Gudel reinforces and is reinforced by the relational contracts perspective.

A critical perspective on the law

Legal education should not be a matter of students' passively absorbing rules of law nor even of learning that form of analysis, built around analogizing and distinguishing, which we call "thinking like a lawyer." It is equally important for students to gain a perspective from which they can criticize and evaluate our legal system – that they become aware of what it means to be implicated in and responsible for its processes and results. The actual nature of the critical standpoint itself is less important – although, of course, I think that a relational contract perspective is the most revealing and realistic way to approach the teaching of Contracts.

On the very first day of class, I set a hypothetical problem for the students: three people in the restaurant business come to you, a lawyer, and ask you to draw up all the necessary contractual documents for them to start a fast food franchise together. Can you represent all three of them? The reading assignment for the problem is the Model Rules of Professional Conduct (MRPC) provisions relating to conflicts of interest. The students quickly come to see that the most relevant applicable rule is MRPC 2.2, "Lawyer as Intermediary."

Section 2.2 allows a lawyer to act as an intermediary (the comment specifically refers to a situation of "helping to organize a business in which two or more clients are entrepreneurs"). The lawyer must, of course, reasonably believe the matter can be resolved without "material prejudice to the interest" of any client and that the lawyer's "representation can be undertaken impartially." But in addition, Rule 2.2 requires that the lawyer "consult with each client concerning the implications of common representation," and obtain the clients' consent to it. To protect himself or herself, the lawyer will naturally have to spell out to the prospective clients all the potential areas of conflict of interest between them and then obtain their consent.

The important issue here is the effect that either *refusing* to represent all three *or* representing them all but complying with the disclosure and consultation provisions will have on the relations between these parties. *Either* will *heighten* their sense of conflicting interest. Refusing to represent them speaks for itself, as indeed does having to tell them that they should all get separate legal representation! On the other hand, the type of disclosure necessary to protect the lawyer's interest is easy to imagine. "I can represent all three of you, but you must understand that there are all these possible areas of conflict between you . . ." Some students think that is all to the good; all parties should enter into these relationships with their eyes fully open. Other students are horrified by the extent to which the Rules force the lawyer to "sow dissension" among the parties. Is the MRPC approach in the best interest of the parties?

I do not suggest that either reaction is necessarily the right one. This does raise, however, very early on, one of the themes of the course: if our legal system is meant to facilitate the system of exchange on which our economy and society depend, are the legal rules that we have the ones best suited to doing that? Or might it be the case that our legal rules encapsulate an overly discrete conception of contracts which creates problems when applied to a relational world?

Structure of the casebook and the course

Almost all contracts casebooks are organized in the same way. They are structured according to "*the life cycle of a contract*." They therefore begin with chapters on formation: agreement and consideration. A contract now being born, they move on to the *content* of the contract – interpretation, parole evidence, conditions vs. promises – and then on to the death of the contract – breach, materiality of breach, mistake, impracticability. Generally, right around here in the casebook there is a chapter on another way contractual relations can be terminated – capacity, duress, unconscionability, etc. Then comes remedies. Usually there is then tacked on to the end, rather as an afterthought, chapters on third party beneficiaries and/or assignment. Even casebooks which in other ways try to take a novel, ground breaking approach to teaching contracts stick very closely to this structure (e.g. Kastely *et al* 1996). I have always liked the title of this casebook, *Contracting Law*, with its overtone of "contracting malaria." Kastely *et al* (1996) mix their legal materials with excerpts from literature and popular culture, ranging from Arthur Miller's *Death of a Salesman* to Abbott and Costello's *Who's on First?* This definitely does give the student a glimpse into the human meaning and impact of legal rules. But the organization of Kastely *et al* is rigidly traditional, beginning with formation and ending with remedies, with "third party interests," which encompasses both assignment and third party beneficiaries, tacked on at the end.

Macneil planned his first edition of his casebook by asking: how does our legal system facilitate the exchange on which our capitalist society and economy are based? It is possible for what we often call less "developed" societies to have quite complex systems of exchange without having anything like an institution of "contract law." So, what does our law do? How does our legal system reinforce exchange? The most basic answer, applicable to all contracts, is that the law protects contracts as property from tortious harm and provides remedies for breach of contract. Therefore, this second chapter contains materials on the tort of interference with contractual relations and (the bulk of the chapter) on remedies. The materials here provide a basic overview of contract remedies and their limitations. The emphasis here is on the three "contract interests" (expectancy, reliance, restitution) and their interrelation.

Chapter 3 is where Macneil and Gudel begins to differ dramatically from traditional casebooks. The question raised in this chapter is: given that the world we live in is a world of highly relational contracts, what specific demands do relational contracts place on our legal system? What must our legal system do *besides* providing a set of remedies for breach?

This chapter begins with non-case materials *describing* three very relational contracts. The point of these is to give students a feel for the characteristics of relational contracts, why they have developed, i.e. the types of planning problems they have evolved to deal with and their sometimes uneasy relationship to the law. The materials are: Stewart Macaulay's article on automobile blanket supply contracts, Gillian Hadfield's "Problematic Relations: Franchising and the Law of Incomplete Contracts" (Hadfield 1990) (this section also includes a large chunk of a real franchise agreement, that of Evelyn Wood Reading Dynamics), and a lengthy excerpt from Elizabeth and Robert Scott's "Marriage as Relational Contract" (Scott and Scott 1998).

These excerpts have tremendous intrinsic interest, but in addition the articles by Hadfield and the Scotts provide a wonderful contrast of views about how courts should treat relational contracts. Hadfield is very close to what Eric Posner, above, calls the "Macneil approach." She argues that when disputes arise courts should enforce the *norms* inherent in the (conflict-laden) franchising relationship rather than the contract as written. The Scotts, on the other hand, approach the problem of what the legal rules governing marriage should be through "the familiar heuristic of the hypothetical ex ante bargain." Their discussion introduces students to the very important notion of a "default rule," which we rely on throughout the remainder of the course. (*Can* all the rules of contract law be described as default rules?) By including the Scotts' excerpt, we try to show that there are different ways to approach the problem of how courts should deal with relational contracts.

After this introductory material, Chapter 3 goes on to explore three ways (and these are not meant to be comprehensive, merely illustrative) in which contract relations make specific demands on the legal system:

1 The law must provide a means for the resolution of disputes *within* an ongoing contract relation, not merely *after* the relation is over.
2 The law must reinforce norms of cooperation and good faith (to the extent that it is able to).
3 The law must take account of the multi-polar aspects of many complex contractual relations.

These three sections provide an opportunity to explore aspects of the relationship of exchange and the law which seemed to Macneil and me to be very important but which are slighted, if not ignored, in traditional contracts curricula. In the first section, we begin by reading materials by Melvin Eisenberg (1976) on the difference between dispute *adjudication* (represented by what the students learn in Civil Procedure) and dispute *negotiation* (represented by Eisenberg's retelling of the delightful "Kadume's case," an anthropological account of dispute resolution by negotiation among the Arusha of West Africa – the students love reading this). Next, we read a labor arbitration decision, focusing on the ways that its approach to the dispute between company and union differs from the approach that courts take – the arbitration decision is much closer to dispute negotiation, although it does retain aspects of dispute adjudication. We then read the U.S. Supreme Court's opinion in *United Steelworkers v Warrior and Gulf* 363 U.S. 574, 80 S. Ct. 1347 (1960), in which the Court adopts a very pro-arbitration stance in regard to the issue of when and how courts should decide whether labor/management disputes are or are not arbitrable.

Justice Douglas' opinion is an excellent meditation on the need in labor relations for a type of dispute resolution that is more relationship-sensitive than the parties can get from the court system. He links this need with the necessary incompleteness and open-endedness of the collective bargaining agreement itself, an agreement that Douglas correctly characterizes as a highly abstract document that can only be given meaning through the concrete behavior of the parties, what labor lawyers call "the law of the shop."

In addition, the open-ended, abstract collective bargaining agreement can only be given meaning *by* the resolution by disputes through arbitration. Compare an abstract constitutional standard like the fourteenth amendment's equal protection clause. How do we know just what this very general norm of equality means, concretely? We learn what "equal protection" means through the process of the resolution of challenges to state action under that clause. It might be our ideal never to have disputes arise under the equal protection clause, but then we'd never know what equal protection *meant*. The same is true for, say, "good cause" in a collective bargaining agreement. Dispute resolution is the way of giving *content* to the contract, so it cannot be a process which heralds the end of the contract, as court adjudication usually does.

The second section in Chapter 3 is devoted to the concept of "good faith." We begin with a case illustrating the classic example of a violation of the norm of "good faith" – behavior which deprives the other party of the expected fruits of the bargain. We then move to an examination of the sources of "good faith" in the UCC (under §607(3)(a) and §306). We finish with a close reading of the case of *Foley v Interactive Data* 47 Cal. 3d 654, 765 P. 2d 373 (1988), a deeply divided California Supreme Court decision holding that California would *not* extend the tort of "bad faith breach of contract" from the insurance context, where it was well established, to the employment context, to which several California appellate courts had extended it. This decision raises profound questions about the nature of the employment contract – is it just like an ordinary commercial contract, except that what is being exchanged for money is human labor instead of widgets? Or is the employment relation in fact more like insurance, in that what the employee seeks to obtain is not monetary or even monetizable? To what extent are we willing to treat human labor as a commodity?

All through the materials, we emphasize the importance to the legal system of some concept of "good faith" as a "safety valve." That is, in a world in which contracts generally *are* incomplete and open-ended, it is necessary to have a notion of "good faith" as a way both to provide norms to police party behavior which cannot be constrained by the written instrument and to fill in necessary gaps in the contract.

The final section of Chapter 3 concerns *multipolarity*, which is an important characteristic of relational contracts, but which in traditional curricula is tucked into a separate chapter, usually at the end of the course. In our course, we provide a note section on the basic rules of third party beneficiary law, one of which, of course, is that any defenses the promisor has against the promisee are also good against the third party beneficiary. One of the things we emphasize is how difficult it is to make sense out of all the illustration from Restatement (2d) Contracts §302 (Intended and Incidental Beneficiaries). The discrete notion of "intent" is simply too narrow to account for all the factors that have to be taken with account in deciding whether it is reasonable to allow a third party to sue on a contract. If I am teaching for California Western School of Law, I can ask it to pay my salary directly to my son, Kenneth, rather than to me. If I materially breach my contract and stop teaching, the students can easily see that the only fair result is that CWSL has no obligation to keep paying my salary to Kenneth. But in the one case we read, *Lewis v Benedict Coal Corp.* 361 U.S. 459, 80 S. Ct. 489 (1960), the U.S. Supreme Court comes to an absolutely opposite conclusion: the coal company is *not* permitted to use the union's breach of the collective bargaining agreement (by an illegal strike) as an excuse to reduce its payments to the Union Pension and Welfare Fund, which the CBA sets up as a third party beneficiary within the Steelworkers/Benedict Coal contract. What is going on here?

I begin our treatment of this case by putting up on the whiteboard a diagram of all the contracts and parties involved in this case. This gets very complicated, since it consists not only of the basic trio of Benedict Coal-Steelworkers-Pension Fund, but also other coal companies (connected to Benedict by a multi-employer bargaining agreement), Benedict's employees, the employees of the other companies (both of those are also union members, so connected to the union by membership agreements) and the dependents of both of those groups. When Benedict Coal argued that the Steelworkers' breach excused it from paying money to the third party beneficiary Pension Fund, the Supreme Court replied that the collective bargaining agreement is not "a typical third party beneficiary contract." The Court demonstrates that it is not a "typical" third party agreement *precisely* by filling in the rest of the parties and relationships into the simple triangular company-union-pension fund structure. For example, the Court says:

> The promisor's interest in the third party here goes far beyond the mere performance of its promise to that third party, i.e., beyond the payment of royalty. It is a commonplace of modern industrial relations for employers to provide security for employees and their families to enable them to meet problems arising from unemployment, illness, old age or death. . . . Not only has Benedict entered into a long-term relationship with the union in this regard, but . . . it has assumed equal responsibility with the union for the management of the fund. In a very real sense Benedict's interest in the soundness of the fund and its management is in no way less than that of the promisee union.

> Moreover, unlike the usual third-party beneficiary contract, this is an industry-wide agreement involving many promisors. If Benedict and other coal operators having damage claims against the union for its breaches may curtail royalty payments, the burden will fall in the first instance upon the employees and their families across the country. Ultimately this might result in pressures upon the other coal operators to increase their royalty payments to maintain the planned schedule of benefits. The application of the suggested rule of construction to this contract would require us to assume that the other coal operators who are parties to the agreement were willing to risk the threat of diminution of the fund in order to protect those of their number who might have become involved in local labor difficulties.

"Multipolarity" in traditional contract law means adding a "third party" to the assumed "normal" two party relationship. In *Benedict Coal*, the court adds *additional* parties to the traditional, "typical" *three* party relationship! The students are easily able to see that expanding the scope of the contract relationships in *Benedict Coal* really does make a difference in what they intuitively see as the fair and just result in *Benedict Coal*, as compared to my hypothetical concerning my son.

One of the things that make the Macneil and Gudel casebook unique is that contracts casebooks generally do not contain cases in labor law, such as *Benedict Coal* or *Warrior Gulf*. It has often been noted that the evolution of contract law is the story of the continuing "spinning off" of different contractual areas into their own autonomous areas of law. So union-management contracts spin off into labor law, insurance contracts spin off into insurance law, etc. The "spinning off" is usually marked by the appearance of statutory regulation of the area in question, which takes the specific type of contract out of the realm of the common law. The subject of the first year Contracts course is seen as consisting of the common law (with the exception of the UCC Article 2, which is itself only a codification of common law principles and so not a "regulatory statute" like the Labor/Management Relations Act or Title VII of the Civil Rights Act of 1964). Therefore, the subject matter of the typical Contracts course keeps shrinking.

As it shrinks, the typical Contracts course becomes more discrete. This is because the regulatory regimes governing the "spun off" contracts are much more sensitive to the relational nature of those contracts – as both *Warrior and Gulf* and *Benedict Coal* illustrate. Indeed, one could argue that the need for a more relational treatment of varying types of contracts is the reason for the creation of all these spun off regulatory regimes. Macneil (2000: 897) has said:

> Relational contract law is so all-pervasive that one feels almost foolish in giving examples. A few examples from but one type of contractual relation, employment, will do: workmen's compensation, numerous anti-discrimination laws, social security taxation and benefits, ERISA, OSHA, other workplace regulations, wage and hours legislation. All of these are

> relational contract law. And all are part of almost any American employment relation. To which needs to be added where collective bargaining is in place, the NLRA, LMRA, and a wide range of law governing unions and other aspects of collective bargaining.

Elizabeth Mertz (2000: 917) has expanded on Macneil's idea:

> As both Macneil and Feinman note . . . one of the clearest vindications of relational contract theory in actual legal developments is the successive spinning-off of distinct branches of law to deal with distinctive kinds of relationships – ranging from varying kinds of employment relations to landlord-tenant and insurance law.

Why should these marvelously relational, context-sensitive contracts cases be banished from the first year course? Mertz (2000: 917) argues that instead of taking the "cordoning off" of, e.g. labor law, for granted, we could use it to open up "another possible vista." Macneil and Gudel is committed to the idea that supplementing neo-classical contract law by more relational areas such as labor law, insurance law or family law not only gives students a more realistic picture of the way the world of exchange actually operates but also opens up for them "new vistas" of the way the law might facilitate *all* contracts in a relational world. Need the courts' approach to labor relations be *limited* to collective bargaining agreements? Or can it be used to open up new perspectives on commercial contracts?

Chapter 4, which is the third substantive chapter of Part I, is entitled, "Social Utilization of Contract Relations." One focus here is on limiting the effect given party purposes in order to promote certain social norms. Here we find the standard doctrines: illegality, capacity, duress, undue influence, misrepresentation and unconscionability. In Macneil and Gudel, however, we give the interaction of social norms and contracting behavior a different spin. In the traditional casebook, the emphasis is all on *limitation* of freedom on contract. The "social control" doctrines normally are implicitly conceived as limitations on a pre-existing realm of "freedom of contract." The distinctive thing about contractual obligations, as opposed to those of tort and criminal law, are that they are not imposed by law but exist *only* as assumed voluntarily by the parties. Therefore, the various limitations are generally conceived as ensuring that exchanges *are* voluntary, since the "voidable" doctrines are all based on the idea that the "agreements" at issue are not truly voluntary in one way or another. But Macneil and Gudel stresses that there is no such realm of "freedom of contract" existing *apart from* the legal institutions and norms which make contracts possible in the first place. As David Campbell (2001) has put it:

> As it has been put as recently as 1993: "The distinguishing feature of contractual obligations is that they are not imposed by the law but undertaken by the parties." This is right in a sense which must be stressed, for it goes

> to the heart of the freedom provided by the market. But it is also wrong in a sense, and this sense is far less well understood. It is the explanation of this aspect of contract that is at the heart of what now is interesting in contracts scholarship. For parties can make contracts only in certain ways – not by claimed telepathic communication, or through exercise of physical force or fraud, etc. – and this is because they must express their undertakings through social institutions. As Macneil put it in 1960: "contract is an edifice partly built by the parties but also partly built by society, by the law."

As a result, Chapter 4, in addition to the "voidability" doctrines, includes material on state specification of contract terms and conferral of contract rights on parties (as, for example, in insurance regulations which specify the minimum things that a health insurance policy must cover), state control of contracting parties (as in, for example, licensing participants in economic activity, from lawyers to barbers), imposing contracts on unwilling parties (as in, for example, the public policy exception to a party's ability to terminate a contract-at-will, or the judicial reinstatement of victims of employment discrimination), and the NLRA-imposed duty of labor and management to "bargain in good faith." This last topic is of particular interest, because the manifest difficulty in actually imposing an effective duty to bargain in good faith raises the question: *can* good faith be mandated by the state? Good faith imposed by the state is *not* the same thing as good faith arising naturally in the relationship. Even if the values and norms of the relationship can be identified, how well can the legal system enforce them?

In commenting on the doctrines which refuse to give effect to agreements, Macneil (1960: 177) has said:

> These . . . appear as exceptions to some general rule permitting the parties fully to define their legal status [but] if the role of the law in creating contracts were more completely presented this distortion would not occur, and these matters would be seen not as exceptions to freedom of contract but a simply part of the law's definition of contract.

It is important that the students not be seduced by the myth that the world of contract is a purely "private" realm existing independent of legal and social institutions. This myth leads to the unfortunate attitude that every state intervention into the "private realm" must be separately justified.

The final chapter in Part I is entitled, "Basic Contract Law Concepts Continued: Consideration, Agreement, Litigation Content [i.e. contract interpretation and parole evidence], Conditions, Assignment." This connecting chapter explains that treatment of these very central doctrines has been put off until now partly because treatment of them in isolation from some knowledge of the real workings of contract would tend to reinforce discrete models of contract in students' minds.

There is a second reason for placing these materials just in this place in the book. This chapter is followed immediately by Part II, which is a treatment of various functional problems in contract *planning*. It is very striking to notice the extent to which various problems arising in contract planning have been traditionally dealt with by the legal system by various applications of and derivations from the law's classical doctrines of consideration, agreement, interpretation and conditions. Thus, this chapter forms a perfect introduction to Part II. Because many of the applications of these concepts are developed in Part II, the materials here provide only a very basic introduction to the concepts.

The treatments of these basic doctrines are relatively short. Just enough material is provided to allow students to grasp the limitations of the doctrines as classically conceived, and to gain a sense that the legal world is moving in the direction of a more realistic application of them. Let me give just one example: consideration. We first begin with that chestnut, *Hamer v. Sidway* 124 N.Y. 538, 27 N.E. 256 (1891), then *Ricketts v Scotthorn* 51 Neb. 51, 77 N.W. 365 (1898) (intrafamilial promise lacks consideration but is enforceable by detrimental reliance). Then we have students read *Feinberg v Pfeiffer Co.* 322 S.W. 2d 163 (Mo. App. 1959), in which a company's board voted to award a pension to Feinberg whenever she retired "in consideration of her long [over thirty] years of service." Feinberg retired two years later. After paying the promised pension payments for five years, the company then stopped them. Feinberg sued for breach of contract, and the court held that Pfeiffer's promise lacked consideration. The question raised is: was Pfeiffer's promise part of an exchange relationship, or was it (as the court held) a gratuitous promise?

In *Feinberg*, the company's promise to pay Mrs. Feinberg $200 a month upon retirement is clearly part of a complex, on-going exchange relation, in which all sorts of things, some monetary, some not monetary but monetizable, some not monetizable, were flowing back and forth between Mrs. Feinberg and Pfeiffer Co., and had been for over thirty years. Yet the court puts the promise to pay the pension on the gift side of the gift/exchange line. The *only* thing that could make sense of this is the idea that you have to take the Feinberg/Pfeiffer relation, break it into its smallest component parts and then try to match up each little bit going from Mrs. Feinberg to a corresponding bargained-for little bit coming back from Pfeiffer. Any little bits that can't be successfully matched up in this way are "gratuities" and are tossed out as not part of the exchange relation. I ask the students: can you imagine any long-term relational contract surviving for long if the parties involved took that attitude to the relationship? ("Honey, would you take out the garbage?" "What will you do for me?") Union members know that a quick way to bring a company to its knees is by "working to rule," i.e. only doing what your job description specifies and no more – anything beyond that the company would have to pay me extra for. But that is the attitude that *Feinberg* takes to be normal. This extremely discrete view reflects actual contractual behavior very poorly.

The consideration materials go on to encompass one of the employee handbook cases, in which the court nicely finesses the consideration issue and holds the terms of the handbook binding on the employer despite the clear lack of the traditional "bargained for" element. We then go on to the famous plant closing/promissory estoppel case, *Local 1330, United Steel Worker v United States Steel* 631, F.2d 1204 (6th Cir. 1980), which is presented in conjunction with Farber and Matheson's (1985: 903) proposal for a new Section 71 for a future Restatement (Third) of Contracts: Section 71. Enforceability of Promises:

> A Promise is enforceable when made in furtherance of an economic activity.

Comment:

a Rationale and Relation to Other Rules. This section deals with what has traditionally been called consideration – namely, the legal conclusion that a promise is enforceable. Prior rules tested every promise or modification to determine whether the promise was conditioned on some tangible bargained-for-exchange. The present section eliminates the need for finding a specific bargained-for promise or performance for each promise or modification. Rather, the key determination is whether the promise is designed to induce the creation of or to aid in the continuation of economic activity, . . .

This leads to a discussion of whether, if Farber and Matheson's proposal were adopted, any of *Hamer*, *Feinberg* and *Local 1330* would come out the way they did.

Our treatments of agreement, conditions, interpretation and parole evidence and assignments are similar to that of consideration. Our treatment of none of these is neutral or purely descriptive. In every case, we contrast neo-classical law with relational reality. In each instance, we do try, as with consideration, to make the point that a discrete neo-classical contract law is moving in a more relational direction. Just enough material is given to allow the students to grasp the essentials of the doctrines. (For example, we read only one case on conditions.)

Contract planning

Part II of Macneil and Gudel is devoted to a series of specific problems in contract planning. As mentioned, the first chapter of this part is devoted to *performance* planning, while the remaining five chapters are devoted to *risk* planning.

The chapter on performance planning is given over to two specific planning problems. The first is planning to combine *flexibility*, in order to be able to deal with changing circumstances, with the *certainty* provided by long-range planning. The second is planning for the problem of *adjusting* contractual relationships where circumstances demand it. (Contract *planning* is not to be confused with contract *drafting*, which is a wholly different subject, and about which there are a number of good books. Drafting generally concerns putting an already planned contract into language.)

The section in planning for flexibility has first a section on the *use of standards* to build flexibility into a long-term contract (for example, use of the consumer price index in a collective bargaining agreement rather than an attempt to specify what wage increases will be given three years from now). This section includes a brief excerpt by the economist Victor Goldberg on the problems of coming up with a workable standard in more complex situations. This section is, I think, a good illustration of the way a planning approach gives the students a different look at the transactional practice of law than is given by traditional casebooks, since students have already seen cases in which a fixed price futures contract has created trouble.

This section moves on to the use of *third party* determinations of contract performance. A main emphasis here is in the use of conditions involving the insertion into the relation of experts like architects (i.e. *Nolan v Whitney*, 88 N.Y. 648 (1882)), and such devices as interest arbitration (with some fun materials on the pros and cons of salary arbitration in major league baseball). The final section treats *one party* control of contract performance – here we have *Wood v Lucy, Lady Duff-Gordon*, 222 N.Y. 88, 118 N.E. 214 (1917), §2–305 of the UCC (open price terms), conditions of satisfaction, no oral modification clauses and a marvelous article on a fashionable London restaurant which does not set prices for its meals but allows patrons to pay whatever they like. This section ends with a discussion of the usefulness and dangers of deliberate gaps in planning and agreements to agree.

The second section of Chapter 6 concerns planning for adjusting contractual relationships. Here we have voluntary settlement of disputes (the substituted agreement/executory accord distinction), the pre-existing duty rule and its decline (see UCC 2–209, Restatement (2d) Contracts § 89D), and economic duress.

From the standpoint of the traditional casebook, the topics in Macneil and Gudel seem all scrambled up. The important thing about Chapter 6 is that it deals with numerous issues that traditionally are dealt with as *doctrines* (i.e. the "hold up game" is almost always part of a chapter on consideration, agreements to agree are in a chapter on agreement, *Nolan v Whitney* in a chapter on conditions). All these are present in Macneil and Gudel, but organized according to the contract planning problem (certainty vs. flexibility) within which they are likely to arise or become relevant to the contract planning lawyer.

The large remainder of Part II (five more chapters), is devoted to risk planning. This is because traditionally lawyers are supposed to be experts in risk planning – and they are. They are in particular experts in one specific risk – the risk of a dispute between the parties, a dispute that might wind up in the legal system. The task of the lawyer here is to ensure that if a dispute does go to the courts, his or her client is in the best position to prevail.

Therefore, after an introductory section on the battle of the forms (since no risk planning provision is effective if it is not part of the contract), the course goes on to consider limitations on liability, exclusion of warranties, limitations on remedies and stipulated remedies. One unique aspect of Macneil and Gudel here is the presence of a whole section on planning for *self-help*, which groups together anticipatory repudiation (since the whole point of identifying an anticipatory repudiation is to identify when the victim of a repudiation can engage in appropriate self-help), progress payments, UCC §§ 2–601, 606, 608 ("giving the stuff back"), the uncertain duty risk ("has the other party *materially* breached, so that my client may stop performing?"), UCC § 2–609 (request for adequate assurances), and acceleration clauses.

Another thing which distinguishes Macneil and Gudel is a complete, separate chapter in the risk planning section on Indemnity, Suretyship, Insurance – tremendously important planning techniques which are rarely given any thematic treatment in contracts courses. We do not attempt to cover the complex law related to these areas, but rather try to lead students to understand how these three work and how they differ.

Part II of the casebook ends with a chapter on what happens when things that have not been planned for occur, as they inevitably do. Here we cover impossibility, impracticability, mistake, frustration of purpose and equitable conversion.

The final case decision we discuss in this section is *Alcoa v Essex Group, Inc.* 499 F. Supp. 53 (W.D. Pa 1980), which presented what at the time was the cutting edge issue in relational theory: court adjustment of long-term contracts as a remedy in cases of impracticability, mistake, etc. In *Alcoa*, after it found the contract was void for impracticality, the district court did *not* hold that defendant Alcoa was discharged of its contract duties (since time immemorial the traditional remedy for impracticality) but reformed the contract with a pricing formula that the court felt was fair to both parties and then enforced the reformed contract. The court's rationale was that simply "to decree recession in this case would be to grant Alcoa a windfall profit," and also to leave Essex Group high and dry without the assured long-term aluminum supply it had expected under the contract. The court's decision was tremendously controversial. The case was appealed but settled before the appellate court's decision (see Speidel 1982).

This final topic allows the class to discuss, for one last time, what has been one of our main themes: how should the courts respond to disputes arising in highly relational contracts?

Conclusion

The Contracts course I teach is somewhat more demanding on students than the traditional contracts course because there are more balls in the air at any one time. The class is constantly dealing with the complex nature of contracts and exchange in a highly complex and relational society, with the rules of law governing such exchange (and their underlying rationales), the question of how many of these rules can be considered to be "default rules," the criticism of existing contract law from a relational perspective, the recognition of alternative perspectives (especially that of law and economics), and the importance and the difficulty of contract planning as the primary way lawyers serve their clients. I have found, however, the students react very positively to the high degree of *unity* which the course presents. Contracts as it appears in Macneil and Gudel is not a succession of separate topics or doctrines but the working out of an intertwined set of themes which appear in the first week of the course and which persist to the end. I think the intellectual satisfaction and practical impact of this very high degree of thematic unity makes the course worth teaching in this way, even if the students do not end up fully committed to the relational theory of contracts.

References

Bernstein, L., 1996. Merchant Law in a Merchant Court: Rethinking the Code's Search for Immanent Business Norms. U. Pa. L. Rev., 144, 1765–1821.

Campbell, D., 2001. Ian Macneil and the Relational Theory of Contract In: Macneil, I. and Campbell, D., eds., *The Relational Theory of Contract: Selected Works of Ian MacNeil*. Sweet and Maxwell, London.

Eisenberg, M.A., 1976. Private Ordering Through Negotiation: Dispute-Settlement and Rulemaking. *Harv. L. Rev.*, 89, 637–681.

Farber, D.A. and Matheson, J.H., 1985. Beyond Promissory Estoppel: Contract Law and the "Invisible Handshake". *U. Chi. L. Rev.*, 52, 903–947.

Goetz, C.J. and Scott, R.E., 1981. Principles of Relational Contracts. *Va. L. Rev.*, 67, 1089–1150.

Hadfield, G.K., 1990. Problematic Relations: Franchising and the Law of Incomplete Contracts. *Stan. L. Rev.*, 47, 927–992.

Kastely, A.H., Post, D.W. and Hom, S.K., 1996. *Contracting Law*. Carolina Academic Press, Durham.

Macaulay, S., Kidwell, J. and Whitford, W.C., 1995. *Contracts: Law in Action: The Concise Course*. LexisNexis, Australia.

Macneil, I., 1960. Review of H. Shepherd and B.O. Sher, Law in Society: An Introduction to Freedom of Contract. *Cornell L. Q.*, 46, 176–179.

Macneil, I.R., 2000. Relational Contract Theory: Challenges and Queries. *Nw. U. L. Rev.*, 94, 877–908.

Macneil, I.R. and Gudel, P.J., 2001. *Contracts: Exchange Transactions and Relations: Cases and Materials*. 3rd ed. Foundation Press, New York.

Mertz, E., 2000. An Afterword: Tapping the Promise of Relational Contract Theory – "Real" Legal Language and a New Legal Realism. *Nw. U. L. Rev.*, 94, 909–936.

Posner, E.A., 2000. A Theory of Contract Law Under Conditions of Radical Judicial Error. *Nw. U.L. Rev.*, 94, 749–774.

Schwartz, A., 1992. Relational Contracts in the Courts: An Analysis of Incomplete Agreements and Judicial Strategies. *J. Legal Stud.*, 21, 271–318.

Scott, E.S. and Scott, R.E., 1998. Marriage as Relational Contract. *Va. L. Rev.*, 84, 1225–1334.

Scott, R.E., 2000. The Case for Formalism in Relational Contract. *Nw. UL Rev.*, 94, 847–887.

Speidel, R.E., 1982. The New Spirit of Contract. *J. L. Com.*, 2, 193–210.

Chapter 11

Human rights reasoning and the contract law scholar

Paul Wragg

Introduction

At first glance, this chapter may be anathema to some and foolhardy to others. What has human rights to do with contract law? They are hardly natural bedfellows. UK contract law commentators have not clamoured to join ranks with their European colleagues who see value in applying human rights scholarship to private law (Micklitz 2014). The heavyweight contract lawyers Atiyah (Smith and Atiyah 2006) and Treitel (2004) made little or no mention of human rights in their last major works at the beginning of the century. (Although by the sixth edition of Patrick Atiyah's *Introduction to the Law of Contract* (Clarendon Law Series), Stephen Smith had taken over writing responsibilities – as Atiyah mentions in the preface – nevertheless, Atiyah says he 'commented extensively' on Smith's draft and, presumably, had opportunity to suggest discussion of the Human Rights Act 1998.) Those commentators who have engaged with human rights law have been less than fulsome in their praise of its virtues; indeed, the reception has been decidedly mixed, ranging from passive ambivalence, to mistrust, to something like outright contempt (e.g., Campbell 2000a, 2002, 2015; Halson 2013; McKendrick 2017 – Collins (2011), however, strikes a more conciliatory tone toward human rights reasoning in contract law). With that in mind, I ask the reader to indulge me: by claiming that human rights can aid the study of contract law, I do not pretend that human rights scholarship is in any way superior; quite the opposite, I agree with those contract law scholars who have challenged its shortcomings (e.g., Campbell 2015). Instead, I hope to show complementary modes of thinking between contract law and human rights law.

This, to my mind, is valuable for the novice contract law scholar because it provides a parallel to aid them through the unfamiliar. After all, contract law tends to be problematic for the novice because both the terminology (e.g., consideration, vitiating factors, frustration, revocation, promissory estoppel, unconscionability, *uberrimae fidei*, *res extincta*, *res sua*, *restitution in integrum*, *quantum meriut*, etc.) and scenarios (e.g., complicated financial transactions, insurance policies, shipping arrangements, hire-purchase agreements, etc.) are likely to seem alien to the average 18-year-old. Judicial reasoning in such cases can also seem odd; it will not always follow the pre-legal intuitions with which novice lawyers tend to approach the study of law. I seek to show, in this chapter, that human rights theory (a term I shall define and defend shortly) offers a ready means of understanding the judicial mindset in what is otherwise unfamiliar territory. Not only that, I will also argue that this dual approach, in which the contract lawyer sees the parallels with constitutional rights may benefit the discipline in the longer term. I seek to demonstrate this by showing the value of human rights thinking in wider contract law practice.

I should add that the thoughts expressed here are personal reflections on teaching contract law over the past decade. They do not necessarily reflect the views of the School of Law at the University of Leeds, or other institutions at which I have taught.

Human rights theory

As with the theory of contract law, human rights theory is a richly textured, contested, multi-disciplined area of academic interest. It is (relatively) uncontroversial to claim that human rights are moral guarantees that a state ought to recognise. The nature of these rights, though, is more contested, including, e.g., whether the rights are limited to civil and political guarantees (such as the right to self-determination) or extend to socio-economic rights (e.g., a right to water, to employment or to adequate housing), or whether they exist by virtue of natural law or not, etc. Likewise, the content of rights may be interpreted differently in different jurisdictions. For example, the Netherlands, the United Kingdom, Austria and China all recognise that the right to freedom of expression can be curtailed, legitimately, when national security or public safety is threatened. But there is much disagreement between these jurisdictions as to what counts as national security or public safety. The Netherlands, being a more socially left society, would be less likely to interfere with that right than, say, China; in China, criticism of government can itself count as a legitimate reason to interfere, something unheard of in the Netherlands.

To keep the discussion manageable, the term human rights theory is used mainly to convey such understandings of human rights as the novice contract law scholar is likely to encounter in their first-year studies on the law programme in England and Wales – though I think the general thrust of the argument has wider appeal, certainly in the US and Commonwealth countries. In England and Wales, first-years will learn about constitutional rights and the European Convention on Human Rights ('the Convention'), which is given further effect through the Human Rights Act 1998, in their public law or constitutional law module. This introduces students to the basic notion of human rights as civil and political claims (rather than the more advanced, and contested, claim of socio-economic rights). That module will also introduce the novice to the difference between absolute rights (such as the right to life) and qualified rights (such as the right to privacy or freedom of expression) as well as the legal framework, by which conflicting qualified rights claims are determined by a process of judicial balancing, where interferences with rights must be for a legitimate purpose (as stated in the Convention) and proportionate to the achievement of that purpose. Proportionality, in its Convention sense, will also become familiar to first-years when they study grounds for judicial review.

For the purposes of this discussion, it is also helpful to discuss some elementary political philosophy which students may encounter either through their lectures or through wider reading on the subject, specifically, the notion of rights claims as understood in classic liberalism. The chief point to which I wish to draw attention is liberalism's aversion to paternalism. This is apparent not only in the works of, say, Adam Smith (Campbell and Skinner 1976) and John Stuart Mill (Robson 1977), but also in those of more modern liberals such as Friedrich Hayek (Caldwell 2007) and Joel Feinberg (1989). Indeed, Feinberg expresses the point well: liberalism 'denies that the need to protect a free, informed and competent actor from the harmful consequences of his own voluntary conduct is ever a good reason for restricting his liberty' (Feinberg 1989: 3). Harm to others is a legitimate reason for judicial interference, but it is not sufficient of itself: it must be shown, in the words of Feinberg (1984: 26) again, that 'there is probably no other means that is equally effective at no greater cost to other values'. Something like this finds expression in common law contract decisions: the law should not protect the individual from her own bad judgment and need not always protect her from losses she incurs through contracting.

My chief claim, established in the next section, is that since the essence of liberty, rooted in its overriding concern to protect the autonomous individual from the paternalistic state, mirrors the *laissez faire* philosophy of classical contract law doctrine, the elementary political philosophy and human rights framework introduced in the public or constitutional law module can be put to good effect in the contract law classroom to explain the law's more mysterious or counter-intuitive moments (that is, mysterious and counter-intuitive to the novice convinced that justice and fairness are welfarist in nature). Just as John Stuart Mill railed against the 'tyrannous majority' who think they know what is best, so too Hayek condemned economic decision-making through state planning. This prioritisation of heterogeneity over homogeneity in determining the 'good life' is the essence of the ideas of those beginning their study of contract. The classic model of freedom of contract (which draws on notions of reciprocity, the solemnity of agreement, the sanctity of contract, the priority of express terms over implied terms, the limited availability of injunctive relief) speaks of a system in which judges treat the law as rules-based not principles-based (in Dworkin's sense of the distinction), and are loath to permit judicial discretion for fear of its effect on legal certainty. In other words, I use human rights as a proxy for classic liberalism which defends civil and political rights from undue interference by the state. In doing so, I seek to tease out the underpinnings of classic contract law theory which treats state inference, be that regulation or legal paternalism, with disdain.

Admittedly, this parallel can only take scholarly understanding of contract law so far and at some point needs jettisoning so that the mature scholar can appreciate the existence of other contract law theories, including notions of the relational contract and, of course, welfarist notions of contract (see e.g., Campbell 2000b; Vincent-Jones 2006; MacNeil 1980) as well as the consumerist and welfarist additions that statutes provide (e.g., Consumer Rights Act 2015, Unfair Contract Terms Act 1977, Sale of Goods Act 1979, Employment Rights Act 1996). Clearly, I am presupposing that a sort of rigid, simplistic view of contract law as solely rules-based (in ignorance of these wider conceptions and extensions of law) is (initially, at least) valuable to the students' better understanding of contract law. That is a view that cannot be defended fully here, though I recognise it is controversial – although perhaps made less controversial by the focus here on common law (to the exclusion of statute). This also speaks to a personal view that the study of contract law would be improved if the first-year law student could do no more than articulate the various legal issues arising in the life cycle of the contract, focusing specifically on terms, performance and the remedies available for non-performance, to the detriment of knowing about complex vitiating factors, or the metaphysics of what a contract really is in law. I have seen too many students sap their energy for critical study on the question of what consideration means, the rule in *Scotson v Pegg* (1861) 6 Hurl & N 295, the availability of promissory estoppel or the niceties of the postal rule – questions that any practitioner will say almost never crop up in real life litigation – such that they feel thoroughly disenchanted, if not lost, by the time the course reaches interpretation of the contract, performance and remedies.

Human rights reasoning in contract law

Anti-paternalism, liberty and the classic model of contract law

Typically, first-year law students struggle to identify with contract law. As noted, this is partly a matter of familiarity. The road traffic accident in tort, the theft or murder case in criminal law, public protest and the passing of statutes in public or constitutional law, all come with ready points of reference that easily engage the underlying law. But the problem also relates to a failure to understand the judicial mindset in contract law. It is alien to them. Unlike other typical first-year subjects, it does not readily match their pre-legal intuitions about law. Seeing decisions through the lens of liberalism can help resolve some of these difficulties. Reasons of space prevent a full appraisal of the contract law diet; but the point can be seen by examining some of the trickier problems that law students encounter.

For example, the common law approach to mistake often baffles students. The distinction between a case like *Hartog v Colin and Shields* [1939] 3 All

ER 566 (where the contract was void because the buyers were snatching at a bargain they ought to have known the sellers had not intended to make) and *Bell v Lever Bros* [1932] AC 161 (where the compromise agreement between employee and employer was not void even though the employer could have dismissed the employee for nothing) or *Lewis v Averay* [1972] 1 QB 198 (where the seller was duped into believing the buyer of his car was a famous actor, and therefore creditworthy) is usually not easily perceived. Why, students often ask, is it that only the seller in *Hartog* can rely upon the buyer's presumed knowledge when the defendant in *Bell* and the rogue in *Lewis* would also have known, or ought to have known, that the actor was acting on mistaken information?

These sorts of conceptual difficulties arise across the contract law course, and the tutor's role is to toughen the student so that they recognise the difference between pre-legal, intuitive 'fairness' and the common law's *laissez faire* underpinnings. This may explain why students tend to lionise Lord Denning, since his notions of fairness often match the pre-legal intuition students have. For example, his solution to the problem of mistaken identity, that the third party is usually the more innocent of the two duped parties, is more understandable to the contract law scholar than the law's (convoluted) distinction between mistake as to identity and mistake as to attributes. Likewise, students tend to prefer Lord Justice Devlin's suggestion in *Ingram v Little* [1961] 1 QB 31, 73–74 that in such cases the value of the property should be shared between the parties:

> The plain answer is that the loss should be divided between them in such proportion as is just in all the circumstances. If it be pure misfortune, the loss should be borne equally; if the fault or imprudence of either party has caused or contributed to the loss, it should be borne by that party in the whole or in the greater part.

This solution, though, was rejected by the Law Reform Committee in its *Twelfth Report on Transfer of Title to Chattels* (Cmnd 2958 (1966)), who thought it would give judges too much discretion and therefore would undermine legal certainty (although see the criticism of Atiyah 1966). Arguably, this conclusion makes sense if the scholar recognises it as a sign of anti-paternalism of the sort seen in classical liberalism. In this way, students can better understand the mind of the contract law judge.

The common law's treatment of agreement also speaks to this theme. For example, *caveat emptor* remains a meaningful rule (to the extent that the Consumer Rights Act 2015, Sale of Goods Act 1979 or Supply of Goods and Services Act 1982 are not engaged). This can be seen in the rule that the false representation must induce the contract. In *Horsfall v Thomas* (1862) 1 H & C 90, the seller concealed a serious defect in the gun (through use of a metal plug), but the purchaser could not rely on the deception because he had not inspected the gun prior to purchase. The contract law judge is not concerned to punish the seller or protect the buyer from a bad bargain. She is concerned only with the statements made about the subject matter. If there is no term incorporated into the contract and no actionable misrepresentation, the buyer is left with no remedy. This attitude is apparent in other misrepresentation cases. For example, in *Roscorla v Thomas* (1842) 3 QB 234, the claimant was unable to enforce the (false) post-contract claim by the defendant that the horse (the subject of the contract) was sound. That claim was unsupported by consideration. Similarly, the law will not protect the promise to pay where the promisee is under an existing duty to perform it (see, e.g., *Collins v Godefroy* (1831) 1 B & Ad 950). Nor will it protect the promise to accept less in full satisfaction of a debt (*Foakes v Beer* (1884) 9 App Cas 605) (although, cf, *MWB Business Exchange Centres Ltd v Rock Advertising Ltd* [2016] EWCA Civ 553). To understand the doctrine, the contract lawyer must think, not about what is best or right for the parties in the circumstances, but whether the rules have been complied with. This process focuses the mind on the nature of exchange in the minimal sense of whether something sufficient (but not adequate) passes between the parties.

Contractual alterations involving the promise to pay more challenge this thesis but do not disprove it. In *Williams v Roffey* [1991] 1 QB 1, the Court of Appeal was rather generous toward the change of circumstances that caused the sub-contractor claimants to ask for more money from the main contractor to complete the work they had previously promised to do. The court could have dismissed the claimant's case by applying the rule in *Stilk v Myrick* (1809) 2 Camp 317 that the promise to pay more for the performance of a pre-existing contractual duty will be unenforceable for want of fresh consideration. Yet the court was clearly sympathetic to the claimant's view that the promise to pay more if the work was done on time allowed the defendant to avoid paying compensation for late completion under the main contract. So, although it chimes less with the strict *laissez faire* of *Stilk v Myrick*, it does contain the decision within the framework of traditional consideration doctrine; it simply alters our understanding of what counts as a valuable exchange.

This liberal approach is also apparent in the way the common law treats exemption clauses. It is unconcerned with whether such clauses are 'fair' *per se* (statute has assumed that role), but rather whether they have been incorporated into the contract prior to, or at the point of, contracting and whether, strictly interpreted, they apply to the circumstances. This is not to deny the existence of (what may be construed as) result-pulled decisions (e.g., *Interfoto Picture Library Ltd v Stiletto Visual Programmes Ltd* [1989] QB 433, *Thornton v Shoe Lane Parking Ltd* [1971] 2 QB 163).

Public policy and human rights: the contract law judge as rights champion

Narrowing our gaze, we can also see the liberal principle animating public policy decision-making in contract law. For example, in the classic case of *De Francesco v Barnum* (1890) 45 Ch D 430, the High Court refused to grant an order of specific performance to compel the (child) actor to fulfil the contract of services. *Per* Fry LJ:

> For my own part, I should be very unwilling to extend decisions the effect of which is to compel persons who are not desirous of maintaining continuous personal relations with one another to continue those personal relations. I have a strong impression and a strong feeling that it is not in the interest of mankind that the rule of specific performance should be extended to such cases. I think the Courts are bound to be jealous, lest they should turn contracts of service into contracts of slavery . . .
>
> (438)

As Treitel (2004) notes, 'To order an employee to work would unduly interfere with his personal liberty'. Indeed, Peel argues that this position is now guaranteed by the Human Rights Act 1998 by virtue of the obligation on courts (under s 6) to comply with the Convention as public authorities (Peel 2015: 11–061). In this way, the common law judge acts as an important champion for liberty across the spectrum of public and private law. The protection of liberty informs the judge's task when asked to grant remedies that would undermine a party's integrity as an autonomous being.

But this is an area where courts tread very carefully. Orders for specific performance in a contract for personal service are an egregious interference with liberty because of the unjustified coercion that would otherwise be involved. Likewise, on the flip side, the court will not imply a positive obligation on the parties to act unless it is of necessity. For example, in *Liverpool City Council v Irwin* [1977] AC 239, the House of Lords recognised that the landlords of a block of flats were under a legal obligation (not mentioned in the contract) to maintain the common parts in a 'reasonable' state of repair. Lord Wilberforce held that the court could imply a term by law, but only where necessary: 'In my opinion such obligation should be read into the contract as the nature of the contract itself implicitly requires, no more, no less: a test, in other words, of necessity'. This approach differed from Lord Denning, MR (in the Court of Appeal [1976] 1 QB 319), who was prepared to imply the term as a matter of expediency (albeit he would have found for the council):

> Some people seem to think that now that there is a Law Commission the judges should leave it to them to put right any defect and to make any new development. The judges must no longer play a constructive role. They must be automatons applying the existing rules. Just think what this means. The law must stand still until the Law Commission have reported and Parliament passed a statute on it: and, meanwhile, every litigant must have his case decided by the dead hand of the past. I decline to reduce the judges to such a sterile role. They should develop the law, case by case, as they have done in the past; so that the litigants before them can have their differences decided by the law as it should be.

The liberty principle helps explain the subtle difference between Lord Wilberforce's decision and Lord Denning's: the common law does not imply terms by law because they are 'fair' or 'good' but because as a matter of necessity they must 'exist' (the law student develops a clearer understanding of this distinction if they study employment law, where they will encounter, e.g., the implied term of mutual trust and confidence) (see Halson 2013). Admittedly, this description of contract law is exaggerated (for effect); this is the classic law position, which is doubtful today (assuming it was ever true). But, for first-year contract law study, it is sufficient (arguably). To put it differently, for contract law judges 'justice' is determined by legal precedent, the meetings of the minds and the solemn bonds of contractual agreement, not by paternalism, welfarism or consumerism.

This simplistic approach has pedagogical value. Interpreting the judicial power to imply terms in this narrow way ought to help the student understand why it is the role of Parliament and not the judge to introduce 'fairness' into the contract. As Halson (2013) puts it:

> It is exactly because contract law still has a core that is at least in part justifiable in terms of mutual consent that the courts feel embarrassed to openly reserve to themselves a general power to overturn or supplement the unambiguously expressed intentions of the parties.
>
> (297)

Likewise, the liberal approach can help explain why the common law recognises no general duty to act in good faith or *uberrimae fidei* in the formation and performance of the contract. This sort of legal moralism (to hold contracts to a standard beyond its terms) interferes with the autonomy of the parties to negotiate protections for themselves prior to contract (see Smith and Atiyah 2006).

Cost of cure and proportionality

Finally, an understanding of human rights practices can help explain contract law at a micro-level. For example, Halson (2013) has noted that the similarity between the calculation of compensation under the Convention and the expectation measure in traditional contract law damages.

Perhaps the clearest example of this use can be seen in the context of the law's treatment of the cost of cure. At the University of Leeds, we use an example in seminars that always provokes extreme reactions from our students. In fact, such is the level of outrage (a term not used lightly) that this provokes, that these seminars have been a constant source of joy. It is as follows:

> Adrian, a lawyer, engages Dora to design and build a summer house for construction in the large garden of Adrian's country mansion. Adrian insists upon recording the terms of their agreement in writing. These terms state that (i) the windows of the summer house will be double-glazed

> throughout with glass manufactured by an American firm, Coolglaze Inc [there are other terms] . . .
>
> Adrian . . . discovers that the glass used in the double-glazing has not been manufactured by Coolglaze Inc, but by a local firm. The glass used is just as good quality, but Dora saved herself £10,000 by switching manufacturers. Adrian demands that Dora replace all the windows with glass manufactured by Coolglaze Inc.(Dr David Pearce of the University of Leeds is the author of this example).

Invariably, (indeed, in almost every instance in which I teach this seminar), there is at least one student (but often several) who becomes quite animated in favour of a (supposed) right of Adrian to his 'Coolglaze Inc' window. It cannot be fair, they say, that Dora can ride roughshod over the terms of the contract: what about the sanctity of contract? To which I say, yes, but . . . Students often do not perceive that these facts replicate those in the US decision, *Jacob & Youngs v Kent* 129 NE 889 (1921), in which the contract stipulated the pipework (in the building of a new house) should be of 'Reading manufacture', but which the builder overlooked in installing a different product of the same quality. Cardozo J held that:

> the cost of replacement is the [usual] measure. . . . The owner is entitled to the money which will permit him to complete, unless the cost of completion is grossly and unfairly out of proportion to the good to be attained. When that is true, the measure is the difference in value [even if it is a nominal amount].

This finding was approved, and applied, by the House of Lords in *Ruxley Electronics and Construction Ltd v Forsyth* [1996] 1 AC 344.

In one sense, it may be said the use of proportionality here has no special or esoteric meaning. It is used in its ordinary way and can be interchanged with the terms 'commensurate', 'relative', 'comparable', etc. In so far as it goes, this is fine, but it does not explain *why* damages need be proportionate. Granted, we would hope the rule that damages compensate not punish would be sufficient explanation but, returning to the 'Coolglaze Inc' scenario, clarity is not always achieved because many students believe replacement with 'Coolglaze Inc' windows *is* compensation (that is, the fulfilment of the binding promise).

By drawing the student's attention to its use in human rights law, these pedagogical problems may be overcome. Specifically, an understanding of proportionality helps the student understand the nature of rights. In their public law module, they will encounter Lord Diplock's memorable understanding of proportionality, that a sledgehammer is not needed to crack a nut (*CCSU v Minister for the Civil Service* [1985] AC 374), and, in the application of the Human Rights Act 1998, that any interferences with rights must be proportionate to the legitimate aim pursued. This learning is valuable to understanding cost of cure. It introduces students to the distinction between absolute and qualified rights. In this way, students may understand why Adrian's claim to replacement of his windows is disproportionate to the nature of his rights. He cannot insist upon fulfilment of the term, either as specific performance or the cost of using an alternative contractor, where the net benefit to him is marginal (the interested scholar can be directed to Barak (2012) and Alexy (2002)). He does not have an absolute right to performance of a contract term, but a qualified right to what is reasonable in respect of that performance.

Lessons for the future?

Inculcating human rights thinking into the study of contract law is not merely window-dressing. It can have (and has had) real value in contract law practice, despite an unpromising start. When the HRA was introduced, the clamour to realise its implications for contract law practice quickly dissipated after the disappointing decision in *Wilson v First County Trust Ltd (No 2)* [2003] UKHL 40, in which the House of Lords overturned the Court of Appeal's decision that provisions of the Consumer Credit Act 1974 were incompatible with the right to a fair trial under Article 6 of the Convention (see Beale 2015: 1-066-1-068). But more recently, the invocation of Art 6 proved decisive in UNISON's successful claim that the (outrageous) Employment Tribunal fees scheme, in which fees were in the thousands for even a simple unfair dismissal claim, was unlawful (*R (on the application of UNISON) v Lord Chancellor* [2017] UKSC 51). It may be that similar success could be achieved if the Civil Court fees scheme is challenged, where the issue fee is 5% of the value of the claim (on claims over £10,000, subject to a maximum of a £10,000 court fee). This is a staggering amount of money to charge claimants in pursuance of their legal rights. (Although the normal rule is that successful claimants recover their costs from the other side, incurring costs in pursuit of a claim is always a litigation risk given that a) those costs are (ordinarily) only recoverable at the conclusion of the claim, which may be years ahead, and b) the defendant may lack the means to pay them. Thus, the high level of costs adds greatly to that risk.)

One area where increased engagement with human rights law would be most profitable is employment law. Employment Tribunal and Employment Appeal Tribunal judges have so far demonstrated little sympathy – or understanding – of human rights law when asked to rule on its applicability to employment law issues. This is disappointing since the right to respect for privacy and family life under Article 8 of the Convention and the right to freedom of expression under Article 10 are two important areas in which the powers of the public authority are (rightly) subdued but those of the private employer are not (see, e.g., Mantouvalou (2008) and Wragg (2015)). The legal protection afforded to free speech rights is especially weak. Tribunals are generally sympathetic to the employer who dismisses the opinionated employee for fear that negativity surrounding their public comments (usually disseminated through social media) reflects badly upon them (the employer). Moreover, tribunals have been too quick to assume that since freedom of speech is a valuable social and political good, the 'value' of speech for democratic purposes is the metric by which free speech rights is judged. This has found its poorest expression in one Employment Tribunal judgment which concluded the right to freedom of speech is one that must be exercised 'judiciously, responsibly and not recklessly' (*Hill v Great Tey Primary School* [2013] ICL 691, [44]).

Human rights law is also relevant to the formation of contracts, particularly where the parties seek to restrict access to the courts when there is a dispute. There is a rich source of case law in this area. Granted, the prospect of an arbitration agreement that binds the parties (and prevents further judicial consideration of the matter) is not, of itself, incompatible with Art 6 (see, e.g., *Broda Agro Trade (Cyprus) Ltd v Alfred C Toepfer International Gmbh* [2010] EWCA Civ 1100), but, nonetheless, drafters must be careful not to be too heavy-handed in the treatment of any restrictions on resolution by court trial. For example, the right to a fair trial may be at stake if one party was forced to agree to arbitration as the only means of resolving disputes in circumstances where the coercion fell short of the standard required for duress (see, e.g., *El Nasharty v J Sainsbury Plc* [2007] EWHC 2618 (Comm) where this argument failed on the facts of the case).

Conclusion

These claims about contract law pedagogy betray the academy in an important sense. The study of contract law has been treated here as an exercise in practical, not academic, understanding of the subject. I am treating the student as a future practitioner and not an exemplar of studying for its own sake. Moreover, I have argued for the use of theory found elsewhere (constitutional law) rather than engagement with contract law's own rich literature on theory. I defend this as a pragmatic solution. In my experience, the typical first-year student finds the study of contract law hard because of its unfamiliarity; as a subject, it is an outlier, compared to the more familiar scenarios and terms found in constitutional law (politics), torts (road traffic accidents) and criminal law (theft and murder). Moreover, the opportunity to discover the rich, underlying theoretical literature is minimal in contract law: the typical syllabus is vast, as it progresses, at a canter, through the three fundamentals of contract law (formation, performance and vitiating factors). In this way, my appeal to knowledge learnt elsewhere in the first-year diet is a 'cheat', an attempt to advocate conceptual understanding of contract law without requiring more work.

In the UK, the Solicitors Regulation Authority seems determined to ruin the study of law by removing the requirement of a qualifying law degree as a preliminary to entering the profession, in favour of the mysterious 'solicitor qualification examination' (mysterious in that no one asked for this fundamental change and no one seriously believes it will cure whatever wrong the SRA thinks exists in the current process of entering the profession). It may be that this affords an opportunity to rethink contract law pedagogy: to shrink the black-letter aspect of the syllabus and allow for greater conceptual engagement from within. But even this may not cure the issues identified above. If it is a matter of familiarity that the first-year student struggles to understand, then further engagement with the literature may not help if the student perceives it to be esoteric.

But I defend this pragmatic solution on the grounds that it is of wider benefit to contract law, in practice and theory. Not only do I think contract law practice has much to gain from a deeper understanding of human rights principles (particularly on the question of proportionality and the right to a fair trial), but also, within the academy, in engaging with the intellectual movement that calls for the unity of the legal order: the 'total constitution' (Collins 2012). For my generation, which studied law at the moment of the Human Rights Act 1998's enactment, one corollary is that we are all human rights lawyers (in an important sense) and are prepared to see all law through that lens, regardless of whether the UK retains the HRA or replaces it with a UK bill of rights.

References

Alexy, R., 2002. *A Theory of Constitutional Rights*. Oxford University Press, Oxford.

Atiyah, P.S., 1966. Law Reform Committee: Twelfth Report. *Mod. L. Rev.*, 29, 541–545.

Barak, A., 2012. *Proportionality: Constitutional Rights and their Limitations*. Cambridge University Press, Cambridge.

Beale, H., 2015. *Chitty on Contracts: General Principles*. 32nd ed. (Vol. 1). Sweet & Maxwell, London.

Caldwell, B., 2007. *The Road to Serfdom: Text and Documents: The Definitive Edition* (Vol. 2). University of Chicago Press, Chicago.

Campbell, D., 2000a. The Limits of Concept Formation in Legal Science. *Soc. Legal Stud.*, 9, 439–447.

Campbell, D., 2000b. Reflexivity and Welfarism in the Modern Law of Contract. *Oxford J. Legal Stud.*, 20, 477–498.

Campbell, D., 2002. Bringing Law and Lawyers to the People: Statism and Anarchy in Left-Wing Legal Thought. *Soc. & Legal Stud.*, 11, 413–424.

Campbell, D., 2015. "Catgate" and the Challenge to Parliamentary Sovereignty in Immigration Law. *Public Law*, 426–439.

Campbell, R.H. and Skinner, A.S., 1976. *The Glasgow Edition of the Works and Correspondence of Adam Smith: An Inquiry Into the Nature and Causes of the Wealth of Nations* (Vol. 1 & 2). Oxford University Press, Oxford.

Collins, H., 2011. Impact of Human Rights Law on Contract Law in Europe. *Eur. Bus. L. Rev.*, 22, 425.

Collins, H., 2012. Cosmopolitanism and Transnational Private Law. *Eur. Rev. Contract L.*, 8, 311.

Feinberg, J., 1984. *The Moral Limits of the Criminal Law: Volume 1: Harm to Others*. Oxford University Press, Oxford.

Feinberg, J., 1989. *The Moral Limits of the Criminal Law: Volume 4: Harmless Wrongdoing*. Oxford University Press, Oxford.

Halson, R., 2013. *Contract Law*. 2nd ed. Pearson Education Limited, Harlow.
Macneil, I.R., 1980. *The New Social Contract: An Inquiry Into Modern Contractual Relations*. Yale University Press, New Haven.
Mantouvalou, V., 2008. Human Rights and Unfair Dismissal: Private Acts in Public Spaces. *Mod. L. Rev.*, 71, 912–939.
McKendrick, E., 2017. *Contract Law*. 12th ed. Palgrave Macmillan, London.
Micklitz, H.W. ed., 2014. *Constitutionalization of European Private Law* (Vol. 22). Collected Courses of the Acade. Oxford University Press, Oxford.
Peel, E., 2015. *Treitel: The Law of Contract*. 14th ed. Sweet & Maxwell, London.
Robson, J.M., 1977. *Collected Works of John Stuart Mill* (Vol. XVIII) Essays on Politics and Society Part I. University of Toronto Press, Toronto.
Smith, S.A. and Atiyah, P.S., 2006. *Atiyah's Introduction to the Law of Contract*. Clarendon Press, Oxford.
Treitel, G., 2004. *An Outline of the Law of Contract*. 6th ed. Oxford University Press, Oxford.
Vincent-Jones, P., 2006. *The New Public Contracting: Regulation, Responsiveness, Relationality*. Oxford University Press, Oxford.
Wragg, P., 2015. Free Speech Rights at Work: Resolving the Differences Between Practice and Liberal Principle. *Indus. L.J.*, 44, 1–28.

Chapter 12

Contract law teaching

Teaching from the case law

David Capper

Introduction

General contract law, the body of principles applying to the vast majority of contracts, remains an overwhelmingly common law case law-based system of jurisprudence in most parts of the common law world. As the editing and general production of this book is being undertaken in New Zealand where the Contract and Commercial Law Act 2017 provides a relatively comprehensive set of rules in this subject area that caveat must be acknowledged. It does not detract from the general point made above. Certain parts of the contract law empire have been codified in statute, such as the Bills of Exchange Act 1882, the Marine Insurance Act 1906, the Consumer Credit Act 1974 and the Sale of Goods Act 1979, but these enactments relate mainly to certain specific kinds of contracts. Within the general contract law some statutes deal with specific issues, such as the Unfair Contract Terms Act 1977 (dealing with exclusion clauses) and the Law Reform (Frustrated Contracts) Act 1943 (providing for the unscrambling of contracts terminated by frustration). But beyond these few discrete examples the corpus of general contract law consists almost entirely of judicial decisions from superior courts that have to a greater or lesser extent crystallised into a reasonably stable system of law. As this system of law is composed of decided cases it follows that any contract law teacher and all contract law students must engage with case law if they are to understand the subject satisfactorily.

Contract law cannot realistically be taught exclusively through case law. This is not just because statutes such as those referred to above are of crucial importance and must be given their place, but also because a completely case law perspective would be far too narrow. Students would not acquire a sufficient understanding of the general principles of contract law, the policy considerations on which those principles are based and the wider theoretical context in which contract law operates, were this approach adopted. They would not get the bigger picture that gives what they learn from studying contract cases true value. This collection of essays certainly cannot be accused of any failure to appreciate the bigger picture. The essay occupying the next several pages of this collection is in harmony with the collection's overall objectives. In celebrating the more traditional, doctrinal approach to contract law teaching and scholarship, it does not yearn for the return of a golden age when this was the pathway usually followed. It fully endorses those wider perspectives that other contributors bring to the table, while maintaining that there is much good in the old which should be retained and incorporated into the more holistic approach advocated by this collection. The argument that will be presented is that, of course, we cannot teach contract law *entirely* from the case law, but we must use the case law creatively and realistically to foster key skills and to develop an understanding of the way that the common law works. In contrast to civilian and other code-based systems of law which operate top down, from general code provisions to particular rules, the common law moves from the bottom up. Judicial decisions harden into rules and principles once a significant body of precedent relating to a particular issue accumulates. Cases must be studied to understand how this dynamic of the common law works (for a particularly celebrated study of this process see Cardozo 1921).

The essay begins with a fairly lengthy discussion of the case method of legal education that has predominated in the United States for most of the last century and a half. This is where teaching contract law *from* the cases truly began in earnest. This is where it was practised in its purest form and where a vast body of experience has been accumulated. In order to understand both what is good about teaching contract law from the cases and the drawbacks associated with this method some delving into the American literature on this subject is essential. Once the essay has described and explained the American case method, and discussed its pluses and minuses, the essay will go on to suggest how teaching from the cases can make a very positive contribution to contract law pedagogy in the years to come. This last section of the essay will draw upon the author's own personal experiences in teaching contract law in the United Kingdom for over 25 years, and a year teaching contract law *the American way* as a visiting professor of law at an accredited United States' law school in the early 1990s.

Langdell's case method

When recommending how contract law should be taught from case law, it must surely be instructive to begin by considering how and why United States' law schools came to teach contract law, and indeed almost everything else, in this way. In 1870 Christopher Columbus Langdell was appointed to the Dane Professorship of Law and the first Dean of Harvard Law School (Gilmore 1977: 41–48; Weaver 1991). His most enduring contribution to legal education was his institution of the case method of instruction. This involved the preparation of printed materials (extracts from law reports) for students to read prior to class. In class the instructor would call upon individual students and engage in a process of Socratic questioning about key aspects of a case – facts, case history up to the court which delivered the final judgment, the arguments of the parties, the decision of the court and whether it was consistent with other decisions on the same issue. As Hall has pointed out this was not the first time law students had been taught through cases; it appears that the Inns of Court in London taught through cases during the Middle Ages and later on (Hall 1955). However Langdell's preparation of printed materials represented a much more systematic way of engaging in this kind of instruction.

The case method replaced earlier instruction models used in the universities at that time, mainly those based on lectures and textbook (Austin 1965), and also the apprenticeship system that operated outside of formal educational institutions. Langdell appears to have wanted to secure the place of the law school within Harvard University itself. Law was perceived to be a craft that did not belong within the university (Weaver 1991: 529; Moskovitz 1992: 243–224). Langdell claimed that law was a science and that the library was the lawyer's laboratory. In a speech he delivered some 17 years after his election to the Deanship at Harvard Langdell (1887: 124) declared:

> [t]he library is the proper workshop of [law] professors and students alike; . . . it is to us all that the laboratories of the university are to the chemists and physicists, the museum of natural history to the zoologists, the botanical garden to the botanists.

By viewing law as a science Langdell sought to legitimise its inclusion among the wider academic curriculum. Langdell described his method in the preface to his casebook on contract law (Langdell 1871: vi):

> Law, considered as a science, consists of certain principles or doctrines. To have such a mastery of these as to be able to apply them with constant facility and certainty to the ever-tangled skein of human affairs, is what constitutes a true lawyer; and hence to acquire that mastery should be the business of every earnest student of the law. Each of these doctrines has arrived at its present state by slow degrees; in other words, it is a growth, extending in many cases through centuries. This growth is to be traced in the main through a series of cases; and much the shortest and best, if not the only way of mastering the doctrine effectually is by studying the cases in which it is embodied. But the cases which are useful and necessary for this purpose at the present day bear an exceedingly small proportion to all that have been reported. The vast majority are useless and worse than useless for any purpose of systematic study. Moreover, the number of fundamental legal doctrines is much less than is commonly supposed; the many different guises in which the same doctrine is constantly making its appearance, and the great extent to which legal treatises are a repetition of each other, being the case of much misapprehension. If these doctrines could be so classified and arranged that each should be found in its proper place, and nowhere else, they would cease to be formidable from the number.

Gilmore described the period in American legal history from which this statement hails as 'The Age of Faith' (Gilmore 1977: ch 3). There is a definite other-worldly, hopelessly naïve quality to it. The common law is presented as timeless and unchanging, and judicial determination as a mechanical choice-free process. Only a few selected cases are useful but how these are to be identified is far from clear. There seems to be little room for any new cases to add to the general understanding of the law. The reader of this essay may well wonder why an author apparently recommending the case method as a teaching tool should start with a quotation like this. The explanation lies in the desirability of showing why the case method was originally adopted. Whether other American law schools bought into Langdell's orthodoxy in full measure admits of some doubt, but what there is no doubt about is that the case method of instruction became and remained the established law school teaching method throughout the United States until comparatively recent times. As Weaver has pointed out candidates for teaching positions and junior faculty seeking tenure were not likely to disparage it; many indeed had prospered under it when they were at law school (Weaver 1991: 544). The Socratic method appears to have been used in tandem with the case method, although there seems no reason to believe that teaching law from the cases necessarily required Socratic exposition. There certainly are signs of the Socratic method being used in a somewhat diluted fashion in more recent times (Kerr 1999, pointing out that a mixture of quasi-Socratic, lecturing and group discussion teaching methods were in use at Harvard Law School in the late 1990s), although it is worthwhile stating that when the author taught in the United States in the early 1990s it was still alive and kicking.

What is good about the case method?

It seems trite to say that if the case method prospered for the considerable time it evidently did it must have had something going for it. Indeed there is testimony to the value of the case method in its adoption, in adumbrated form, in the common law systems of the British Isles for well over half a century now. One of the pioneers of the case method in contract law in the British Isles was the late Professor Sir John Smith who used this method with his former colleague Professor JAC Thomas at Nottingham University in the 1960s (Smith 1967). It is worth noting that Socratic style teaching does not seem to have been a feature of the way they taught.

So what are the benefits of teaching contract law from the cases? The list below contains most of the generally accepted benefits of teaching contract law this way but is not claimed to be completely comprehensive.

First, where students actually read cases their learning is likely to be more in depth (Smith 1967). At a relatively basic level they will learn how to read cases properly, extracting the law from the judgments and reading those judgments adversarially so as to spot ambiguities, vagueness and gaps (Weaver 1991: 549–550; Slawson 2000). These may not be everyday skills for every lawyer and may not specifically involve anything that a law graduate who enters a non-law career may be required to do. But the art of reading something densely written deeply and carefully can only be valuable whatever one's walk of life. In addition to the deep reading skill fostered by reading cases, cases often have human interest stories that can make the law memorable, and on the interpretation of statutes (a crucial task in other legal areas) they can provide examples to clarify what the statute means (Knapp 2013: 1361).

Second, reading cases helps students to get to grips with common law methodology and doctrine, and how lawyers develop arguments in light of it. In the introduction to this essay attention was drawn to the difference between the top down and bottom up processes of developing legal rules depicted by the civilian and common law systems respectively (Cardozo 1921; and text). Two important aspects of common law methodology are the ways in which the law develops case by case and the restrictions that precedent places upon this process (Weaver 1991: 553–561; Strasser 1981). Langdell would have had us believe that the judicial role in any new case involved no law making at all (Langdell 1887: 1871). Just over a century after the first edition of Langdell's contract casebook Lord Reid castigated this sort of thinking as a fairy tale (Reid 1972):

> There was a time when it was thought almost indecent to suggest that judges make law – they only declare it. Those with a taste for fairy tales seem to have thought that in some Aladdin's cave there is hidden the Common Law in all its splendour and that on a judge's appointment there descends on him knowledge of the magic words Open Sesame. Bad decisions are given when the judge had muddled the pass word and the wrong door opens. But we do not believe in fairy tales any more.

In *National Westminster Bank v Spectrum Plus* [2005] 2 AC 680 at [22] Lord Nicholls had this to say about the judicial role in new cases that come before the superior courts:

> The common law is judge-made law. For centuries judges have been charged with the responsibility of keeping this law abreast of current social conditions and expectations. That is still the position. Continuing but limited development of the common law in this fashion is an integral part of the constitutional function of the judiciary. Had the judges not discharged this responsibility, the common law would be the same now as it was in the reign of King Henry II. It is because of this that the common law is a living instrument of law, reacting to new events and new ideas, and so capable of providing the citizens of this country with a system of practical justice relevant to the times in which they live.

One area of contract law that is developing uncertainly at present concerns the variation of contracts. Is consideration required to support a promise by

A to pay more to B for the same contractual performance in return; together with the related question of whether a promise by creditor (C) to accept part payment from debtor (D) must be supported by fresh consideration. *Williams v Roffey Brothers* [1991] 1 QB 1 now recognises any 'practical benefit' acquired by A as sufficient consideration to make A's promise to pay more enforceable. Can this be extended to the analogous issue of part payment of debt? Students who have read *Foakes v Beer* (1884) LR 9 App Cas 605 would be better placed than those who had not to appreciate the difficulty the doctrine of precedent presents in this connection and to appreciate whether promissory estoppel might offer an alternative solution. These issues were most recently considered by the Court of Appeal in *MWB v Rock Advertising* [2016] EWCA Civ 553. The hoped for resolution by the Supreme Court did not materialise, the case eventually being decided on another ground ([2018] UKSC 24). They concern one of the most significant contemporary problems in English contract law. A law teacher, no matter how experienced and lucid in his or her explanation of the problem, cannot simply tell students all they need to know about it. To acquire the clearest understanding of the issues, the kind of arguments a lawyer might present to a court with law making power and a sense of where the law might go, there is no real substitute for rolling up the sleeves and reading the relevant judgments carefully. This is one area of law that needs to be taught *from* the cases.

Third, as Professor Charles L. Knapp, a very experienced contract law teacher and distinguished authority on commercial law, has pointed out, the case method is an excellent way of bringing out those aspects of contract law cases that frequently lie hidden unless the reader digs down deeply into the judicial opinions (Knapp 2013). Appellate cases demonstrate that there is frequently no clearly correct answer to a legal question (Knapp 2013: 1362). The mere fact that the losing party in the court below thought that another tribunal could take a different view is often enough in itself to demonstrate this. In the appellate court there may be majority and dissenting opinions and even within these there may be different reasons and nuances. An excellent illustration of this is the decision of the House of Lords in *White and Carter (Councils) Ltd v McGregor* [1962] AC 413. The Inner and Outer Houses of the Court of Session in Scotland both found in favour of the respondents and would not permit the appellants to affirm the contract in the face of the former's anticipatory breach. In the House of Lords two judges (Lords Hodson and Tucker) strongly favoured the right to affirm, treating an unaccepted repudiation as 'a thing writ in water ... [that] confers no legal rights of any sort or kind' (*Howard v Pickford Tool Co Ltd* [1951] 1 KB 417, 421 (Asquith LJ)). Two other judges (Lords Morton and Keith) were equally strongly of opinion that the Scottish courts had taken the correct view. In determining the outcome of the appeal the speech of Lord Reid proved to be the all-important one. He concurred with Lords Hodson and Tucker as to the result but suggested that the right to affirm may be subject to two possible limitations. One was where the affirming party required the co-operation of the breaching party to enable the affirming party to complete its own contractual obligations (*White and Carter*: 429). The other was where the affirming party had absolutely no legitimate interest in performing the contract as opposed to claiming damages (Ibid: 431). Lord Reid's speech containing these two exceptions has come to be understood as the *ratio decidendi* of *White and Carter v McGregor*. The clear understanding of these conflicting views and the conflicting policy considerations (Knapp 2013: 1368) which ground them would definitely be facilitated by a reading of the case itself.

In the same article Professor Knapp also points out that studying the judicial opinions in a case may indicate the presence of factors other than those expressly acknowledged in arriving at the decision of the court (Ibid: 1367). A study of the less reliable Espinasse report of *Stilk v Myrick* (1809) 170 ER 1168 appears to ground the decision to refuse the deserting sailors' pay to the remaining crew on duress, whereas the more highly respected report (from Campbell) grounds it on consideration. Yet it is difficult to imagine that a fear of encouraging sailors to demand more pay in times of national crisis had nothing to do with the decision (for a fascinating contextual account of *Stilk v Myrick* see Luther 1999). Again, a study of the two reports would surely be instructive about this phenomenon in judicial reasoning.

Knapp also points out how studying the report of a case can help one to appreciate the tactical decisions lawyers make in presenting a case (Knapp 2013: 1372). Another near to home example illustrates this. In *Ruxley Electronics & Construction Co Ltd v Forsyth* [1996] AC 344 Mr Forsyth offered the House of Lords an undertaking that if he were awarded damages measured by the cost of reinstating his swimming pool to the correct depth he would spend that sum on actually doing the work. The House of Lords restricted his damages to the difference in value between the contractual performance he received and the performance he should have received, so his reasons for offering this undertaking appear understandable in that light. Once again a careful study of the speeches in the House of Lords would bring out the tactical moves the parties made and the several policy reasons for the decision.

So clearly the case method of instruction still has much to offer from a pedagogical point of view. We turn now to its drawbacks.

What is not so good about the case method

The first and most obvious problem about the case method is that it provides depth at the expense of breadth. Professor Smith quickly realised this after he introduced a case method of instruction at Nottingham University in place of the lecture system that had been used before (Smith 1967). The case method allowed teacher and students to study the material in more depth, it generated better discussion, enabled students to learn more as they went along, and produced more thoughtful and analytical examination answers. But it did not allow anything like as much ground to be covered as could be covered by lectures and textbook. If one taught by cases alone there would likely be whole swathes of contract law that students learned little about.

American perspectives are in agreement with Professor Smith. Professor Slawson has pointed out that for all the case method's advantages in terms of the development of analytical skills it is ineffective in teaching *the law*. To do that textbooks should be used to provide students with an overall framework into which the cases may be inserted. The textbook should be studied first before proceeding to the cases. Casebooks themselves need to include commentary and explanation sections, and cases should be selected for specific reasons, such as illustrating the application of legal principle and to flag up areas of difficulty in the subject. A regular diet of appellate court decisions unsupported by material like this is not likely to provide students with a true grounding in the subject (Slawson 2000). This approach would seem to have one eye on the multi-state examination common to all state bar examinations in the United States. The emphasis is placed here on substantive knowledge as opposed to analytical or reasoning skills, but that is what the customer (fee paying student) is paying for.

The second 'not so good' feature of the case method tends to be its over-concentration on legal doctrine. Students do not obtain from a case method instruction model much of a sense of the goals and objectives of the law (Weaver 1991: 581–583). It is true that Langdell's casebook has now been replaced by 'Cases and Materials' books providing extracts and references to law review articles and other literature which motivated students could delve into. But rarely, it seems, has much effort been made by instructors to place contract law in its political, social, economic or business context (Austin 1965: 164; Friedman and Macaulay 1967). This seems something of a missed opportunity because if these objectives and contexts were given greater emphasis students might better understand what they were learning. When I was teaching Contracts in the United States in the early 1990s a colleague gave a guest lecture on law and economics but that was it by way of policy context. Perhaps the location of Contracts in the first year of the curriculum goes some way to explaining the neglect of context. It is a foundational year, grades are so important to securing employment in law firms both while studying and after graduation, and examinations rarely test for this kind of knowledge. This criticism of contract law teaching is not confined to the United States. On this side of the Atlantic, where a pure case method of instruction has not been the fashion, the level of focus on the law's objectives and context has not traditionally been much greater (Tillotson 1976; Lewis 1982).

The third way in which the case method of teaching contract law in the United States comes up a little short is in relation to its commitment to skills development. The case method is not a skills-free zone as we have seen. The skills of reading cases deeply and adversarially have already been emphasised (Slawson 2000; and text). But as Judge Jerome Frank complained more than three quarters of a century ago the Socratic case method is overly academic and library-focused (Frank 1933). More recently there have been calls for greater clinical education in contract law courses, developing skills such as contract drafting, negotiating and interpretation (Rubin 2007: 642; Chomsky 2015: 887). It has been plausibly argued that students learn better by doing (Chomsky 2015: 887). What the work of these more contemporary scholars confirms is that Frank's criticism of the Langdellian model of law schools still largely holds true. Clinical education is more extensive today through moot court, trial practice and law clinic classes, but there is surely room for bringing clinical elements into the more traditional legal doctrine courses.

One way of developing clinical skills without revolutionising teaching methods or requiring the investment of significant additional resources would be through the greater use of problem exercises in contract law classes. My recollection of teaching Contracts and Federal Bankruptcy in the United States in the early 1990s is that the Bankruptcy casebook had plenty of problem exercises to illuminate the meaning of the Bankruptcy Code but the Contracts casebook did not use problems at all. Only a decade ago Professors Rakoff and Minow observed that cases were used in classroom instruction, but law students were examined by problem exercises (Rakoff and Minow 2007). Professor Moskovitz has strongly endorsed the problem method of teaching as a better way of developing students' analytical and problem-solving skills. His recommendation is that cases and problems should be used in tandem. Students should do the problem exercises as homework preparation for class along with assigned reading of cases. The problems give meaning and purpose to the case assignments and consequently that material is more effectively absorbed (Moskovitz 1992).

It is acknowledged that this has been a lengthy discussion of the case method in but one jurisdiction. But this jurisdiction is where contract law has been taught most extensively *from* the cases and where a plentiful supply of lessons about the good and the not so good about this instruction method can be sourced. We now move on to some recommendations about how the cases can best be used to teach contract law going forward.

How to teach contract law from cases now

Despite the lengthy section just completed, this essay is not about reforming the North American JD or the place of contract law within it. It is about teaching contract law *from* the cases across the common law world (this includes Scotland). Of course, context, specifically the kind of law degree students are pursuing, goes to the use that is made of cases in teaching contract law. The wise teacher would not use contract law cases in exactly the same way in an LLB course in Britain as (s)he would in a Contracts class in the JD program at a North American law school. Obvious differences with the latter are that students are mostly graduates and the course lasts for an entire academic year, in contrast to the UK and Ireland where most law students are undergraduates and quite a few law schools teach Contract Law through a one-semester module. One important similarity, however, is that few, if any, of the students in either of these examples would have studied law in an academic setting before.

To give a sense of the different levels at which contract law is taught at a United Kingdom law school take my own school at Queen's University Belfast. We teach a one-semester (12 teaching weeks) contract law module to second and third year undergraduates; another one-semester module to second year MLAW students, an extended version of the English Graduate Diploma in Law; and a full academic year course to international JD students.

The lessons to be learned from our study of teaching contract law through cases in the United States have to be fitted into the above framework as well as the North American JD. The case method in America is excellent at endowing students with all those qualities for which Professors Weaver, Slawson and Knapp have complimented it. But this is all that it does. Why, asks Professor Weaver (1991: 562), should students have to experience this kind of teaching in every course for three years? This was written about the case method generally, but it also serves as a pertinent observation about contract law. In theory, law schools could select contract law as the course where the skill of case analysis was to be developed. It would be easier to do that in a North American JD, which adheres to a more or less general template, than in the myriad of contract law courses that are offered across a much wider range of primary law degrees in Britain and Ireland. But to target contract law as the case analysis course risks missing out in that subject on so much that is valuable in other teaching methods and perspectives on contract law. Students would not acquire as broad a sense of the wider panoply of contract law as they would if textbooks and lectures were used to explain the general doctrines and overall subject matter of contract law. They would not learn as much as they should about the important role that contract law plays in facilitating business transactions, its connection with economics, and the question of when the legislature or the courts have to intervene to regulate certain contracts on the ground that a consumer needs protection and cannot be treated as one who has to live with the consequences of choices made. There are extremely valuable skills, such as reading, drafting and interpreting contracts and other legal documentation, that can be developed in a contracts law course better than most other curricular offerings. These skills, together with problem solving, are of immense value to graduates entering a whole host of occupations. This matters particularly in the United Kingdom where many law graduates do not enter the legal profession. Law teachers should be in the business of developing general transferable skills, not just those of value to practising lawyers.

The problem with the case method in the United States appears to be a tendency to try to teach everything, or at least too many things, via that method. This comes at the expense of teaching what the law is, appropriate context and skills development. However, if we were to try and ensure that all contract law courses included these undeveloped aspects of contract law teaching in addition to retaining a commitment to developing students' skills in reading and analysing cases, we might end up trying to do too much. Instead of an excess of case method, we could be doing everything so superficially that ultimately students would learn very little. In deciding how much contract law should be taught *from* the cases we need also to take account of the different levels at which contract law is taught because this will affect what the true priorities are and what realistically can be done.

The bottom line is that we have to teach the general doctrine of contract law and this will not simply emerge from studying cases alone. So lectures and textbooks will remain integral parts of our pedagogical toolkit. Many of our students will want to be professional lawyers so they will need to have at least some general framework of this critical subject going into the profession. Students entering other occupations would also benefit from acquiring this 'big picture'. The need to teach the general doctrine will remain after the Solicitors' Qualifying Examination (SQE) replaces the qualifying law degree as the certificate that students have satisfied the academic stage of professional training because most students will likely continue to learn their law at university. Lectures and textbooks can provide some guidance to students as to the functions of contract law, the policy considerations underlying the rules and the wider context, but at undergraduate level, particularly in modular courses, it would be sufficient to do this at a mostly introductory level.

Skills such as problem solving and contractual interpretation can be the focus of smaller group tutorials. What then of cases? As my friend and colleague John Stannard has said, contract law contains a great many cases it is important to know *about* but not many cases one actually needs to know in depth. Students at all of the relevant levels above could probably cope tolerably well with problem exercises without an in-depth knowledge of many cases. Professor Moskovitz's argument that problem exercises give meaning and purpose to assigned readings of cases is certainly sound and offers a way in which contract law can be taught *from* the cases. My suggestion would be that contract law teachers should ensure that at least a few of their tutorial problem exercises cover areas of law where the subject is 'on the move' (this was Lord Phillips' description of the law of vicarious liability in *Various Claimants v Catholic Child Welfare Society* [2012] UKSC 56 at [19]). One such area in contract law is consideration in the context of contractual modifications. If students could be given one or two problem exercises with a short and discrete list of cases that clearly address the issues raised by those problems, they could really learn a lot from this exercise. Our reading lists are frequently much too long and, because contract law contains mainly cases that students need to know *about*, they seldom see much point in trying to undertake an unmanageable task. Explain the benefits that will be derived from reading a discrete and manageable list of cases and there is a far better chance of students actually doing the work and deriving some real benefit from it.

What are some other ways in which contract law can be taught *from* cases? One is mooting, but this is a very labour intensive task to undertake in a curriculum course. Mooters undoubtedly have to dig down deeply into legal authorities in constructing their arguments, so they would get a lot out of it, but mostly mooting is something to be undertaken in a specially designed course or as a CV building extra-curricular activity. Something I have tried with a modicum of success is to assign the presentation of key cases to students in class. It operates reasonably successfully in relatively small groups of up to 20 students. I use it in my JD Contracts course (and also JD Torts) and in a final year optional undergraduate module, Remedies in Private Law. A week in advance I will ask some members of the class to present on selected cases, giving a steer as to what I think would be helpful for the student to highlight. The presentation is incorporated into class discussion and I respond to anything arising out of the student's presentation. Since the JD course lasts for a full academic year there is the opportunity to do a lot more work with cases. Case presentations force students to read cases, usually the entire report, and offer spin-off benefits in terms of developing oral communication skills. A casebook can be useful in the year-long courses because there is more opportunity to study the various aspects of contract law in depth. But even here the observation about there being not that many cases one needs to know in depth has cast a shadow over the venerable casebook. Professor Knapp has pointedly posed the question whether online resources are now going to supplant traditional casebooks altogether (Knapp 2013: 1357).

Conclusion

Cases still have much to offer as a pedagogical tool in contract law. But we cannot operate on the assumption that seems to have prevailed in the United States for a very long time that *everything* can be learned from studying cases. Langdell was correct in saying that only a few contracts cases have true value as teaching tools. However this is not because there are only a few cases illustrative of the fundamental doctrines from which the law is distilled. On the contrary it is those cases addressing contemporary issues where the law is on the move that should be studied carefully. Contract law contains a lot of cases the student needs to know *about*, but only a few that need to be known thoroughly.

So how should we, the contract law teachers of today, use cases in our teaching? We need to ensure to begin with that we are teaching the key doctrines and principles of contract law. We need to supplement this with explanations of the underlying policy issues and objectives of contract law. Into this lecture and textbook framework, key skills such as interpretation, problem solving and case analysis should be inserted. We need to appreciate that for the average law student, whether an undergraduate or a graduate student taking a primary law degree, reading cases is a time consuming and intellectually demanding exercise. To engender the kind of commitment to this exercise that we would want to see, we have to sell it thoughtfully. We need to be honest about the number of cases students really need to read; we need to appreciate that a little reading done well is much more beneficial than a larger amount done badly; and we need to explain to our students why we want them to read cases and what the potential benefits are for them if they undertake the task conscientiously. We also need to avoid a 'one size fits all' model. How much we use cases and the way we use them necessarily varies between contract law courses and the nature of the student cohort we are teaching.

References

Austin, A.D., 1965. Is The Casebook Method Obsolete? *Wm. & Mary L. Rev.*, 6, 157–166.

Cardozo, B.N., 1921. *The Nature of the Judicial Process*. Yale University Press, New Haven.

Chomsky, C.L., 2015. Casebooks and the Future of Contracts Pedagogy. *Hastings L.J.*, 66, 879–898.

Frank, J., 1933. Why Not a Clinical Lawyer-School?. *U. Pa. L. Rev.*, 81, 907–923.

Friedman, L.M. and Macaulay, S., 1967. Contract Law and Contract Teaching: Past, Present, and Future. *Wis. L. Rev.*, 805–821.

Gilmore, G., 1977. *The Ages of American Law*. Yale University Press, New Haven.

Hall, J., 1955. Teaching Law by Case Method and Lecture. *J. Soc'y Pub. Tchrs. L. NS*, 3, 99–106.

Kerr, O.S., 1999. The decline of the Socratic method at Harvard. *Neb. L. Rev.*, 78, 113–134.

Knapp, C.L., 2013. Cases and Controversies: Some Things to Do with Contracts Cases. *Wash. L. Rev.*, 88, 1357–1394.

Langdell, C.C., 1871. *A Selection of Cases on the Law of Contracts: With References and Citations*. Little, Brown, Boston.

Langdell, C.C., 1887. Harvard Celebration Speeches. *Law Q. Rev.*, 3, 123–124.

Lewis, R., 1982. Criticisms of the Traditional Contract Course. *Law Tchr.*, 16, 111–121.

Lord, Reid, 1972. The Judge as Law Maker. *J. Soc'y Pub. Tchrs. L.*, 12, 22–29.

Luther, P., 1999. Campbell, Espinasse and the Sailors: Text and Context in the Common Law. *Legal Stud.*, 19, 526–551.

Moskovitz, M., 1992. Beyond the Case Method: It's Time to Teach with Problems. *J. Legal Educ.*, 42, 241–270.

Rakoff, T.D. and Minow, M., 2007. A Case for Another Case Method. *Vand. L. Rev.*, 60, 597–608.

Rubin, E., 2007. What's Wrong with Langdell's Method, and What to Do About It. *Vand. L. Rev.*, 60, 609–666.

Slawson, W.D., 2000. Changing How We Teach: A Critique of the Case Method. *S. Cal. L. Rev.*, 74, 343–346.

Smith, J.C., 1967. The Case Method of Teaching Law. *Law Tchr.*, 1, 17–23.

Strasser, K.A., 1981. Teaching Contracts—Present Criticism and a Modest Proposal for Reform. *J. Legal Educ.*, 31, 63–86.

Tillotson, J., 1976. Anyone for Contract?. *Law Tchr.*, 10, 135–145.

Weaver, R.L., 1991. Langdell's Legacy: Living with the Case Method. *Vill. L. Rev.*, 36, 517–596.

Chapter 13

Making use of new technology

Jessica Viven-Wilksch

Introduction

Murphy (Murphy 1996) wrote that

> this new form of learning will be shared with smart machines and will extend beyond the school, beyond the static roles of teacher and learner and beyond the school years. Smart environments, interactive hypermedia systems, biomedical and brain technology, and a 'communication infrastructure that makes all knowledge accessible to anyone, anywhere, anytime': these are the 'four threads' of hyperlearning technology. The impacts of the 'HL revolution' will include greater accessibility of learning through distance education, smart environments that make learning characteristic of everyday situations, expertise as a property of 'systems and networks' rather than persons, and people of all ages and levels learning together and throughout their entire lives.

While this quotation could be taken from a recent article, it actually was written 25 years ago. Yet it captures an important debate in legal education today. The way we teach has changed dramatically in the last 15 years, and the development of Learning Management Systems (LMS) and other technological innovations are likely to continue to change our pedagogy. Digital capabilities are currently a buzzword in higher education. Lecturers across universities in Australia and around the world are told teaching needs to reflect the needs of the "digital natives". Some institutions have decided not to lecture any longer (Freyer 2017: 1), and many record lectures (though some refuse to do so for example, (Melbourne Law School, n.d.). So what do these trends mean for contract law teaching?

A review of the course outlines of the 39 Australian law schools shows one thing to be clear: teaching contracts is first and foremost about delivering content. The author wholeheartedly agrees with this position. This chapter will discuss not *what* to teach, but *how* to possibly teach, and will reflect on how technology can help students understand contract law and develop the critical skills needed to become a successful legal professional. In essence, this chapter will explore the possibility of technology leading to re-imagining contract law pedagogy by asking the following question: How could embedding technology benefit the student's understanding and the lecturer's teaching of contract law? This is not a chapter about how we *must* teach but a reflection on how we *could* teach.

The chapter will first present an overview of the current teaching of Australian contract law as it is presented to prospective and current students online. The chapter will then discuss how technology is transforming the needs and wants of both the student cohort and the lecturer. This part will debunk the myth of the *digital native* and explore the responsibility of the lecturer in developing skills regarding both the content of contract law and the way to engage with that content. Contract law lecturers do not *have to* use technology in an active manner, but whilst it may well become mandatory, it could also be used because it is interactive, engaging and fun! The chapter moves on to discuss relevant legal education scholarship on some innovative initiatives in this area. It will present some of the tools available today which can be used to better engage the students by providing an enriched experience for both students and lecturers. Drawing on personal experience, the author will provide some insights into some of the tools which are now used and the possibilities which lie ahead.

This chapter has three main aims: to provide a review of the literature on teaching with technology; to provide information on where to start in designing and using digital tools in contract law teaching; and to start a broader conversation on the need to share, with the legal education community, initiatives taken in this space. It is not about surrendering to educational technology fashion and "trend of the season" but instead determining how making *effective* use of technology can in fact provide students with a stronger and deeper understanding of contract law notions.

Teaching contract law

"To imagine" is defined in the *Macquarie Dictionary* as "to form a mental image of (something not actually present to the senses)" (Macquarie Dictionary Online). Therefore it is relevant to look at what approaches are currently used in legal education in relation to contract law teaching before re-imagining the pedagogy around teaching this course as the title of this collection suggests we should. This part of this chapter will provide an overview of freely available online course outlines which will show that, whilst the content of the teaching is, of course, described to future students, information on the methods of teaching and use of technology, if any, is generally scarce.

Teaching contracts at an Australian law school

In Australia, to become a registered lawyer, students need to complete a Graduate Diploma of Legal Practice. During their practical legal training, students will have to demonstrate their competencies in prescribed areas (Law Admissions

Consultative Committee 2017). However, before undertaking this training, students must first complete a law degree and be able to demonstrate knowledge, ethics and professional responsibility, thinking skills, research skills, communication and collaboration, and self-management (McKeough 2012). As part of their degree, and to be able to enrol in the GDLP, students must have studied particular topics, the so-called Priestley 11 (Law Admissions Consultative Committee 2002; Law Council 2016). One of these is Contracts. The Priestley 11 focus exclusively on the content of the course. The Law Admissions Committee stipulates the following academic requirements for admission in relation to Contracts: "formation, including capacity, formalities, privity and consideration; [c]ontent and construction of contract; [v]itiating factors; [d]ischarge; [r]emedies; [a]ssignment" (Law Admissions Consultative Committee 2016: 2). While

> [s]ome variation may be expected in the breadth and detail of the topics. In general, however, knowledge of the formal requirements for concluding contracts, capacity, the content and interpretation of contracts, their performance and discharge, available remedies, together with an understanding of the broad theoretical basis of contract would be expected.
>
> (ibid)

The focus is clearly on substantive notions to be learnt and not yet on the association with particular professional skills (Law Society of New South Wales 2017).

From the course outlines of the Australian law schools, it is clear that it is the content rather than the method of teaching that is "advertised", in line with the prescriptive guidelines in the Priestley 11. The QUT course outline for Contract Law is one notable exception in that it clearly describes the pedagogy of the course as follows: "Student learning is supported with online materials, including quizzes, to provide feedback on the understanding of the principles and skills of the unit" (QUT, n.d.).

The focus on content is also reflected in the learning outcomes prescribed for the courses on Contracts, which generally ask students to be able to demonstrate that they can identify and articulate the different notions encountered in the course. A review of the course outlines also shows that Australian law schools split the material over two courses and across two semesters. For students who enrol to complete a single degree in law, online study plans show that it is one of the first courses a student in a law degree will have to complete. The format across Australian law schools is generally one weekly two-hour lecture and one weekly one-hour tutorial. Some institutions however offer trimester courses, including the University of South Australia, Griffith University, the University of New England and Deakin University (University of South Australia, n.d.; Griffith University, n.d.; the University of New England, n.d.; Deakin University, n.d.). Most law schools use delivery on campus, though some also provide online delivery such as the University of New England and Edith Cowan University (University of New England, n.d.; Edith Cowan University, n.d.b).

Contracts certainly is a technical course and grasping the different notions and articulating them in practical situations can be difficult for students who are just beginning their law degree (Yin and Moore 2017: 203). This is because the notions are challenging and in particular because the presence of many "grey zones" (the factual matrix, good faith) is often perceived to be so difficult and obscure concepts as to be overwhelming. Contract pedagogy is, or should be, of the greatest importance in facilitating the learning experience of new undergraduate students. While methods of teaching are not widely advertised or explained in course outlines, legal education scholarship shows that there have been attempts to discuss the pedagogy of contract law but only in an ad hoc manner (Butler 2007, 2008, 2011, 2012a, 2012b; Xynas 2011). Generally speaking, Australian law schools have adopted a Socratic style of teaching which includes some forms of interaction with the cohort during the lecture before students are divided into seminars to work on particular problem questions and to practice their communication and problem-solving skills. The focus of teaching Contracts is therefore mostly on face-to-face interactions.

The context in which contract law applies and is taught is changing

Many important social developments, including globalisation (McKeough 2012: 1) and the growth of artificial intelligence (Bennett Moses 2017: 561), have led to calls for reform of the law degree. Digital capabilities (University of Adelaide 2017; Deakin University 2015) or the development of digital skills for the 'digital native' are current buzzwords. Interestingly, back in 2010, the Australian Learning and Teaching Council (2010), referring to international sources and experiences, considered whether graduates of a bachelor of laws degree should be required to demonstrate intellectual and practical research skills, including the "capacity to use necessary technology for information searches in the course of conducting, and keeping up to date in, a legal practice" (Australian Learning and Teaching Council 2010: 42).

The development of technology has, of course, had a considerable impact on both the content of the law and the access to legal information (Bennett Moses 2017: 561). Successive communications technologies (the postal system, telephones, facsimiles, email) have increased the speed and decreased the cost of communicating with clients and other parties (Bennett Moses 2017: 561). Legal information is more easily available through online platforms including Austlii, Thomson Reuters, law firms' and government departments' websites which may provide information sheets and finally automated online citators (Freudenberg 2017: 389). Contracts are also changing, and so is contract law. The development of e-commerce and online transactions, smart contracts and blockchain technology have been revolutionising the concept of agreement (Giancaspro 2017: 825). Yet most contracts still take the form of words written on a page, whether those words be handwritten on paper or appear in a Word document on the screen or on a web page. Contract law notions typically envisage paper documents, with the four corner rule a case in point. To this day, a lot of what a contract lawyer produces takes the written form of letters, memoranda, submissions, etc. While the disruptive impact of technology is yet to be fully felt by the legal professional of today, there are clear signs of changes to come tomorrow.

Questions such as, "Which existing processes are repetitive and time-consuming? What scope is there for automating these processes? Are you still drafting documents the old fashioned way?" (Digital Lawyer (the) 2017) lead us to wonder about the place of the contract lawyer in tomorrow's world. The connection between contract law, legal practice and legal study needs to be made stronger than ever before. Students enrolled in Contracts need to be taught to think and work like a lawyer in the 21st century.

'A meeting of the minds' of students and lecturers, profiling current students and future graduates

Students who enrol in a law degree are part of a diverse cohort (Hewitt and Stubbs 2017: 1), from school leaver to mature aged student and from social media addict to technophobe. Many of our students are millennials, meaning they are "typically comfortable with technology, having been born into an age of exponential change, and who are usually forced to juggle study with other commitments such as work commitments" (Butler 2007: 20). Many are born after 1984 and therefore fall into the category of "digital natives" (Race and Pickford 2007: 98). This expression was first coined by Prensky (2001) who distinguished this group from digital immigrants born before 1984. The main point of difference between the two groups is the fact that digital natives "have been exposed and immersed in digital technologies and are therefore natives" (Kirschner and De Bruyckere 2017: 136). Others have also highlighted the particularities of this generation of "homo zappiens" (Veen and Vrakking 2006).

Yet recent studies show that the digital native may be only a myth (Kirschner and De Bruyckere 2017: 137) and that students are not *actually* digitally literate. While students may be familiar with social media, they are not necessarily versed in using technology in a professional setting. There are implications of busting this myth; we should avoid both the pitfall of assuming that "students possess talents and abilities that they do not actually have" and "the widely held notion that if there is a generation of digital natives, there is also a generation of digital immigrants", obliging us to recognise that "digital literacy *is* an important subject in education for present students" (Kirschner and De Bruyckere 2017: 137 emphasis added).

The law students of today are the graduates of tomorrow. The attributes it is expected that graduates will develop will depend on the particular degrees awarded by particular institutions, and these attributes include being proficient with technology. For instance, at Flinders University, graduates of a bachelor of laws must be able to use recent technologies (Flinders University, n.d.). Melbourne JD graduates must be aware "of advanced communications technologies and modalities, sound working skills in the application of computer systems and software, and receptiveness to the expanding opportunities of the 'information revolution'" (The University of Melbourne, n.d.). Any graduate of the University of Adelaide must be "technology savvy" (University of Adelaide, n.d.). The University of Canberra also refers to the ability to "evaluate and adopt new technologies"(University of Canberra, n.d.). Charles Sturt focuses on making graduates who are "digitally literate citizens, able to harness technologies for professional practice and participate independently in online learning communities" (Charles Sturt University, n.d.). Other universities, including Curtin University, CQ University and Edith Cowan University, refer to the graduates' ability to use technology appropriately (Curtin University, n.d.; CQ University, n.d.; Edith Cowan University, n.d.a). Deakin University has developed a *Digital Literacy Framework*, which also includes assessing the use of digital technology (Deakin University 2015). One institution explicitly asks their graduates to have digital literacy (University of Southern Queensland, n.d.). While some of these universities provide online delivery of the Contracts course, the majority of Australian law schools provide an on-campus course either exclusively or alongside online delivery. Contract law, being taught early in the law degree, gives an opportunity to the lecturer, as part of a team teaching in the whole degree, to think about the ways they can design courses such as Contracts to build the digital and legal skills of the legal professional of tomorrow. The first step is for students to familiarise themselves with technology within a professional setting (Brescia, 2016). Once they understand it, then they can learn not only how to use it professionally but also as a tool to innovate.

Profiling the lecturer of today and of tomorrow

A lecturer is defined, in the *Macquarie Dictionary*, as someone who "imparts knowledge [or] skill [by giving] instruction in a particular topic". The Bloom taxonomy is an educational framework that emphasises the different steps of student learning and is widely used (Clark. n.d.; Anderson *et al* 2000). Based on this framework, the qualities of a contract law lecturer therefore should include knowledge of the topic, an ability to convey information and an ability to articulate the notions in such a way students can gain knowledge, understand it, apply it, analyse it, combine it and evaluate it. Traditional lectures have shortcomings, and these have been recognised across many disciplines worldwide. A Dutch review of the literature in the area highlights the issue of low attendance, the lack of engagement and critical thinking skills development, and a short attention span (Schmidt *et al* 2015: 12). There are shortcomings in delivery of knowledge by means of one-way traffic in which information is given to an ideal cohort of fully attentive students by the "almighty" lecturer. The use of a Socratic style in Australian higher education has alternatively set the scene for a conversation between the students and their lecturers, where the lecturer is a facilitator of the student's learning, drawing connections between different situations and contract law. Therefore, whilst lecturers must think about how to teach the content of contracts, they should also think about becoming 'digitally competent teachers' (Instefjord and Munthe: 2017: 37) and building students' digital literacy.

Using technology to gain digital literacy

> New technologies provide a range of new learning possibilities that can be beneficial to student outcomes – however, these possibilities typically require new skills in TEL and teaching for both educators and students.
>
> – (Keppell *et al* 2015: 8)

To understand what it means for students to be digitally literate and how lecturers can help them to become so (de Bruin and van Merriënboer 2017: 4) new initiatives were created such as Jisc in the UK and The Digital Capabilities Framework in Australia. These institutions advanced the argument that higher education needs to provide these skills to graduates of the twenty-first century. This means that both students *and* staff need to be proficient in:

> downloading and uploading files to cloud spaces, the internet etc.; organising, managing and backing up digital files; choosing relevant software, apps and services for the subject of study and being able to use digital tools to make learning more efficient (calendar; tasks lists). Students must be able to innovate, meaning using technologies to develop new ideas, projects and opportunities and collaborate digitally using file sharing, shared writing tools and project management tools.
>
> (The University of Adelaide 2017: 2–4)

Many will recognise that these skills are some of the most basic of any legal professional. To ensure students gain these skills, staff are required to facilitate learning in digital settings (e.g. online, blended, technology-rich classrooms), use digital technologies to support in-class learning (e.g. polling tools, digital presentation), develop and adapt digital learning resources according to students' needs, and guide students to use their own digital devices (University of Adelaide 2017: 6). Current LMS allow these skills to be practiced and have been used to enhance problem-based learning within the law degree (McCall 2010: 50).

While not every university and program requires that our graduates become "tech savvy" there is a clear movement towards this development in higher education and in the legal profession (Castan and Hyams 2017: 2). A recent commission of inquiry in Australia also stated that the graduate of the future needs to have the skills in and knowledge of technology which would enable them to use it and to innovate with it (Law Society of New South Wales 2017: 6). This clear, definitive and recent evolution of teaching has led lecturers across a wide range of disciplines to "blend" learning by recording lectures, encouraging active learning and "flipping" the classroom to better encourage students to use technology. While these changes do not necessarily mean that each course of the legal degree should be taught with digital literacy in mind, it is clear that due to the changing context in which contract law operates, it is probably wise to integrate technology. This is so for the following reasons: first, as we saw earlier, how contract law will operate is changing due to advances in technology; second, students are not necessarily digitally literate for the professional world; and third, using technology can help improve students' long-term engagement with the content of the course – since they are likely to revisit some concepts in other courses during their law degree (Castan and Hyams 2017: 19). But the lecturer must understand how to integrate technology successfully and efficiently. This is where contract pedagogy can be re-imagined.

Re-imagining contract pedagogy using the blended approach

It is no small endeavour to successfully lead students to engage with the content of contract law, to facilitate their handling of complex notions and to start teaching them the skills necessary for them to become digitally literate. Add to this the new languages of flipping the classroom and of online teaching tools, and revisiting the design of the contracts course can feel overwhelming and time consuming. This chapter is not about describing the many and sometimes complex tools available, partly because there are too many tools available and the list would be outdated too quickly, but also because not every tool is appropriate to teaching contract law, for instance because of their more scientific focus. Furthermore, some of these tools may be fashionable today but are unlikely to persist into the long term, not least because some institutions may mandate the use of a particular platform which limits the use of those tools. However, there are tools which are readily available and easy to learn, and their use could help us to rethink contract pedagogy.

From the first use of an LMS in Australian higher education more than 15 years ago (Parish 2011: 423) to the more recent development of MOOCS (Massive Open Online Courses), contract law pedagogy has already been obliged to change. Today students can access PowerPoint slides of the lectures at any time and can also complete a self-paced course on contract law, such as that taught by Charles Fried at the Harvard Law School, for free and in the comfort of their homes (Harvard University. n.d.). There are tools available today which will engage the students more fully and provide an enriched experience of what is often presented as the dry topic of contracts. The questions which arise are how could embedding technology benefit the Contracts student of today and better prepare the legal professional of tomorrow? How could the lecturer embed technology in teaching Contracts? Technology should not be used for the sake of it but to actually enhance students' learning. There are "innovative law teachers [who] continue to explore the vast potential that emerging technologies hold for effective and engaging teaching of law that meets the needs of modern students" (Butler 2011: 496), no matter the students' level of digital literacy. This is because using technology in teaching contracts has the potential, not only to encourage a better grasp of notions, but also to reach students in an interactive and engaging way. Research has shown that "multisensory interactions can be exploited to yield more efficient learning of sensory information and suggest that multisensory training programs would be most effective acquisition of skills" (Seitz *et al* 2006 as cited in Doyle 2011: 108). Whilst we should not add the visual for the sake of it, a picture or a short video linked to a particular case or notion has the potential to lead to better student engagement with the material taught (Doyle 2011: 113).

Technology can be used in different ways to improve the quality of the insight that students gain during face-to-face interactions. This is what the blended approach is about. Adopting a blended approach means that a course will include "some online aspects . . . plus some face to face" (Parish 2011: 427) interactions. Carefully thought out and produced online learning "has the capacity to be reliable, efficient of time, accountable, accessible, enabling, cost effective, auditable, adaptable, customisable, flexible, democratic" (Race and Pickford, 2007: 97). The advantage of taking a blended approach to teaching is that it allows the lecturer to reach out to students who may be off as well as on campus (Crawford and Jenkins 2017: 63). It also responds to the demand from 'university students for a flexible, innovative and engaging learning experiences provided with technologies that they commonly use or will be expected to use in today's professional, academic and social environments' (Spiliotopoulos 2011 as cited in Crawford and Jenkins 2017: 53). There are different models of blended learning depending on whether one looks at one course or an entire degree (Crawford and Jenkins 2017: 55). The approach proposed by the author is the *rotation model*, which "prescribes that students motion through learning activities that cover different modalities, with at least one of these activities being administered online" (Crawford and Jenkins 2017: 55). As Crawford and Jenkins point out, "Opportunities for increased communication and resources, peer collaboration and networking and flexible learning . . . [are] aspects of blended learning that appeared to be valued by the students" (Crawford and Jenkins 2017: 63). When students engage with software, internet and cloud-based system in online activities, they will build their digital literacy.

Students enrolled in a contract law course must first and foremost be able to articulate their understanding of formation, performance and termination of contracts as per the Priestley 11. However, using a blended approach could help students develop their academic communication and writing skills, as well as their critical thinking, and allow them to penetrate deeper within the content of the course.

Traditionally, students would meet their lecturers and tutors on campus, either in a lecture theatre or in the classroom. This is no longer the case (Size, 2016:4). Today, some law degrees can be completed online, and students are often not present in classes because those classes are recorded. These students nevertheless interact with the material taught, but in their own time and space. The Australasian Survey of Student Engagement "reveals that less than a quarter of students in Australia and New Zealand spend significant amounts of time on campus – in class or in other ways" (ACER 2008; Cameron 2009: 3). This has been precipitated by the development of LMS intendedly built to improve the relationship between students, course materials, lectures, lecturers and tutors. This has led to the construction of new online meeting places where students and lecturers meet asynchronously. An argument has been made that such online tools and asynchronous technologies could better help students in learning the Priestley 11, since these "require mastery of complex concepts [and these] [a]synchronous approaches may provide better opportunities for reflection, exploration, integration and resolution than even the traditional on-campus classroom-based approach" (Parish 2011: 428). The creation of Canvas, Blackboard, Moodle and other LMS reflects the move towards a more student-centred approach in higher education pedagogy (Butler 2011: 470). It is worth noting that there are many ways to engage beyond the use of LMS. For instance, in the USA, a new application, titled "contracts is a beach", is available for Android phones in which blank questions appear as a game by the playing of which students review contracts law notions. It is worth noting that there are many ways to engage beyond the use of LMS. For instance, in the USA, a new application is available for Android phones in which blank questions appear as a game by the playing of which students review contracts law notions. Other examples include "online business simulations, medical simulations, virtual site visits, [and] online study-skills coaching" (Race and Pickford, 2007: 102). Many of these can be done using the LMS platform and are therefore readily available and supported by institutions' frameworks.

Today, students will log on to their LMS to access course information, readings and PowerPoint slides as made available by the lecturers. They might also complete online quizzes and submit assignments electronically. In more recent times, students have been able to access lecture recordings in many institutions. Yet, there is more to technology and digital literacy than this. Careful design of a blended learning approach should be paramount. The first steps are to identify and take advantage of the opportunities available. A well thought out design that includes online learning, face-to-face interactions, reflective learning practice and instructor engagement can positively impact on students and their learning (Castan and Hyams 2017: 6).

Pre-class: online reading and activities

Pre-class activities were once limited to readings and preparation of tutorials. Today, with the emergence of the flipped classroom, students can be asked to view videos and read materials prior to attending the lecture. During face-to-face interactions, the role of the lecturer is to facilitate understanding of and reflection on the content assimilated before class and no longer to deliver content. The research on the use of technology in higher education shows that technology should be used but that it must be carefully designed and not overused. Done well, it can enhance the student experience both on campus and online. Not every student is a visual learner. Nevertheless, challenging students by asking them to engage with different media throughout a course and ultimately a degree can positively impact on students' emotional intelligence (Kauffman 2015: 7). A recent study by Melissa Castan and Ross Hyams (2017) presents an interesting outlook on how university policy is changing the method of teaching. After adopting a blended approach to teaching an introductory law course, new resources were created. These included videos posted on a private YouTube channel with links from the LMS. The authors argued that "where blended learning approaches offer the opportunity for students to scaffold their knowledge and to develop reflective learning practices and . . . put these to use in a supportive class environment, it is likely to show enhanced learning outcomes" (Castan and Hyams 2017: 19).

Videos and other digital multimedia can "allow the depiction of material in a form that takes advantage of the cognitive power of story-telling, makes connections with real-world settings and facilitates discussion in face-to-face classes" (Butler 2011: 472). At QUT, one institution the Contracts Course outline of which implies blended learning, the use of multimedia led to the creation of contract vignettes. These video podcasts of 10–15 minutes of narrated PowerPoint slides "provide an overview of the topic, explain difficult concepts and provide tips for understanding" (Butler 2011: 471). These were part of a broader redesign of the course that also included a workbook with case authorities, legislation and checkpoint questions throughout. Butler accurately points out that

> law teachers currently teaching using a traditional approach should visualise how, within the financial and other demands of their schools, their subjects could be taught if lectures were removed from the learning and teaching strategy. How might technology provide a better means of learning particular topics? Could, for example, major cases or general principles, be more effectively and efficiently covered by use of audio or video podcasts?

These podcasts have the advantage of relieving the need to go over the meaning of basic concepts that might otherwise have taken up valuable class time and can help to advance class discussions by providing a consistent foundation for understanding (Butler 2007: 20). The cost can be minimal as commonly available software can be used (Castan and Hyams 2017: 9).

Before starting to produce videos, a lecturer should carefully decide upon the content of those videos. Pistone (2017) provides insightful advice on this matter: identify the topics that you typically cover (cf. Mirriahi 2015: 7); don't think you have to produce all the videos; plan what you want to do with the additional face-to-face time with students that blended learning will afford; produce chunked, short video content of 5–8 minutes; and hold the students responsible for watching the videos. The language used also needs to be carefully considered. For instance, videos should not include expressions such as "this hot issue", "today" or "last year". It is important to "create teaching methodologies that can be repeated" (Castan and Hyams 2017: 18). Doing so will ensure the videos can be reused "which may offer long-term institutional cost savings" (Hewitt 2015: 97).

The author has experience of the student response to fifteen 5–8-minute videos created for an elective in comparative law. These "capsules" were used either as an introduction to a topic, a teaser for the lecture to come or as a way to prepare students by giving them particular perspective before class. Some videos included the author navigating through slides; others were interviews with colleagues and legal practitioners which provided an opportunity for students to hear from professionals they may not have been able to connect with otherwise. These videos were scripted for accessibility. Similar tools could be used in contract law teaching more widely across law schools in Australia and around the world.

During class: active learning

Once students have acquired information in their own time, they attend the lecture ready with some basic understandings of what is to come. While some students do not necessarily come prepared (Schmidt *et al* 2015: 13), the willingness to do well and be able to engage might compel students to indeed complete pre-class readings and activities. As a colleague told me, "Keep it engaging and they will come"! This is where active learning comes into play. So what is active learning? In the Australian Survey of Student Engagement:

> Active learning is defined as the extent to which students are involved in experiences that involve actively constructing new knowledge and understanding . . . including the frequency with which students ask questions or contribute to discussions in class or online, make presentations, work with other students during and outside of class, tutor other students, discuss ideas

> from classes outside of class and extend learning beyond formal classroom contexts.
>
> (Radloff and Coates 2009: 17)

Once students have engaged with the material prior to class, it is important to build on this experience in class and not revert to a lecture format which is only about delivering content when it should be more of a conversation. However, finding the balance between content delivery and student engagement can be challenging. The Contracts cohort is generally made up of undergraduate students (although there is a notable expectation as students enrolled on the Juris Doctor at the University of Melbourne are part of the postgraduate cohort). "Most undergraduates are novice learners. Their ability to recognise patterns within the subjects we teach is limited by their background knowledge and the kinds of educational training they received before entering [university]" (Doyle 2008: 55; Doyle 2011: 123–125.) During the lecture, the students can start to recognise such patterns in the material that has just been explained. This will create new pathways in students' minds and contribute to their understanding of the course.

LMS have been updated to include a broad variety of tools to help with active learning. Where one might have asked a question and then for a show of hands, used clickers or employed websites such as Survey Monkey and Votapedia in order to rapidly assess response in class, new LMS "add-ons" have allowed for these to be more widely supported. Echo360, previously known as LectureTools, a system that allows for the recording of lectures, is now used by more than 57% of the 47 Australasian ACODE member universities (Australasian Council on Open Distance and e-Learning 2013). In 2017, the University of Adelaide moved to this platform and its built-in active learning platform, Echo360ALP. A lecturer can now show a question on the screen in the lecture theatre and the question will simultaneously appear on students' laptops, tablets and phones. Students choose their answer and the lecturer then has the opportunity to show the results to the class before showing the right answer and explaining the concept again if necessary. The advantage of this tool is that it provides very quick feedback on students' understanding. Such feedback is essential to successful teaching; the lecturer must engage with the notion and explain why the other answers are not correct. Students can anonymously check their understanding during these activities as only the lecturer can use analytics to identify the student afterwards.

The author trialled some of these activities with the Contracts cohort in semester 1, 2017. After presenting a particular case or principle, a slide would appear and a question be asked. It was often a multiple choice question, but sometimes was a short problem scenario. Students participated by answering on their devices, without having to put their hand up. The question reached students who would not contribute for fear of being singled out or plainly wrong. In engaging with the software, students can feel connected to the lecturer even though the activity took place in a large theatre, and they will have the capacity to benchmark themselves within the cohort and so have a feeling of unity (Shaw 2015: 10). Surveys have shown that this is a valuable tool (Nielsen *et al* 2013: 4).

There are however clear limitations. First, it takes time to go through the activity. Time freed by pre-class videos, readings and activities can however alleviate this issue. Timing the activity is also a way to keep the class on track. Furthermore, technology itself comes with limitations; it is a fantastic tool when it functions well, but it can also be more than an inconvenience when students cannot log in or the internet is not working. Students must also be taught beforehand and then be regularly reminded of the need to connect to the app on their phone or tablet, or the LMS on their laptops so that they are ready to contribute. However, the fact that students can also answer by sms at no cost can help with these technological glitches. However no analytics will be recorded if sms are sent which can limit possible future empirical research. In the author's experience, making regular announcements on the LMS and dedicating a short time at the start of some lectures to go through the process can help students engage with the activities.

A word of warning,

> Students were highly critical of lecturers who cannot use IT processes efficiently and fumble about at the beginning of a lecture. It is apparent that lecturers need to be more consistently trained in a range of IT techniques for supporting the lecture, so they can skilfully use these.
>
> (Cameron 2009: 8)

It is therefore imperative to trial the activities before class. The lecturer must also be committed and consistent in using the tool to ensure the creation of patterns for the students and an atmosphere of caring for the student's learning experience (Nielsen *et al* 2013: 5).

Post class: reflecting

After the lecture, either before the tutorial or the exam, students are likely to revisit slides and recorded lectures and videos to help strengthen their understanding: "Lecture-recording enables students to personalise their learning by allowing them to supplement (or replace) their face-to-face lectures; to study and revise differently for exams; to take fewer notes and to focus on listening during lectures knowing they can revisit the difficult parts of the lecture in their own time" (Dona *et al* 2016: 131).

Beyond this, LMS also have discussion boards that could be used for students to post not only questions but also examples of contract clauses. Rather than showing them an Apple iTunes contract clause, or the clause famously added by Van Halen, why not let students find these themselves and post it on the forum?

Another tool is mind maps. These word maps of concepts and links could be used to help students draw connections between different concepts in contract law, but a recent article also calls for them to be used in written agreement (Mitchell 2018: 1).

Finally, optional modules can be added in which students may further explore and challenge their understanding, should they want to. This is the purpose of the OO files in Contracts at QUT – a suite of eight modules with a continuing narrative and multiple choice questions (Butler 2012a: 1; Deane and Bozin 2016: 1). Such online activities can be summative and graded, or formative and optional, and by using them, and blended learning more generally, students are able to oversee their studies with a flexibility which they value (Hewitt and Stubbs 2017: 11). They also enable the student to identify the learning experience in which they prefer to engage, whilst also improving their legal skills and their digital literacy. The time spent in gaining new skills can be perceived as stressful, and the ability to revise materials online and feel supported during that time can effectively reduce this stress (Hewitt and Stubbs 2017: 21). This could improve students' understanding of the impact and opportunities technology offers them in learning and later working as a legal professional.

Conclusion

Re-imagining contract pedagogy does not have to mean re-creating from scratch, but it does mean adaptation. Change is inevitable, and as lecturers we have the capacity, and arguably the duty, to prepare future graduates for the world of tomorrow. This does not mean that lecturers need to rethink and completely remodel their way of teaching. Technology is already part of our teaching. Current challenges in contract law and technology are opportunities for re-imagining contract pedagogy. This chapter has identified where the use of technology could enhance the student experience. A program of practical legal training should, among other skills, "include practical experience in the use of current information technology" (Law Admissions Consultative Committee 2002: 37). Core Priestley 11 and practical legal training can complement themselves in developing students' digital literacy. Contract being one of the first courses students enrolled on a law degree will undertake, and since technology is greatly impacting on its content and future, Contract is the perfect setting for lecturers to make *effective* use of technology that can "support new types of learning experiences, . . . enhance existing learning contexts" (Keppell *et al* 2015: 3) and prepare the legal professional of the future.

References

Anderson, L. W. and Krathwohl, D. R., et al., 2000., *A Taxonomy for Learning, Teaching, and Assessing: A revision of Bloom's Taxonomy of Educational Objectives*. Pearson, Allyn & Bacon, NY.

Australasian Council on Open Distance and e-Learning, 2013. *Lecture Capture in Australasian Universities*. Retrieved December 21, 2017, from www.acode.edu.au/pluginfile.php/419/mod_resource/content/1/ACODE_Lecture_Capture_Report_2013.pdf

Australian Learning and Teaching Council, 2010. Bachelor Of Laws Learning and Teaching Academic Standards Statement. *Learning and Teaching Academic Standards Project*. Retrieved December 20, 2017, from http://cald.asn.au/assets/lists/Education/LLB%20TLOsKiftetalLTASStandardsStatement2010%20TLOs%20LLB%5b2%5d.pdf

Brescia, R.H., 2016. Law and Social Innovation: Lawyering in the Conceptual Age. *Alb. L. Rev.*, 80, 235–309.

Butler, D.A., 2007. The Contracts Vignettes: Cost-effective Podcasting Producing Quality Learning Outcomes in First Year Contract Law. In: Proceedings *62nd Annual ALTA Conference – Law and Public Policy: Taming the Unruly Horse?* University of Western Australia, Perth, Western Australia. Retrieved December 21, 2017, from https://eprints.qut.edu.au/14393/1/14393.pdf

Butler, D.A., 2008. Air Gondwana: Teaching Basic Negotiation Skills Using Multimedia. *J. Aus. L. Tchrs. Assoc.*, 1, 213–226.

Butler, D.A., 2011. Technology: New Horizons in Teaching Law. In: Kift, S. et al., eds., *Excellence and Innovation in Legal Education*. LexisNexis, Australia, pp. 459–496.

Butler, D.A., 2012a. The OO Files: Providing Online Formative Feedback on Contract Law Learning in a Narrative Setting. *J. Aus. L. Tchr Assoc.*, 5, 1–12. Retrieved December 20, 2017, from https://eprints.qut.edu.au/59496/1/Butler_JALTA.pdf

Butler, D., 2012b. Second Life Machinima Enhancing the Learning of Law: Lessons from Successful Endeavours. *Aus. J. Educ. Technol.*, 28, 383–399.

Cameron, H., 2009. Passion or Podcasts? Students' Views About University Lectures. *The Student Experience* Proceedings of the 32nd HERDSA Annual Conference 6–9 July 2009 Darwin, Australia School of Social Work & Social Policy. Retrieved December 21, 2017, from www.herdsa.org.au/publications/conference-proceedings/research-and-development-higher-education-student-experience-7

Castan, M. and Hyams, R., 2017. Blended Learning in the Law Classroom: Design, Implementation and Evaluation of an Intervention in the First Year Curriculum Design. *Legal Educ. Rev.*, 27, 1–19.

Crawford, R. and Jenkins, L., 2017. Blended Learning and Team Teaching: Adapting Pedagogy in Response to the Changing Digital Tertiary Environment. *Aus. J. Educ. Technol.*, 33, 51–72.

de Bruin, A.B. and van Merriënboer, J.J., 2017. Bridging Cognitive Load and Self-Regulated Learning Research: A Complementary Approach to Contemporary Issues in Educational Research. *Learn. Instruct.*, 51, 1–9.

Deane, F. and Bozin, D., 2016. Using Guiding Principles to Construct Effective Multiple Choice Exams to Assess Legal Reasoning. *Legal Educ. Rev.*, 26, 1–17.

Digital Lawyer (the), 2017. Why Lawyers' Work Ethic Means Legal Practice Is Ripe for Disruption. Retrieved December 21, 2017, from https://digitallawyer.news/articles/why-lawyers-work-ethic-means-legal-practice-is-ripe-for-disruption

Dona, K.L., Gregory, J. and Pechenkina, E., 2016. Lecture-Recording Technology in Higher Education: Exploring Lecturer and Student Views Across the Disciplines. *Aus. J. Educ. Technol.*, 33, 122–133.

Doyle, T., 2008. *Helping Students Learn in a Learner-Centered Environment: A Guide to Facilitating Learning in Higher Education*. Stylus Publishing, LLC Sterling Virginia.

Doyle, T., 2011. *Learner-Centered Teaching: Putting the Research on Learning IntoPractice*. Stylus Publishing, LLC Sterling Virginia.

Freudenberg, B., 2017. Beyond Lawyers: Legal Literacy for the Future. *Aus. Busi. L. Rev.*, 45, 387–404.

Freyer, F.J., 2017. Who Needs Lectures? Vermont Medical School Chooses Other Ways to Teach. Retrieved December 20, 2017, from www.bostonglobe.com/metro/2017/01/31/who-needs-lectures-vermont-medical-school-chooses-other-ways-teach/NnVNKxLGF9dqYtXDoctBhO/story.html

Giancaspro, M., 2017. Is a "smart contract" Really a Smart Idea? Insights from a Legal Perspective. *Comp. L. Sec. Rev.*, 33, 825–835.

Hewitt, A. and Stubbs, M., 2017. Supporting Law Students' Skills Development Online – A Strategy to Improve Skills and Reduce Student Stress? *Res. Learn. Technol.*, 25, 1–24.

Hewitt, A., 2015. Can You Learn to Lawyer Online? A Blended Learning Environment Case Study. *L. Tchr.*, 49, 92–121.

Instefjord, E.J. and Munthe, E., 2017. Educating Digitally Competent Teachers: A Study of Integration of Professional Digital Competence in Teacher Education. *Teach. Tchr Educ.*, 67, 37–45.

Kauffman, H., 2015. A Review of Predictive Factors of Student Success in and Satisfaction with Online Learning. *Res. Learn. Technol.*, 23, 26507 Retrieved December 20, 2017, from https://journal.alt.ac.uk/index.php/rlt/article/view/1648/html_12

Keppell, M., Suddaby, G. and Hard, N., 2015. Assuring Best Practice in Technology-Enhanced Learning Environments. *Res. Learn. Technol.*, 23, 25728, 1–13.

Kirschner, P.A. and De Bruyckere, P., 2017. The Myths of the Digital Native and the Multitasker. *Teach, Tchr Educ.*, 67, 135–142.

Law Admissions Consultative Committee, 2002. "Appendix A" *Towards a National Legal Profession Revised Uniform Admission*. Retrieved December 20, 2017, from http://cald.asn.au/assets/lists/Resources/Revised%20Uniform%20Admission%20Rules%5B1%5D.pdf

Law Admissions Consultative Committee, 2017. *Practical Legal Training Competency Standards For Entry-Level Lawyers*. Retrieved December 20, 2017, from www.lawcouncil.asn.au/files/web-pdf/LACC%20docs/224336988_10_LACC%20-%20PLT.pdf

Law Council, 2016. *Prescribed Academic Areas of Knowledge*. Retrieved December 20, 2017, from www.lawcouncil.asn.au/files/web-pdf/LACC%20docs/243473563_1_Prescribed_Academic_Areas_of_Knowledge.pdf

Law Society of New South Wales Commission of Inquiry, 2017. *The Future of Law and Innovation in the Profession*. Retrieved December 23, 2017, from www.lawsociety.com.au/cs/groups/public/documents/internetcontent/1272952.pdf

Macquarie Dictionary Online., *Macmillan Publishers Australia*. Retrieved December 21, 2017, from www.macquariedictionary.com

McCall, I., 2010. Online Enhanced Problem-Based Learning: Assessing a Blended Learning Framework. *L. Tchr.*, 44, 42–58.

McKeough, J., 2012. Graduate Attributes – The Priestley Areas of Knowledge and the Broader Educational Context. *Internationalising the Australian Law Curriculum for Enhanced Global Legal Education and Practice* (National Symposium March 16, 2012, Canberra) Retrieved December 20, 2017, from http://curriculum.cald.asn.au/media/uploads/9_8_Graduate_attributes.pdf

Mirriahi, N., Alonzo, D. and Fox, B., 2015. A Blended Learning Framework for Curriculum Design and Professional Development. *Res. Learn. Technol.*, 23(1) 28451, 1–14.

Mitchell, J.A., 2018. Whiteboard and Black-Letter: Visual Communication in Commercial Contracts. *U. Pa. J. Bus. L.* (forthcoming).

Moses, L.B., 2017. Artificial Intelligence in the Courts, Legal Academia and Legal Practice. *Aus. L.J.*, 91, 561–574.

Murphy, E., 1996. 'School's Out: Hyperlearning, The New Technology, And the End of Education by Lewis Perelman, Avon Books, 1992' Retrieved December 20, 2017, from www.ucs.mun.ca/~emurphy/stemnet/school.html

Nielsen, K.L., Hansen, G. and Stav, J.B., 2013. Teaching with Student Response Systems (SRS): Teacher-Centric Aspects That Can Negatively Affect Students' Experience of Using SRS. *Res. Learn. Technol.*, 21(1), 18989.

Parish, K., 2011. Flexible, Blended and Intensive Learning in Law. In: Kift, S. et al., eds., *Excellence and Innovation in Legal Education*. LexisNexis, Australia pp. 421–458.

Pistone, M., 2017. *Blended Learning for Law Schools*. Retrieved December 18, 2017, from https://bestpracticeslegaled.albanylawblogs.org/2017/07/14/blended-learning-for-law-schools/

Prensky, M., 2001. Digital Natives, Digital Immigrants Part 1. *On the Horizon*, 9(5), 1–6. Retrieved December 22, 2017, from www.marcprensky.com/writing/Prensky%20-%20Digital%20Natives,%20Digital%20Immigrants%20-%20Part1.pdf

Race, P. and Pickford, R., 2007. *Making Teaching Work: Teaching Smarter in Post-Compulsory Education*. Sage, London.

Radloff, A. and Coates, H., 2009. Doing More for Learning: Enhancing Engagement and Outcomes: Australasian Survey of Student Engagement: Australasian Student Engagement Report. Retrieved December 22, 2017, from https://research.acer.edu.au/ausse/12/

Schmidt, H.G., Wagener, S.L., Smeets, G.A., Keemink, L.M. and van der Molen, H.T., 2015. On the Use and Misuse of Lectures in Higher Education. *Health Prof. Educ.*, 1, 12–18.

Shaw, J., Kominko, S. and Terrion, J.L., 2015. Using LectureTools to Enhance Student – Instructor Relations and Student Engagement in the Large Class. *Res. Learn. Technol.*, 23: 27197, 1–14.

Size, R., 2016. Taking Advantage of Advances in Technology to Enhance the Rule of Law. *Aus. L.J.*, 91, 575–587.

University of Adelaide, 2017. Developing digitally capable graduates Retrieved December 20, 2017, from www.adelaide.edu.au/library/digital-capabilities/docs/FINAL_Digital_Capabilites_framework.pdf

Veen, W. and Vrakking, B., 2006. *Homo Zappiens: Growing up in a Digital Age*. Network Continuum Education, London.

Xynas, L., 2011. Approaching Legal Education in the Online Teaching and E-learning Environment: A Case Study-Taxation Law. *J. Aus. L. Tchr Assoc.*, 4, 81–97.

Yin, K. and Moore, J., 2017. Hypothetical Cases as a Pedagogical Tool in Contract Law Studies. *J. Aus. L. Tchr Assoc.*, 10, 203–220.

Websites

Charles Sturt University, (n.d.). *Graduate Attributes Policy*. Retrieved December 22, 2017, from https://policy.csu.edu.au/view.current.php?id=00257https://policy.csu.edu.au/view.current.php?id=00257

Clark, D. (n.d.). *Bloom's Taxonomy of Learning Domains*. Retrieved December 22, 2017, from www.nwlink.com/~donclark/hrd/bloom.html *Contracts is a beach*. (n.d.). Retrieved December 22, 2017, from www.youtube.com/watch?v=rwUgj43EGbA.

CQ University, (n.d.). *Graduate Attributes*. Retrieved December 22, 2017, from www.cqu.edu.au/policy/sharepoint-document-download?file_uri=%7BBE8380F3-F86D-4C55-AC0D-84A81EAFD6A2%7D/Graduate%20Attributes.pdf.

Curtin University, (n.d.). *Curtin Graduate Attributes*. Retrieved December 22, 2017, from https://clt.curtin.edu.au/teaching_learning_practice/graduate_capabilities.cfm

Deakin University, (n.d.). *Contract*. Retrieved December 22, 2017, from www.deakin.edu.au/current-students-courses/unit.php?unit=MLL111

Deakin University. (2015). *Deakin University Digital Literacy Framework, Graduate Learning Outcome 3*. Retrieved December 22, 2017, from www.deakin.edu.au/__data/assets/pdf_file/0008/268748/DL_framework_2014-CC_rev-_2015.pdf

Edith Cowan University. (n.d.a). *Contract Law I*. Retrieved December 22, 2017, from http://handbook.ecu.edu.au/unit_outline.asp?UCID=1268&V=0.0403.

Edith Cowan University. (n.d.b). *Graduate attributes*. Retrieved December 22, 2017, from http://intranet.ecu.edu.au/learning/teaching-and-learning-support/employability/work-integrated-learning/graduate-attributes

Flinders University, (n.d.). *Bachelor of Laws and Legal Practice*. Retrieved December 22, 2017, from www.flinders.edu.au/courses/rules-2012/undergrad/blawlpg.cfm#learningoutcomes.

Griffith University, (n.d.). *Contracts 1*. Retrieved December22, 2017, from https://degrees.griffith.edu.au/Course/1029LAWhttps://degrees.griffith.edu.au/Course/1029LAW

Harvard University, (n.d.). *Contract Law: From Trust to Promise to Contract*. Retrieved December 22, 2017, from www.mooc-list.com/course/contract-law-trust-promise-contract-edx

Melbourne Law School, (n.d.). *Class recording Policy*. Retrieved December 23, 2017 from http://law.unimelb.edu.au/students/jd/studies/class-recording-policy MOOC ContractsX.(2017) www.edx.org/course/contractsx-2017-harvardx-hls2x

QUT, (n.d.) *Outline Contract Law*. Retrieved 22 December 2017, from www.qut.edu.au/study/unit?unitCode=LLB202

University of Adelaide, (n.d.). *University of Adelaide Graduate Attributes*. Retrieved December 22, 2017, from www.adelaide.edu.au/learning/strategy/gradattributes/

University of Canberra, (n.d.). *Graduate Attributes*. Retrieved December 22, 2017, from www.canberra.edu.au/about-uc/tl/graduate-attributes

The University of Melbourne, (n.d.). *Attributes, Outcomes and Skills*. Retrieved December 22, 2017, from https://handbook.unimelb.edu.au/2017/courses/mc-jurisd/attributes-outcomes-

University of New England, (n.d.). *Law of Contract I*. Retrieved December 22, 2017, from https://my.une.edu.au/courses/units/LAW171

University of South Australia, (n.d.). *Contracts A*. Retrieved December 22, 2017, from https://study.unisa.edu.au/courses/101559/2018

University of Southern Queensland, (n.d.). *Qualities of a Graduate Policy*. Retrieved December 22, 2017, from http://policy.usq.edu.au/documents/13420PL#4_Principleshttp://policy.usq.edu.au/documents/13420PL#4_Principles

Chapter 14

Doing away with the case method

What could go wrong?

Marcus Roberts

Introduction

We are now well into the twenty-first century, and there are calls for the teaching of law to move with the times. The calls include that legal educators focus more on teaching skills to their students, rather than merely transmit dry doctrinal points from the front of a lecture hall to hundreds of bored, passive students (for example Havelock 2013; Tzannes 1997; Sylvester *et al* 2004). There are also calls for change focussed particularly on the teaching of contract law: that the twenty-first century should see lecturers focusing more on what contracts in the real world actually consist of, rather than on marginal issues that get academics excited (for example Lewis 1982; Tillotson 1976; Friedman and Macaulay 1967). According to commentators critical of more traditional methods, contract law teaching in the twenty-first century should be more skills-centred, problem-based, and technologically savvy. What could possibly go wrong if contract law teaching was to move in such a direction?

As shall be seen, I am a teacher of a more traditional bent, both in terms of method and content. In this chapter, I aim to sound a note of caution against leaping into the modern world of contract law teaching. This chapter is not seeking to deny that there are ways that the traditional, casebook method could be improved. Instead, it is simply a reappraisal of the benefits of the traditional casebook method. In Part II I will describe the casebook method that I use when teaching. I will then look at some of the identified shortcomings of this approach and the criticisms directed towards it in Part III before I provide some responses to these criticisms in Part IV, and finally some thoughts on how the casebook method can be improved in Part V. Hopefully this chapter will provide some food for thought for contract law teachers at both the innovative and the more conservative ends of the spectrum. That way, the chance that anything goes wrong by throwing out the casebook method in the twenty-first century will hopefully be minimised.

An example of the casebook method in the twenty-first century

What does a casebook method look like in the twenty-first century? At the University of Auckland, we teach the Law of Contract as a full year course. It counts for a quarter of a normal undergraduate workload of 120 points a year. The course content is primarily delivered in three one-hour lectures a week. In addition, there are eight one-hour tutorials and eight one-hour clinics provided for students to practice problem solving, essay writing and examination techniques. The lectures I give typically involve a discussion of a number of cases which have been assigned for the day and which are contained in a casebook. The cases taught are usually appellate cases from New Zealand or the United Kingdom, with a sprinkling of Australian and American ones. While the vast majority of the casebook is made up of cases handed down in the last 100 years, there are also quite a few older ones. Aside from the nineteenth-century staples like *Hadley v Baxendale* (1854) 9 Exch 341 (Exch) and *Smith v Hughes* (1870–71) LR 6 QB 597, we also include some decidedly ancient cases from the earliest days of contract law such as *Thoroughgood v Cole* (1582) 2 Co Rep 9a, 76 ER 408 (KB) (for the purpose of introducing the concept of *non est factum*) and *Sturlyn v Albany* (1587) Cro Eliz 67, 78 ER 327 (KB) (as a good example of the courts not inquiring into the adequacy of consideration).

The value of such cases is to show the original context in which rules like consideration were developed and the circumstances and concerns that prompted their development (Bix 2012: 4). For example, when we teach the topic of frustration we begin with examples of the original common law rule of absolute obligations (*Paradine v Jane* [1558–1774] All ER Rep 172 (KB) and *Thornborow v Whitacre* (1705) 2 Ld Raym 1164, 92 ER 270 (KB)). We then examine the different types of external intervening circumstances which gave a valid defence against a claim for breach of contract. We do this through reading a number of cases from the latter half of the nineteenth century: *Taylor v Caldwell* (1863) 3 B & S 826, 122 ER 309 (KB) (destruction of the specific, named subject matter of the contract); *Poussard v Spiers* (1876) 1 QBD 410 (incapacitation of a person when that contract was for a personal service); and *Jackson v Union Marine Insurance Co Ltd* [1874–80] All ER Rep 317 (Exch) (delay leading to frustration of common commercial venture). Although we do not usually include one in the casebook, I also mention at least one of the World War One shipping cases, such as *FA Tamplin v Anglo-Mexican Petroleum Products Co Ltd* [1916] 2 AC 397 (HL), as an example of intervening illegality being held to be a valid defence for failure to perform. We then look at how these separate categories of cases in which impossibility of performance was held to be a valid defence were submerged within a wider, more general doctrine which excused both parties from further performance in the twentieth century through the classic English cases of *Krell v Henry* [1903] 2 KB 740 (CA), *Davis Contractors Ltd v Fareham Urban District Council* [1956] 2 All ER 145 (HL) and the recent

New Zealand decision of *Planet Kids Ltd v Auckland Council* [2013] NZSC 147, [2014] 1 NZLR 149. Taking the students through the development of the doctrine not only gives them good examples of frustration, but also gives them some insight into the benefits and disadvantages of having a restrictive, and then gradually more liberal, defence for failure to perform due to circumstances outside the parties' control. This brings forth a discussion of concepts such as foreseeability and allocation of risk during contractual negotiation as well as the extent to which the courts' concept of doing justice to the parties should supplant the expectation that they protect themselves through adequate contractual drafting. These concepts come alive in the facts of the cases studied which are often fascinating tales of disaster from history. For example, one question I like to ask is how Prince Rupert could be both Charles I's leading cavalry general and could also be described as "an enemy to the King and kingdom" in *Paradine v Jane*. But the study of these cases also demonstrates the direction in which the law in this area has been heading for the last 150 years or so.

Frustration is, of course, only one of the topics we cover in our contract law casebook. Over the year we cover the life cycle of a contract: the requirements for formation; interpretation; damages and cancellation for breach or misrepresentation; frustration; illegality; mistake and unconscionability. Although we teach through reading and analysing cases, in New Zealand one cannot ignore the role of statutes. The second half of the course centres on the Contract and Commercial Law Act 2017, a conglomerate statute which amalgamated a number of previous contract law statutes without amending the previous substantive law. The Act covers a number of contract law areas including: relief in the event of a frustrated contract; relief in the event of an illegal contract, especially in the event that an unreasonable restraint of trade is found; relief when a contract is entered into due to a qualifying mistake; remedies for a pre-contractual misrepresentation and for when one party has the right to cancel the contract; and the rules governing when third party beneficiaries are allowed to sue to enforce contractual obligations owed to them.

Students are expected to know these statutes, to be able to interpret them, and to apply them to novel fact problems in an exam setting. Thus, although the course is heavily based upon appellate cases, a large number of these cases in the second half of the year are themselves exploring, defining and interacting with the relevant statutes. For example, the students see how the New Zealand Court of Appeal in *Garratt v Ikeda* [2002] 1 NZLR 577 (CA) grappled with the question whether an unpaid deposit still had to be tendered by the breaching party upon the valid termination of a sale of land contract by the vendor. This, in turn, required the Court to interpret s 8(3)(a) of the Contractual Remedies Act 1979 (now s 42(1)(a) of the Contract and Commercial Law Act 2017 which stated, "So far as the contract remains unperformed at the time of the cancellation, no party shall be obliged or entitled to perform it further". Drawing on the law as it existed prior to the enactment of the relevant legislation and having determined that the framers of the Act did not intend that this earlier law should be overturned, the Court held that s 8(3)(a) did not affect rights that unconditionally accrued prior to cancellation, and thus the deposit was still payable by the purchaser (*Garratt v Ikeda* at [8]-[25]). This case demonstrates to the students the courts interpreting one statutory provision by using a number of different tools: textual analysis of the section in question; exploration of the law prior to the enactment; the stated intention of the drafters of the Act; and consideration of the practical effect of the different interpretations available.

Through the casebook method students are also introduced to the wonders of inconsistent and uncertain statutory drafting. For example, in the section of the course dealing with mistake, students are able to see that there are two inconsistent principles running through the contractual mistakes legislation. The first is to give the courts the power to grant relief to "mitigate the arbitrary effects of mistakes on contracts" (Contracts and Commercial Law Act 2017 section 21(1)). This principle can be seen to strongly influence the expansive definition of a qualifying mistake given by the Court of Appeal shortly after the passing of the Act in *Conlon v Ozolins* [1984] 1 NZLR 489. The second principle is that relief should not be granted in a manner "that prejudices the general security of contractual relationships" (section 21(2)(b)). This principle, as well as section 29 which states that no mistake in the interpretation of the contract itself can qualify for relief, led to the Court of Appeal's subsequent retreat from *Conlon v Ozolins* in *Paulger v Butland Industries Ltd* [1989] 3 NZLR 549 (CA) and *Mechenex Pacific Services Ltd v TCA Airconditioning (New Zealand) Ltd* [1991] 2 NZLR 393 (CA). By discussing these cases and analysing the relevant statutory provisions, students are introduced to the difficulties of successfully balancing contradictory concerns through legislation. The better students often end up asking themselves (and me) whether the New Zealand mistakes legislation actually has any practical effect at all. When we teach students contract law doctrine through the New Zealand cases, we necessarily have to get them to grapple with statutes and statutory interpretation as well (for the problems of neglecting statutory analysis for case law analysis only, see Crespi 2013).

There is no doubt that there is a lot to get through in our Law of Contract course. Seventy-two hours of lectures is not usually enough to get through the material without rushing at the end. The lack of time is exacerbated by public holidays which usually reduce the number of teaching hours to 68. The course as a whole is a good example of what others have termed the "North Platte River Approach" – where, just like the eponymous river, there is an abundance of breadth but not much depth (Tillotson 1976: 143). The question as to whether we are devoting our time wisely in our course will be returned to in the next part of the chapter.

As may be guessed, it can be said that our Law of Contract casebook and my approach to teaching is fairly Langdellian. Although I do not immediately start my first class by asking a shell-shocked student to tell me the facts of the first case in the case book (currently *Denny v Hancock* (1870) LR 6 Ch App 1) as Christopher Langdell apparently did when he taught his first Contracts class at

Harvard in 1870 (Grey 1983: 1), I do usually start asking questions of the students in my second lecture. I seek to encourage classroom discussion through the asking of questions to do with the facts of the case in front of us, its ratio and how it fits more broadly into the topic that we are studying. I encourage students to ask questions throughout the lecture if they do not know something and also invite other students to attempt to answer their peers' questions. Students are expected to have read the cases to be discussed prior to coming to class and in a perfect world they should also be reading them after the class discussion.

Pressures to change for the twenty-first century

Having detailed our Law of Contract course, there may be some readers who are horrified at our traditional, if not downright obsolete, approach. Many commentators have had little to say in favour of the traditional contract course (such as the one described above). Attacks on this method of contract law teaching have usually come from two directions. First, there are those who criticise the traditional casebook material as not sufficiently preparing lawyers to practice once they graduate. Second, there are those who are concerned that the casebook method is not the most effective way of educating students, particularly now that the generation in the lecture halls is composed of "digital natives". Let us look at both of these criticisms in some more detail.

What do we teach in the casebook method?

According to a recent survey of 800 junior lawyers in New Zealand, law school does not prepare students for the real world overly well (800 does represent a very large sample of junior lawyers in New Zealand; there are only about 900 lawyers admitted to the bar each year: see Adlam and Jacombs 2016). While 92.7% of the respondents of the survey thought that law school had given them a good grounding in legal theory and analytical skills, less than half (49.1%) thought that law school had prepared them well for practice. Also, 52.4% disagreed with the statement that law school had given them a good grounding in legal practical skills. At the time they left law school, a vast majority (82.8%) were either not at all informed, or only slightly informed, as to what legal practice actually involved. One interviewee compared practice as akin to driving a car for the first time when they had only read the operating manual (Pemberton 2016). Although this survey was not limited solely to courses in the Law of Contract, many would heartily agree with these sentiments when applied to contract law. Many commentators have expressed the concern that the casebook method does not accurately reflect how contract law actually works in the real world (Friedman and Macaulay 1967: 811). As Professor Richard Lewis once noted, "If an object of the traditional [contract] course is to reflect the practice of commerce and highlight current problems in the work of lawyers, it fails" (Lewis 1982: 113). As was described above, our course spends the year tracking the life cycle of the contract and devotes the better part of half a year to formation and estoppel. However, as many commentators have asked, how often do lawyers or parties actually have a dispute about formation (Ross 1983: 9)? More generally, how often do parties in a dispute reach the stage of a court hearing, let alone reach the higher appellate courts? Yet it is these appellate court decisions, a tiny fraction of all contract disputes in the real world, that our traditional casebook focuses on.

Therefore it has been said that the traditional course focus too heavily on only the formal, expensive, and adversarial trial method of dispute resolution by examining contract law through the lens of (usually appellate) court cases. The traditional casebook bestows on these cases an "antique mythology" that does not reflect their real-world importance (Tillotson 1976: 137). This is at the expense of spending time looking at the less formal, but more commercially realistic, methods of settlement such as diplomacy and negotiation (Lewis 1982: 115; Tillotson 1976: 143). Not only does litigation have the potential to damage a party's reputation in the wider industry, but the relationship may be one which the innocent party has no wish to imperil through a costly legal dispute. Private sanctions between-the-parties often exist and work at a far lower cost than turning to litigation or even threatening to do so. Alternatively, it often will be easier and much cheaper for a business to cut its losses and move on to the next transaction than become bogged down in a lengthy legal dispute (Friedman and Macaulay 1967: 815–816). A student who thinks that beginning legal proceedings is the best (or perhaps only!) response to a contract dispute probably does not realise that resort to the formal legal dispute mechanisms is an indication of a failure of the business relationship and is a course of action which, if taken, is likely to sever all future long-term relationships between the parties. Advising such a course neglects the importance that the relationship might have to the client and which might require some give and take, irrespective of the legal rights (Arup 1987: 134–135).

This difference between strict, traditional contractual legal rights and business practice can be seen in the courts' struggles with how to deal with informal contractual variations. Rather than using one of the traditional means of ensuring that the variation is legally enforceable (such as ensuring that both parties provide some additional consideration), one party often agrees to pay more (or accept less) to help a struggling counterparty. This has led to a shifting approach taken by the courts to the requirement of consideration in variation situations. The redefinition of consideration as including a "practical benefit" (*Williams v Roffey Bros & Nicholls (Contractors) Ltd* [1991] 1 QB 1 (CA)), or doing away with the requirement of consideration in variation situations altogether (*Nav Canada v Greater Fredericton Airport Authority Inc* 2008 NBCA 28, (2008) 329 NBR (2d) 328 and *Antons Trawling Co Ltd v Smith* [2003] 2 NZLR 23 (CA), *Teat v Willcocks* [2013] NZCA 162, [2014] 3 NZLR 129), can be seen to be attempts by the courts to configure the law to the parties' expectations and commercial practices. These cases are good examples of the parties seeking a way through a breach of contract (or potential breach) without immediately resorting to legal action and instead allowing some leeway so that the relationship can continue. These commercial, everyday practices are things that the traditional contract law course does not focus on at all. Instead, the casebook analyses them in light of the courts' attempts to fit them within the traditional contract law forms so that they can be enforceable *post facto*. Students are thus introduced to the effects that these judicial attempts have upon the doctrine of consideration and not to the business practices that the parties are employing outside of the reach of contract law.

Moving from dispute resolution, when it comes to drafting, how often does a traditional casebook actually contain a business agreement? Such a document might be very useful for the students to learn the function of particular clauses, the relationship between various clauses, and what parties negotiate for and what they are silent about (Tillotson 1976: 140). Students are taught about the formation doctrines and the requirements for an enforceable contract at law, but the realities of forming contracts in the world of commercial law are largely passed over. For example, those in business might deem it more prudent to rely on a sense of trust to smooth over potential disputes in the future. The danger of allocating all possible risks by a written contract is that it might expose strains in the relationship between the parties that are best left hidden. Leaving gaps in the contract and hoping that the future will not expose those gaps may seem to be a better option at the time of drafting than trying to tie down a watertight bargain that covers all eventualities. At the very least, the latter option will be more expensive and time consuming, at the worst it may jeopardise the transaction as a whole if negotiations break down (Friedman and Macaulay 1967: 815–816). Despite this, we spend nearly half of our course describing the different ingredients needed to form an enforceable contract (including the increasingly irrelevant postal acceptance rule (*Adams v Lindsell* (1818) 1 B & Ald 681, 106 ER 250 (KB), *Henthorn v Fraser* [1892] 2 Ch 27 (CA) and *Holwell Securities Ltd v Hughes* [1974] 1 All ER 161 (CA)) without exploring how often such doctrines reflect common business practice (Friedman and Macaulay 1967: 820–821).

Finally, despite the fact that the casebook gives the impression that it is an authoritative overview of the entirety of the Law of Contract and that students therefore will know at least something about everything contract-related at the end of the course, this is simply not the case. As statutory regulation covers more of the ground once held by the law of contract, it seems to many that the traditional Law of Contract course involves "teaching more and more about less and less" (Lewis 1982: 117). If students wish to know anything about the specialised rules of insurance and employment contracts, or agreements concerning sale of goods, consumer credit agreements, or consumer contracts then they will have to take courses in those subjects; the Law of Contract course will not teach them anything about these areas (aside, perhaps from saying that "of course, these rules do not apply to a sales of goods contract"). Indeed, in some later courses, such as Insurance Law, the general principles learned in the Law of Contract may be a positive hindrance to students, rather than any helpful base from which to branch into a specialised area (Lewis 1982: 116). As one commentator noted (Unger 1982: 617):

When you add up the exclusions, the exceptions, and the repressions, you begin to wonder in just what sense traditional contract theory dominates at all. It seems like an empire whose claimed or perceived authority vastly outreaches its actual power.

How do we teach with the casebook method?

Having discussed the perceived shortcomings with *what* is taught in a traditional Law of Contract course, let us now turn to the identified problems with *how* the casebook method transmits information to the law student. Sir William Osler once wrote of medical students: "To study the phenomena of disease without books is to sail an uncharted sea, while to study books without patients is not to go to sea at all" (Osler 1925: 220). For many critics of the casebook method, students are invited to study doctrine without ever putting that doctrine to use by "going to sea" and practising what they have learnt through more realistic, problem-based exercises.

First, the casebook method does not prepare students to analyse and sift through irrelevant facts. This is an essential skill since lawyers will be faced with clients who come to them with a number of problems, not all of which will be legal. The lawyer will be expected to be able to sift through the information given to them by the client (often in an incoherent way) in order to identify the relevant areas of the law and the issues involved. At the same time lawyers will also have to assess a number of non-doctrinal points, such as whether or not this client is telling the truth and would be a reliable witness or not (Sylvester *et al* 2004: 48–49). But the casebook method already edits and selects the relevant facts for the students so that there is no need for them to develop this skill. This pre-selection of material happens at a number of different levels. The students know at the broadest level that the course is one dealing with contract law and that any other legal issues will be ignored, or only mentioned in passing, and will not be examinable. The course is then divided up into discrete topics, so the students know that *this* case is relevant for *this* issue before they read it. The cases themselves are typically at the appellate level and thus the relevant facts for the purpose of the dispute have already been separated from the irrelevant at the trial stage and by the appellate judges when they write their judgments. Furthermore, appellate cases are selective in the issues discussed and thus fail to disclose many important parts of the legal controversy as it unfolded and was resolved (Wizner and Curtis 1980: 677–678). Finally, some of the cases in the casebook might be further edited by the course lecturers in order to stay within mandated page limits. When the cases are edited the most relevant parts are selected, further reducing the amount of sifting of facts and arguments that the students must do while reading (see generally Johnson 2016: 598). While there might be some requirement that the students display some ability to identify relevant issues and facts in a problem style exam or essay questions, the number of irrelevant facts that can be included in such a question will never be able to mirror the complexities of real-life disputes. In short, the casebook method does little to develop our students' ability to ask the right questions of their future clients in order to determine what the dispute is actually about.

The wider problem is that law students are "spoon-fed" in a traditional casebook method class. Students are not expected to take ownership of their learning or of a problem given them. They are presented with all the relevant material in the casebook. Essays and exam problems can be answered by students without any research required outside of the cases provided to them in the casebook and the lectures. Information is thus passively received by the students; they do not have to actively look for the answer to problems. This is in contrast to teaching methods such as "problem-based learning" in which the focus is on the student answering problems through their own research. A problem is presented as the first step in the learning process and the student is then expected to answer it through assigned materials and independent research. Students are constantly required to evaluate the material as they encounter it to determine its relevance to answer the problem set (Tzannes 1997; Havelock 2013). Such a research-centred method would more accurately reflect the work that lawyers actually do. It would give students the skills to research areas of law in response to a problem in an area of law that they are not already familiar with (Havelock 2013: 390). Finally, a more active learning method would make students more likely to retain the knowledge they acquire than if they are simply passive, note-taking automatons in a lecture theatre. The breadth of the traditional Law of Contract course makes it more likely that students will acquire a surface knowledge of the material in order to succeed at a particular task (to do well in an essay or an exam) without internalising the material at a deeper level (Fry *et al* 2009). In short, the traditional casebook method is focussed on doctrine at the expense of more useful skills, and the doctrine taught is less likely to be retained by students in the long term.

A defence of the casebook method

There must be some benefit to the casebook method, since it has proven to be so enduringly popular. Nearly 150 years after its introduction, the casebook was still used by about nine in ten lecturers in the United States as the locus of their "primary source materials" at the turn of the millennium; it could still be accurately described as "the written centrepiece of legal education" (Bodie 2007: 10). But, if plagued by problems and shortcomings, why is the casebook method still so popular? This cannot simply be put down to institutional inertia or bloody-mindedness on the part of thousands of academics. Instead, there are benefits to the casebook method, and many of the criticisms of it are either misplaced or overemphasised.

The first and most obvious benefit of the casebook method is that it does instil skills in law students that are necessary for the practice of law. Lawyers and law students will always need to know how to read and analyse cases (Johnson 2016: 632). The Socratic method of teaching based on a casebook develops the students' ability to think analytically and construct logical arguments, especially within our system of case precedence (Bix 2013: 1254). These skills are required to apply the law to a given set of facts, draft legal documents, and effectively represent a client. The analytical thinking that the traditional casebook method fosters is the *sine qua non* of effective advocacy (Lamparello 2016: 408). It teaches students to "think like lawyers" – critically, logically, and carefully – something that the legal market in the twenty-first century still requires (Johnson 2016: 598; Morant 2016: 247; Friedman and Macaulay 1967: 810). Having a course in which students read a lot of appellate cases gives students many examples of the finely balanced policy arguments, interests, and values that lie behind judicial decisions (Bix 2013: 1255). Going through the cases introduces students to the uncertainties of otherwise apparently certain black letter rules which should be embraced as it is dealing with this uncertainty that allows students to become good lawyers (Bix 2013: 1256).

Thus, it is something of a false dichotomy to declare that one must either teach the casebook method or a more "skills-based" method. It is not a choice between a skills-based method or not; it is a choice between different methods of teaching which impart different skills. The casebook method teaches students how to read cases, which is not quite the same as reading other material. Students need to analyse what they read while trying to understand its relationship to prior readings, as well as its potential impact on current and future problems (Montana 2017: 445). If they wish to practice law, then students still need to know how to read cases. In New Zealand, the law of contract is still very much developed by case law; this has not changed even with the proliferation of contract law statutes over the last forty years or so. As students are shown in our Law of Contract course, cases are still extremely important for defining the scope of these statutes. Although there may be some merit to the accusation that contract law as taught does not mirror how parties in the real world order their transactions, lawyers still need to know the actual *law*. It is no failing of a Law of Contract course that it teaches contract law as applied by the courts and contained within statutes rather than teaching business negotiation or general business practice. Perhaps students could be given some insight into such practices in a Law of Contract course, but primarily they should be taught what the law actually *is*, rather than how parties navigate, ignore, or remain ignorant of, the law. After all, as lawyers, they will be expected to advise what the courts will decide if a dispute is to get that far. Even if litigation is not contemplated by the parties, the legal position will be a key piece of information for the purpose of negotiations. The legal position must be provided by lawyers, and lawyers need to learn it in a Law of Contract course.

Indeed, the benefits of the casebook method and forcing students to read a large number of cases is probably increasing, since students in the second decade of the twenty-first century are so ill-equipped to concentrate and read for long periods of time. It goes almost without saying that a weak reader and analyser of the law will struggle to do well at university and later on in practice (Montana 2017: 446). However, the ability to sit down, to read, and to concentrate on lengthy judgments in our students cannot be taken for granted. Instead, it has to be taught. The imperative to do so is greater now than ever due to the technological environment in which our students are immersed. The millennials who populate the lecture halls of the early twenty-first century are digital natives, relying on computers and video for their education and entertainment. For many of them, this digital milieu is not just supplementing the traditional written word in books and hardcopy – it is replacing it. For example, one alarming study in the United States showed that reading is a vanishing recreation, even for the most well educated. It showed that approximately 37% of college-educated readers and 25% of those with a graduate education had not read a single novel, play, or piece of poetry in the previous year (Montana 2017: 435).

In place of the hardcopy, written word, our students are more used to reading in short bites, jumping from link to link to find the information required in the shortest time possible. This habit of reading and processing information is extremely distracting and leads to an attention span which is unaccustomed to work that requires focus, deep thinking, or critical analysis. Many students brought up in the digital world show deficiencies in basic critical reading, thinking, analysis, and writing skills (Boothe-Perry 2016: 62). They are generally not accustomed to the active attention and engagement that reading dense, analytical text entails (Montana 2017: 439–443).

As contract law teachers, we can help our students by introducing them to the skills that they need and that they are not acquiring elsewhere. When in practice, our students will probably read cases and statutes and commentaries online, rather than in hardcopy format. There is still a need, no matter what the medium is, for the students to apply themselves and absorb and learn (Blissenden 2017: 877). They will still need to know how to concentrate, how to read a judgment or legal opinion carefully, and how to analyse it. This is what the casebook method can provide to students – practice in how to read and analyse cases. Problem-solving skills, client-interviewing skills, and drafting skills – these are all valuable for the budding lawyer. But there is no substitute for reading a large number of cases in order to practice how to read and analyse judgments, opinions, statutes, and commentaries as a lawyer. This is what the casebook method can provide. If the teaching of the Law of Contract was to move away from this method in the twenty-first century without adequately safeguarding this benefit for our students, then we will have taken a wrong turning.

Ways to improve what we do

Although I think that the criticisms of the casebook method are not so compelling that we should abandon the approach, I do think that there are ways that the traditional method could be improved. I propose to briefly discuss these ways now to show that keeping the casebook method does not mean to preserve the status quo with no innovation in the twenty-first century whatsoever.

The first way that the casebook method can be enhanced is to strengthen the analytical skills of the students as they read the cases – the key skills that the casebook method imparts to students. This strengthening can be done by first ensuring that they do not come to the readings "cold". That is, that they are given an introduction to the readings for the next class or topic. What are they going to read? How do the cases fit together and into the course as a whole? A brief introduction will help to alleviate the confusion that students might find by reading something with no idea as to how it builds into the structure of contract law that they have learned so far. Such an introduction will help students to understand what they are reading prior to class and to remember what they have read (Montana 2017: 449). The second technique is to cement the readings into the students' minds and memories by conducting quizzes based upon the cases that the students have just read. The quiz should be short in duration, perhaps only a couple of short written answer questions at the beginning of class from time to time such as: What are the facts of the case? What was the decision? How does it build into previous decisions we have looked at? Does this case create an exception, or limit or expand a rule? This forces the students to look at the case more closely and to then think more critically and not to be able to get by with skim reading, which raises the danger of them missing patterns in the law and failing to be able to apply the law to new scenarios (Montana 2017: 453).

Another relatively easy technique that could be introduced into a traditional case method course to increase its practical relevance would be an exercise to be given to students at the end of the formation part of the course. This exercise would consist of a poorly drafted, unenforceable contract that the students are asked to either critique or redraft into an enforceable form. This would be a way to integrate drafting skills into the course in a manner which does not use up too much time while also cementing the knowledge that the students have learned in the formation lectures and readings (Lamparello 2016: 418).

A final point to keep in mind if the casebook method is to be retained in the twenty-first century is that the environment in the lecture hall needs to be a positive one in which students are able to trust the lecturer, and each other, that their contributions will be valued (Boothe-Perry 2016: 63). This is particularly important when one is using the Socratic method and therefore demanding that students participate. If that is the case, then one must foster amongst the students a feeling that they can participate and not have their contributions belittled by other students or the lecturer (Boothe-Perry 2016: 63). As a lecturer, such belittling is probably going to occur unconsciously, but there is always the recurring problem of how to gently but authoritatively tell a student that are wrong before they start to confuse and mislead the entire class. And there are also less obvious pitfalls. I used to walk incessantly during my lectures up the front of my class and down the aisles. This was partly to make the classes more interesting, to keep my students on their toes, but mainly because I get restless. However, I stopped that practice after a senior colleague told me that I could potentially be intimidating students when pacing the aisle or standing in the midst of the aisle to take or ask questions. I had never thought that that could be the case and I certainly did not have that intention, but my colleague noted that my physical presence coupled with my status as lecturer had the potential to make students uncomfortable. This is a salutary warning that we have to be constantly on our guard to protect the lecture space for students, especially if we wish the casebook method to work.

Conclusion

There are ways that the current casebook method could be improved. Teachers who are always seeking to improve their methods and their course should be open to new ideas, and I would hope that the teachers of contract law are no exception. However, as a teacher who uses the casebook method coupled with the Socratic lecture method, I would hope that we do not lose what is useful and important in the case method in the rush to innovate. Students in the twenty-first century will still need to learn how to read, absorb, and critically analyse cases. They will still need to know what contract law doctrine is, even if only for the purposes of avoiding its reach in practice. The case method serves both of these functions. So by all means tweak and adapt, but let us not throw the casebook method baby out with the bath water in the twenty-first century.

References

Adlam, G. and Jacombs, A., 2016. Snapshot of the Profession. *L. Talk*, 883, 17–27.

Arup, C., 1987. Teaching Legal Skills and Substance: The Case of Contract. *L. Tchr.*, 21, 127–138.

Bix, B.H., 2012. *Contract Law: Rules, Theory, and Context*. Cambridge University Press, Cambridge.

Bix, B.H., 2013. Contract Texts, Contract Teaching, Contract Law: Comment on Lawrence Cunningham, Contracts in the Real World. *Wash. L. Rev.*, 88, 1251–1264.

Blissenden, M., 2017. Law Teaching in an Ever Changing World: Are We on the Right Track?: Some Reflections and a Case Study from Western Sydney University. *Univ. Pacific L. Rev.*, 48, 875–886.

Bodie, M., (2007). The Future of the Casebook: An Argument for an Open-Source Approach. *J. Legal Educ.*, 57, 10–35.

Boothe-Perry, N.A., 2016. The New Normal for Educating Lawyers. *BYU J. Pub. L.*, 31, 53.

Crespi, G.S., 2013. Teaching Contract Law Through Common Law Analysis: The UCI Law Experiment. *SMUL Rev.*, 66, 351–362.

Friedman, L.M. and Macaulay, S., 1967. Contract Law and Contract Teaching: Past, Present, and Future. *Wis. L. Rev.*, 805–821.

Fry et al., 2009. *A Handbook for Teaching and Learning – Enhancing Academic Practice*. Routledge, London.

Grey, T.C., 1983. Langdell's Orthodoxy. *U. Pitt. L. Rev.*, 45, 1–54.

Havelock, R., 2013. Law Studies and Active Learning: Friends Not Foes? *Law Tchr.*, 47, 382–403.

Johnson, S.M., 2016. The Course Source: The Casebook Evolved. *Cap. UL Rev.*, 44, 591–654.

Lamparello, A., 2016. The Integrated Law School Curriculum. *Elon L. Rev.*, 8, 407–442.

Lewis, R., 1982. Criticisms of the Traditional Contract Course. *Law Tchr.*, 16, 111–121.

Montana, P.G., 2017. Bridging the Reading Gap in the Law School Classroom. *Cap. UL Rev.*, 45, 433–456.

Morant, B.D., 2016. The Continued Evolution of American Legal Education. *Wake Forest L. Rev.*, 51, 245–258.

Osler, W., 1925. *Aequanimitas*. 6th ed. P. Blakiston's Son & Co, Philadelphia.

Pemberton, J., 2016. *First Steps: The Experience and Retention of New Zealand's Junior Lawyers*. The Law Foundation, Wellington.

Ross, J., 1983. Consideration: The need for re-definition? *L. Tchr.*, 17, 9–16.

Sylvester, C., Hall, J. and Hall, E., 2004. Problem-Based Learning and Clinical Legal Education: What can Clinical Educators Learn from PBL. *Int'l J. Clin. Legal Educ.*, 4, 39–63.

Tillotson, J., 1976. Anyone for Contract? *L. Tchr.*, 10, 135–145.

Tzannes, M., 1997. Problem Based Learning in Legal Education: Intentionally Overlooked or Merely Misunderstood. *L. Tchr.*, 31, 180–197.

Unger, R., 1982. The Critical Legal Studies Movement. *Harv. L. Rev.*, 96, 561–675.

Wizner, S. and Curtis, D., 1980. Here's What We Do: Some Notes About Clinical Legal Education. *Clev. St. L. Rev.*, 29.

Chapter 15

Insights from outside the common law

John Cartwright

Introduction: the value of looking outside the common law

Contract is one of the building blocks of private law in any legal system. However, systems take different approaches to the underlying notion of contract, to the place of contract within private law and even to the territory covered by 'contract' – the definition of contract's border with other parts of private law such as tort and property. Inevitably, these differences may also be reflected in how contract is taught. Common lawyers might know that lawyers from (for example) the continental European civil law tradition have different ideas about contract law, a different style of writing their contracts and different ways of educating their students. But they may say that the background of those civil law systems – their legal and educational culture – is just so different that we cannot sensibly learn anything from it. Or they may say that, in spite of the apparent differences, their law cannot (surely?) in reality be so different from ours, given that we are all part of a common Western culture, so we need not inquire into it anyway. The former view is one of cultural legal isolationism; the latter is a presumption of similarity of the law; and in their most extreme versions they both deny the value of comparative law. Neither should be adopted. Legal education is not simply about learning the law. It must include critical reflection on the law.

Earlier chapters of this book have discussed a range of perspectives that ought to be presented to our students in order to give them the tools necessary to assess contract law critically whilst they are learning its substantive legal rules. Understanding something of how other legal systems think about their own law is another such tool. We do not need to have any grand aim to harmonise or unify the law across systems, nor even to assume that we should in consequence reform our own national law. There is real value in studying another legal system in order to measure our own: to sharpen our understanding and assessment of underlying values which may otherwise be uncritically assumed. English lawyers can, of course, compare the law of contract in other systems in the common law tradition. Indeed, as teachers of English contract law, we naturally include comparisons with selected topics in other common law systems to show how the common law can develop, and therefore how English law might develop, given that the other common law systems have (by definition) a common heritage with English law, and their law of contract will in consequence share to a large extent the underlying principles and values of the English law of contract. For example, comparisons are commonly drawn with jurisdictions such as the United States, Australia and Canada over the potential development of reliance-based liabilities (promissory estoppel) and the doctrine of unconscionability. However, it is in looking outside the common law that we see a greater challenge in comparing systems containing different substantive rules, which appear to reflect different principles and values.

In this chapter, I shall first outline some of the differences of substance between the English law of contract and contract in the continental civil law tradition which it could be useful for students of English law to understand in order to reflect on their own law. It should also, however, be useful for those of us who teach contract law to classes which include students already trained in the civil law – such as the significant body of exchange students who come to us after two or three years' study of their own law. These students know what a contract is in their own system and, if they are not shown at an early stage how English law thinks about contract law, drawing attention to the differences in substance from the approach taken in the civil law, they risk misunderstanding, or making the wrong assumptions about, English law. (See generally Cartwright 2016, which is aimed primarily at such students.) Later, I shall comment briefly on how we might think about using the civil law within our courses on the English law of contract.

Contract law in continental civil law systems: reflections on the substantive law

The basis of contractual obligation may differ between legal systems: in Chapter 2 Martin Hogg began by drawing attention to the different roles of 'agreement' in classical Roman law, early English law and the modern law, and to some related differences in the underlying basis of contract. Indeed, the territory covered by 'contracts' may differ from one legal system to another. The promise of a gift may be a contract in one system but not in another: in the common law, the doctrine of consideration excludes a promise of a pure gift from being a contract (although it may be binding if executed as a deed), but civil law systems generally have no such difficulty (e.g. French law defines a gratuitous contract, '*le contrat à titre gratuit*', as 'where one of the parties provides a benefit to the other without expecting or receiving anything in return': Civil code, art. 1107, translated in Cartwright and Whittaker 2017: 412). And a particular type of transaction may be seen as contractual by one system, but in another it is governed by the law of tort or even by some third category – e.g. the duties of a gratuitous borrower of a movable might be seen as springing from a 'real contract' in the Roman thinking (Nicholas 1962: 167–171; Nicholas 1992: 40–42), but covered by bailment in English law (Bridge 2015: 59–61). It may be said that these examples are taken from the fringe of contract law, and certainly the classic, core cases of contract are equally familiar in all systems. Transactions involving a sale of goods, or the supply of services in return for a price, for example, have a strikingly similar feel in all systems. But even in apparently similar cases, we need to be alert to the fact that there can still be significant underlying differences. I cannot here give an account of the substantive rules of the law of contract in all of the various civil law systems. French law differs significantly from German law – they are often labelled as being different legal 'families' (for one explanation of legal families for the purpose of comparative private law, see Zweigert and Kötz 1998: ch 5); and even systems of the same 'family' – such as France, Belgium, Italy and Spain (the 'Romanistic' family, according to Zweigert and Kötz 1998: 68–69, ch 8) – will differ, just as we know that there are differences amongst the common law systems. But the continental civil law systems share certain features in how they think about contract law: its place within private law and the underlying values which it embodies. These values are reflected in some of the substantive rules that we find in each system's law of contract, and they offer contrasts – sometimes very sharp contrasts – with English law. Seeing these contrasts, our students can be challenged to reflect on the approach taken by English law.

The place of contract within private law

One thing that strikes the common lawyer about the civilian view of contract is that that there is a scheme, a system, within which contract has its natural place. This is one of the legacies of classical Roman law, the 'institutional' scheme set out first by Gaius (Stein 1988; Birks and Descheemaeker 2014: ch 1), in which some writers saw a legal actor's assets (his 'patrimony') as divided into his property rights and the rights he has (or the duties he owes) under obligations; within the law of obligations there are sub-divisions into contract, tort (or 'delict') and some other sources of obligation such as unjustified enrichment. In the modern codified systems in the civil law, this scheme, or some development of it, is generally reinforced by the very structure of the code. The German civil code contains in Book 1 a 'General Part' containing (inter alia) provisions relating generally to legal transactions (including contracts, and some provisions are aimed specifically at contracts), before Book 2 covering the Law of Obligations (which also contains some provisions for contracts generally, as well as many detailed provisions on special types of contract). Book 3 then deals with Ownership, Book 4 Family Law and Book 5 Succession. The original French civil code contained three books, giving a strong patrimonial structure to the civil law: Book 1 on Persons, followed by Book 2 on 'Property and the various modifications of ownership', then Book 3 on 'The different ways by which ownership is acquired' which covers succession, gratuitous transfers of property and obligations (in the modern era, a new Book 4 on Securities was added). But the notion of such a system does not depend on the codification of private law; it was part of the continental *ius commune* before codification (Stein 1988), and some form of it is also found in systems which follow generally the civil law tradition but have not undertaken a full codification of their private law, such as the Nordic countries (Zweigert and Kötz 1998: ch 19; Flodgren and Runesson 2015: 27–49).

English law does not think in such institutional, structural terms about private law. This is not to say that we could not equally draw up a scheme under which a person's 'estate' is composed of her property, together with the benefit of obligations she is owed (less the burden of obligations she owes). 'Contract' belongs in, broadly, the same place in the common law as in the civil law; it is part of the law of obligations, not property, and within obligations it is contrasted with obligations arising to compensate wrongs (torts) or to reverse an unjust enrichment. But we draw up that scheme only when we need to draw up an account: the estate that is gathered in by the trustee in bankruptcy for distribution to the creditors, for example, or by the personal representatives for the distribution of the deceased's assets. Otherwise, we see contract as a separate field of study, and most textbooks (and university courses) are on 'contract', not 'obligations' (subject to exceptions discussed in "Reflections on Teaching" below). There are also some important practical differences in the language of private law. Since the civil lawyer sees contractual rights as one species of the broader genus of obligations, the language of 'creditor' (one with the right under an obligation) and 'debtor' (one with the duty under an obligation) can apply generally, rather than being limited to the common law's notion of the person with the right to receive (or the duty to pay) a sum of money.

Borderlines: tort and property

Other systems may see the different relationships between contract and tort, or between contract and property in ways which can give the common lawyer pause for thought. These days, our students grow up with the idea of free concurrence of actions in contract and tort: let the claimant choose which claim best serves his interests (*Henderson v Merrett Syndicates Ltd* [1995] 2 AC 145, 193–194). Of course, that was not always the approach taken in English law and in the mid-20th century there was a debate about whether a claimant should have the right to circumvent contractual rules by suing in tort. Some civil systems traditionally take a strong anti-concurrence approach: most notably, the rule of '*non-cumul*' (i.e. the non-accumulation of liabilities in contract and tort) in French law generally defines a contracting party's rights by reference exclusively to the contract and therefore prohibits him from bringing an action against the other contracting party in tort where the contractual action exists. Knowing the history of the English rule is useful for our students to examine our current law, but seeing that other systems have had similar concerns reinforces the discussion: indeed, in the authoritative modern case, *Henderson v Merrett Syndicates Ltd* [1995] 2 AC 145, 184–194, Lord Goff drew on comparative material in his discussion. Also, we are used to teaching our students about the essential line between contract and tort; the different interests protected; the different measures of damages; the different defences available. There is a wide range of material in the different European civil law jurisdictions' approaches to add depth to this discussion. Some jurisdictions are much more open than others, including the English law, to awarding damages for intangible losses in contract, seeing the compensation of 'loss' as the general object of the law of obligations (contract and tort) (e.g. French law: Nicholas 1992: 227). And the borderline between contract and tort appears to come under pressure in many legal systems, where rules limiting a tort claim push the courts to finding a contractual solution, or vice versa (e.g. finding a contractual claim to avoid the need for a claimant to prove fault in tort in French law: Nicholas 1992: 190; or to avoid the restrictive rules of vicarious liability in German tort law: Markesinis *et al* 2006: 95–96). English cases where the courts behave similarly may then be less surprising when they are seen within a broader tradition of judicial decision-making (e.g. *Forsikringsaktieselskapet Vesta v Butcher* [1989] AC 852, 858–867, 875, 879 and *Barclays Bank plc v Fairclough Building Ltd (No. 2)* [1995] 44 Con LR 35, allowing the defence of contributory negligence in contract to avoid the claimant having a better claim in contract than in tort).

The relationship between contract and property is also a rich field for comparative study. Two particular issues can be mentioned here: first, the relationship between the contract and the transfer of property effected pursuant to the contract; and second, whether or not the contract transfers the property, what is the position of a purchaser in good faith from a non-owner? Even if we limit ourselves to contracts for the transfer of goods (the doctrine of *Walsh v Lonsdale* (1882) 21 ChD 9, under which the courts regard a (specifically enforceable) contract to convey an interest in land as already having the same effect *in equity* as a completed conveyance, raises issues which cannot be discussed here), all systems have to ask whether the contract itself transfers or creates a property right in the transferee, or whether some other act (delivery, or the execution of a document) is required to complete the transfer. The English contract law books do not always deal with this very satisfactorily, and the question is often left to the law of property. But our students need to understand the approach taken by English law in order to understand the contract cases on mistake of identity – the mistake which renders the contract void also renders the transfer of property void – because this is crucial to their understanding of the significance of the void/voidable distinction. This is one area where the English cases have drawn explicitly on comparison with the civil law: in *Shogun Finance Ltd v Hudson* [2004] 1 AC 919, [85]-[86], Lord Millett said:

> Under German law, too, the innocent third party obtains a good title, though this is a consequence of the law of property rather than the law of

> contract. Article 932 of the German Civil Code provides that a purchaser acting in good faith acquires title where he obtains possession from a seller who has no title. The purchaser is not in good faith if he knew, or by reason of gross negligence did not know, that the goods did not belong to the seller. Thus, under German law, whether or not A obtained title from B, he is able to pass a good title to D.
>
> German law reaches this conclusion by admitting a far wider exception to the *nemo dat quod non habet* rule than we accept, and this enables it to dispense with the need to decide the contractual effect of mistaken identity (and the meaning of 'identity' in this context) or to conduct a fruitless inquiry into the identity of the intended counterparty. Our inability to admit such an exception compels us to adopt a different analysis, but it would be unfortunate if our conclusion proved to be different. Quite apart from anything else, it would make the contemplated harmonisation of the general principles of European contract law very difficult to achieve.

The *nemo dat* rule in English law in principle protects the original owner, at least until the owner's claim is barred by limitation (Limitation Act 1980 (UK), s. 3: the owner's claim in English law is in the tort of conversion – again, an interesting contrast with the civilian systems, which provide the owner of personal property with a proprietary action to recover it). Civil law systems, by contrast, favour the good faith purchaser. The policies underlying this can more easily be explored by English students when they have an understanding of different approaches taken by other systems. Although this is a question of property law for the civil lawyer, it is a necessary element within the law of contract for the English lawyer, given that the *nemo dat* rule pushes the solution (or the lack of it) back into the void/voidable distinction within contract.

Categorising contracts

Even the structure of contract law is seen somewhat differently in civil law systems. The classical Roman heritage of 'special contracts' – under which a transaction is recognised as a contract because it fits a recognised category, rather than because it fulfils a general conception of 'contract' (Nicholas 1962: 165–166) – still lingers in the modern civil law systems. There is now, of course, a general conception of contract in the modern systems – a general definition, together with a list of conditions of existence of the contract, even if the elements vary from one system to another – and it raises some very interesting issues for comparison for the English student. But in the civil law tradition students learn the general law of contract first, but then still have a separate, more advanced course on 'special contracts' (typically focusing on sale, but also other types of contract). This reflects the structure of the modern civil codes, which contain lengthy, detailed sections on the different types of contract.

This structural difference has some significant consequences for the different ways in which civil lawyers think about contracts. In the first place, there is inevitably much more legislative regulation of the content and effects of these different types of contract than the English lawyer would expect. It looks similar to the English approach to terms implied by law into contracts, but we know that our courts are generally rather cautious in implying terms, at least into a detailed commercial contract (*Marks and Spencer plc v BNP Paribas Securities Services Trust Co (Jersey) Ltd* [2015] UKSC 72, [2016] AC 742). There are, of course, areas in which English law has rather extensive legislative regulation, such as in the case of consumer contracts (see, in particular, Consumer Rights Act 2015, Part 1). But these are seen as the exception – as, indeed, legislative intervention is generally the exception in English contract law. A second difference, though, which follows from this greater regulation of contracts in civil law systems is that there tends to be more mandatory regulation. In all systems, where a statute provides for a particular contract to contain a term, there is a question as to whether the term is mandatory or can be varied or excluded by the parties. But the starting point for an English lawyer is that the contract is based on the parties' free negotiation, and therefore the 'implied term' introduced by statute will give way to a contrary express term except in cases where the legislator expressly provides (e.g. Sale of Goods Act 1893 s. 55 as applied in *L'Estrange v Graucob* [1934] 2 KB 394; see now Sale of Goods Act 1979 s. 55, incorporating expressly the limitations of the Unfair Contract Terms Act 1977. The statutory terms imposed for the benefit of the consumer under Part 1 of the Consumer Rights Act 2015 are made expressly non-excludable: ss. 31, 47, 57). There is generally a stronger expectation in the civil law that such terms are mandatory (non-excludable), because of a stronger role for public policy and overriding general principles in contract law. (For a discussion of the position under the reform of French Law in force since 1 October 2016 see Pérès 2017.)

The role of general principle in contract law

In English law, we may say that there are certain general principles of contract law such as freedom of contract and the binding force of contracts. But these 'principles' are statements of values underlying our law – not precepts from which the answer in any particular case can be derived (Beale 2015: para 1–025). They explain the underlying thinking of judges in certain areas: the courts' reluctance to intervene in the terms of the contract can be said to be based on the parties' freedom to determine the terms – the contract is made by the parties, not by the court, and the reluctance to allow mistakes or changes of circumstances to constitute a ground of judicial intervention may be based on some version of the binding force of contracts: see e.g. *Bell v Lever Brothers Ltd* [1932] AC 161, 224: Lord Atkin:

> It is of paramount importance that contracts should be observed, and that if parties honestly comply with the essentials of the formation of contracts – i.e., agree in the same terms on the same subject-matter – they are bound,

> and must rely on the stipulations of the contract for protection from the effect of facts unknown to them.

Although all systems will display some similar general underlying values, articulated by the codes or by the courts, the civil law systems may give such values a more active status, elevating them into tools for the courts to use in deciding cases on their facts (e.g. French civil code arts 1102 (freedom of contract), 1103 (binding force)). The most obvious such case is a general principle which is not recognised as such in English law at all: good faith. In the modern law, the civilian systems have developed the view that the parties must form and perform their contract, and exercise their rights and remedies arising from the contract, in good faith – that is, there is a general norm of behaviour which regulates the relationship between the parties from the negotiations through to the complete performance of the transaction: see, e.g. the French civil code art. 1104 (non-excludable duty to negotiate, form and perform contract in good faith [bonne foi]); the German civil code § 242 (duty to perform an obligation according to good faith [Treu und Glauben]); and the Dutch civil code, book 6, art. 2:1 (obligor and obligee must act in accordance with requirements of reasonableness and fairness [redelijkheid en billijkheid]). This is an objective norm, a standard of conduct which the law expects of each party in their mutual dealings – a general norm which is absent from English law (Beale 2015: para 1–039). This does not, of course, require each party in a civil law system to subordinate its position to that of the other – a contractual relationship is not (in the terms of English law) a fiduciary relationship. But it is still a long way from the core assumption of English law that the parties are entitled generally to look to – and only to – their own interests. The strongest position on this in English law is in relation to the negotiations for a contract, where the absence of any general duty to negotiate in good faith is well attested (*Walford v Miles* [1992] 2 AC 128, 138). This is not to say that solutions are not sometimes found, through the law of tort, contract, unjust enrichment or equity (Cartwright 2016: 83–94). It might look as though this is simply a question of technique: English law uses specific duties, rather than a general principle. This is, indeed, part of the answer. But it goes much deeper than this, to the heart of the contractual relationship. The duty to negotiate in good faith is an articulation of a relationship which the law creates between parties negotiating a contract – indeed, some civilian systems say explicitly that the general duty arises from the moment of entry into the negotiations (e.g. German civil code §311(2).1), even if the scope and intensity of the duty will develop (and ebb and flow) as the negotiations develop. For the English lawyer, the negotiations are not, in this sense, a 'relationship'. But the student reading *Walford v Miles* should ask herself why not: and in this context it is not enough just to say that the civil law systems have a different way of doing things; we need to be able to put some flesh on the bones of the 'good faith' discussion.

Indeed, this has become more important in recent years with ideas being raised in English law about whether (or when) there can be an implied duty to *perform* the contract in good faith. Leggatt J's well-known discussion in *Yam Seng Pte Ltd v International Trade Corp Ltd* [2013] EWHC 111 (QB), [2013] 1 CLC 662, [120]-[155] makes English lawyers ask themselves why we are 'swimming against the tide' (ibid [125]) in continuing to reject a duty to perform a contract in good faith. That judgment made some reference to the civilian approach, but to explore this properly with the students we need to be able to dig more deeply into why it is that civil law systems naturally adopt a duty to perform in good faith – not only, as we have seen, in the broader recognition of general principle in the civil law, but also in the rather different vision that civil law systems appear to have of the very relationship between contracting parties. The traditional English approach – no inherent duty to negotiate in good faith (each party entitled to pursue his or her own interests) (*Walford v Miles* [1992] 2 AC 128, 138); and no duty to perform in good faith, only to do whatever it is that the parties have agreed in their contract to do (cf. *TSG Building Services plc v South Anglia Housing Ltd* [2013] EWHC 1151 (TCC), [2013] BLR 484, [46]) – may seem very stark, and can be either approved or challenged. But a broader understanding of the civil law approach to contract will help us to explain why in fact English law does what it does, given the very different underlying approach to contract and the commercial paradigm which it has adopted (see the section below on "The Paradigm Contract: Commercial, Consumer or Neutral?"), and could support us in rejecting some of the arguments that are used in support of the restrictive English approach, such as the fact that the notion of good faith is too 'uncertain' to be applied by the judges (*Walford v Miles* [1992] 2 AC 128, 138: Lord Ackner: uncertain, because subjective; cf. *Yam Seng Pte Ltd v International Trade Corp Ltd* [2013] EWHC 111 (QB), [2013] 1 CLC 662, [151]: Leggatt J.: objective meaning, definable).

The role of the court in relation to the contract

What we have seen so far should make clear that one very significant difference between the continental civil law systems and English law is found in the latitude given to the court in controlling the contract. Although the details vary from one system to another, the continental judge may have the power to disapply terms of the contract because they are unfair, unreasonable or contrary to good faith; or to refuse to allow a party to exercise the remedies normally available to vindicate her contractual rights because such an exercise would be contrary to good faith; or even to intervene in the contract to modify its terms to take into account changes of circumstances outside the parties' control – all in circumstances where it would be unthinkable for an English judge to do the same. Judges in all systems have to interpret the contract, and interpretation can sometimes be used to cloak judicial intervention in the terms of the contract or in its operation. But overt judicial powers over the contract are notably more limited in English law.

This may be attributed, at least in part, to structural differences between English law and the civil law systems. The division between the common law and statute within English law operates to restrict the courts' own powers over the contract, at least as the courts have interpreted it. The judges did not see their role as interventionist. The modern law of contract as it took its basic shape in the mid-19th century (Ibbetson 2001: ch 12) has an underlying philosophy of the parties' freedom of contract and concomitantly rejects an overt power for the court to override the parties' agreement. There has been, of course, significant development to provide moderating solutions for unfair terms and to protect weaker parties. In earlier times the courts of equity took a role here, but in the modern law such developments have been almost always by statute. And this has reinforced the dichotomy between the role of the judges and the role of the legislature in control over the contract. Judges have deplored the unfairness of contracts but have found that they have no power to intervene (*L'Estrange v Graucob* [1934] 2 KB 394, 405: Maugham LJ), and even when Parliament has intervened in specific contexts to give the courts a power to strike down unfair terms, the courts have seen this as a limited power, not as giving an indication that they should go beyond the statutory powers in other contexts (*Photo Production Ltd v Securicor Transport Ltd* [1980] AC 827, 843 (Lord Wilberforce), 851 (Lord Diplock); *National Westminster Bank plc v Morgan* [1985] AC 686, 708 (Lord Scarman)). This is a natural way for a common law judge to think; the common law is the general law, legislation is of a higher order, but is specific and not to be used as the basis of reasoning 'beyond the statute'. In a civil law system, a judge is much more likely to use legislation – even if it does not confer a more general power by its own language (which civil law systems may well do) – as a pointer towards a general legislative intention that can be given effect beyond the words of the legislation itself. In other words, civil judges tend to exercise powers over the contract – either powers expressly given by the legislator or powers that they interpret for themselves from the legislation – much more significantly than English judges.

The paradigm contract: commercial, consumer or neutral?

What we have seen in the previous paragraphs also illustrates another significant difference between the English law and the civil law of contract: identifying the paradigm. In all legal systems, we have to accommodate a wide range of transactions between different types of parties, including consumer contracts and contracts between purely commercial parties. In the 21st century it is obvious that a consumer contract needs somewhat different regulation from commercial contracts and that there are many other nuances, depending on whether the parties are of (broadly) equal bargaining power or not, combined with the nature of the contract – its subject matter and purpose. By comparing English law with the approach taken in other systems, we can see that laws of contract take some generic style of transaction as their particular paradigm, and the core rules broadly reflect the set of policies appropriate to that paradigm, leaving variations to be dealt with elsewhere. This is often a product of the history of the legal system.

The general paradigm of the English common law – the arm's length exchange between parties of broadly equal bargaining power – is a product of the 19th century liberal philosophy which formed the backdrop to the cases which crystallised the modern English law of contract (e.g. *Smith v Hughes* (1871) LR 6 QB 597; *Taylor v Caldwell* (1863) 3 B & S 826; *Currie v Misa* (1875) 10 Exch. 153; *Tweddle v Atkinson* (1861) 1 B & S 393; *The Moorcock* (1889) 14 PD 64), together with the fact that by that time there was no special law merchant, independent of the common law, nor special commercial courts to determine commercial matters. Continental systems did not see the paradigm contractual relationship as primarily commercial; and some developed a separate commercial law, with separate commercial courts, supported (after the codification of their law) by a separate commercial code. This was the case in France, where the civil code of 1804 was followed swiftly by the commercial code of 1807, and Germany, where the commercial code came into force alongside the civil code in 1900 (for France, contrasting England, see Bell *et al* 2008: 453–454). In any case, the 'consumer' was not defined and given special protection until the last third of the 20th century, too late to form the paradigm transaction. But in the English law, consumer contracts seem to be even more remote from the core, paradigm contract on which the general rules are based, not only because of the inherently commercial paradigm, but also because the judges did not create their own common law of consumer contracts, but left it to the legislature – which is therefore seen as special law, separate from the core, common law rules and not to be drawn on to develop the common law (see the section above on "The Role of the Court in Relation to the Contract").

Contract drafting styles

It should also be noted here that English lawyers take a different approach from civil lawyers to the drafting of their contracts – especially lawyers for commercial parties who write documents which are commonly criticised by civil lawyers as unnecessarily long. But this is not just an innate verbosity, nor an attempt on the English lawyers' part to justify their fees: it is a consequence of the nature of a contract in the eyes of the common law. In a system where the contract is made by the parties, not by the courts (and the courts are reluctant to intervene, and the parties certainly prefer to keep them out); where there is little legislative regulation of the content of contracts which would fill the gaps of the document; where there is no overriding duty of good faith, or fairness, in the formation or performance of the contract on which a party can rely if things go wrong of which the other party had not warned him; and where the contract is defined by reference to its objective wording, albeit interpreted in context (*Investors Compensation Scheme Ltd v West Bromwich Building Society* [1998] 1 WLR 896, 912–913), it is the parties' (or, rather, their lawyers') natural instinct to pin the transaction down to the detailed provisions of the text. The negotiated, written commercial contract is only one form of contract, of course, and hardly the most numerous, but rather it is generally the most economically significant. And the courts continue to set the model by reference to this economically significant transaction. The certainty that it engenders is seen as a hallmark of English contract law and therefore an attraction for commercial parties to make English law the choice of law for their contract (*Wood v Capita Insurance Services Ltd* [2017] UKSC 24, [2017] 2 WLR 24, [15]).

Reflections on teaching

There remains the question of how to bring into our teaching ideas that we can draw from the civil law. This is not easy. Introducing civil law comparisons into the courses on English contract law risks being superficial (and therefore misleading) or, if it is done in sufficient depth, just too difficult for the students. Nor, of course, can we expect all teachers of English contract law to become specialist comparative lawyers with detailed knowledge of any of the civil law systems.

The structure of the teaching of contract law in civil law faculties follows, as might be expected, from the general approach to contract as described above. Courses (and textbooks) will often follow the structure of the civil code, first presenting a common course on the law of 'obligations' (including tort as well as contract, and looking also at the common rules and principles of the law of obligations), and then having a later, more detailed course on special contracts. This does not generally fit our thinking in the common law, where contract is commonly studied independently of tort – and, indeed, these two subjects may be taught and examined in different years of the degree so there is little opportunity to put them together to see the unity of the law of obligations. Some English faculties do seek to address this, either by offering a separate, more advanced course on obligations (as an option) after the basic rules of contract and tort have been assimilated, or by bringing their core teaching of contract and tort together into a module on the law of obligations; some books are published on the (combined) law of obligations, although the core textbooks are still separated into contract and tort (Burrows 2013 attempts to restate English law in a structure following the classical Roman model set by Gaius' and Justinian's Institutes: see also Samuel 2001; Samuel 2010; Cooke and Oughton 2000). Some form of cross-fertilisation between contract and tort is surely to be encouraged: within the normal confines of an English law curriculum we should find a place for a discussion of the relationship between the different sources of obligations, their essential nature and the contrasts between them, even if this is done through 'overlap' topics in the core contract and tort courses.

The idea of going further and making our contract courses inherently comparative is not realistic, although it should be noted that there are some interesting models on the continent, where civil law faculties have begun to offer non-traditional degrees designed to teach students not simply their national law, but a broader 'European' and comparative curriculum, including in contract law. The most radical recent development is in Luxembourg, where the Bachelor in Law now takes a new 'transnational format', taught in French and English (see www.en.uni.lu/studies/fdef/bachelor_en_droit_academic); and for other examples, see the European Law School at Maastricht University (www.maastrichtuniversity.nl/education/bachelor/bachelor-european-law-school) and the Bachelor in International and European Law at the University of Groningen (www.rug.nl/bachelors/international-and-european-law/programme). For us, however, the question is how to introduce our students to ideas from outside the common law, as an integral element of our regular courses.

One inherent limitation in such a venture is language. We cannot expect our students to read European languages in order to find out about the European systems. However, we are fortunate in having much relevant literature available in English, either in its original writing or in translation. And there is a particularly rich resource of comparative material, written in English, which is the product of the European harmonisation projects undertaken over the last 25 years since the European Parliament requested in 1989

> that a start be made on the necessary preparatory work on drawing up a common European Code of Private Law, the Member States being invited, having deliberated the matter, to state whether they wish to be involved in the planned unification.
>
> ([1989] OJ C158/400, 26 May 1989)

We are not here concerned with the harmonisation process itself, which has not succeeded, so far at least: the ultimate proposal for a Regulation on a Common European Sales Law (COM(2011) 635, 11 October 2011) was withdrawn at the end of 2014. But within that process there was very significant academic comparative study of national systems across Europe, including sets of 'soft law' instruments of contract law (models of possible rules of contract law, set out in the form of codes), the notes and comments published as part of two of these: the Principles of European Contract Law ('PECL') (Lando and Beale 2000) and the Draft Common Frame of Reference ('DCFR') (von Bar Clive and Schulte-Nölke 2009), which draws extensively on the PECL. The notes and comments briefly explain the different approaches taken by the national systems – including English law – to each topic, and they distil common approaches or (where there are differences) select preferred solutions for a new European contract law.

This material can be very inspiring for the student of English contract law. Not only can it give in short order a picture of the extent to which English law is similar to, or different from, our European neighbours, but it can give food for thought about the approach taken by English law. The European experience illustrates similar debates that we expect our students to discuss in our own national contract law, such as the tensions between certainty and fairness, between protecting commercial interests and the interests of the weaker party; the underlying basis of contractual obligation and the significance of the parties' intentions; the role of the court in intervening in the contract (in case, for example, of significant changes of circumstances); the range and priority of remedies that the court has at its disposal to secure the performance of the contract for the benefit of the victim of a breach. Giving our students such material is not just about their deciding whether English law is swimming with, or against, the international tide; it is to pursue one of the fundamental approaches – and values – of comparative law: to look outside our own system, to reflect on how others deal with similar issues, and accordingly to measure our own way of doing things.

References

von Bar, C., Clive, E. and Schulte-Nölke, H., 2009. *Principles, Definitions and Model Rules of European Private Law: Draft Common Frame of Reference (DCFR)*. Sellier, Munich.

Beale, H., 2015. *Chitty on Contracts: General Principles*. 32nd ed. (Vol. 1). Sweet & Maxwell, London.

Bell, J., Boyron, S. and Whittaker, S., 2008. *Principles of French Law*. 2nd ed. Oxford University Press, Oxford.

Birks, P. and Descheemaeker, E., 2014. *The Roman Law of Obligations*. Oxford University Press, Oxford.

Bridge, M., 2015. *Personal Property Law*. 4th ed. Oxford University Press, Oxford.

Burrows, A. ed., 2013. *English Private Law*. Oxford University Press, Oxford.

Cartwright, J. and Whittaker, S., eds., 2017. *The Code Napoléon Rewritten: French Contract Law After the 2016 Reforms*. Hart Publishing, Oxford.

Cartwright, J., 2016. *Contract law: An Introduction to the English Law of Contract for the Civil Lawyer*. 3rd ed. Hart Publishing, Oxford.

Cooke, P. and Oughton, J., 2000. *The Common Law of Obligations*. 3rd ed. Butterworths, London.

Flodgren, B. and Runesson, E.M., 2015. *Contract Law in Sweden*. Kluwer Law International, Alphen aan den Rijn.

Ibbetson, D.J., 2001. *A Historical Introduction to the Law of Obligations*. Oxford University Press, Oxford.

Lando, O. and Beale, H.G., eds., 2000. *Principles of European Contract Law: Parts I and II*. Kluwer Law International, The Hague.

Markesinis, B.S., Unberath, H. and Johnston, A.C., 2006. *The German Law of Contract: A Comparative Treatise*. 2nd ed. Hart Publishing, Oxford.

Nicholas, B., 1962. *An Introduction to Roman Law*. Clarendon Press, Oxford.

Nicholas, B., 1992. *The French Law of Contract*. 2nd ed. Clarendon Press, Oxford.

Pérès, C., 2017. Mandatory and Non-Mandatory Rules in the New Law of Contract. In: Cartwright, J. and Whittaker, S., eds., *The Code Napoléon Rewritten: French Contract Law After the 2016 Reforms*. Hart Publishing, Oxford, pp. 167–186.

Samuel, G., 2001. *Law of Obligations & Legal Remedies*. 2nd ed. Cavendish Publishing Ltd, London.

Samuel, G., 2010. *Law of Obligations*. Edward Elgar, Cheltenham.

Stein, P., 1988. The Fate of the Institutional System. In: Stein, P.G., ed., *The Character and Influence of the Roman Civil Law: Historical Essays*. Hambledon Press, London, pp. 73–82.

Zweigert, K. and Kötz, H., 1998. *Introduction to Comparative Law*. 3rd ed. trans. T. Weir. Clarendon Press, Oxford.

Chapter 16

Contract law pedagogy

A new agenda

Warren Swain

Some of the challenges to good legal pedagogy are not discipline-specific. Many of the themes that were identified in the sister volume on criminal law pedagogy (Gledhill and Livings 2016) are just as applicable to the law of contract. The same comment can be made about the future as well as the present. No special insight is needed to predict that technology is likely to have a greater impact on the teaching of law than it generally does today. Nor is it too difficult to make a good pedagogical case for developments of this sort. As Viven-Wilksch shows, technology to some degree is already widely used. Most modern students are digital natives who are not merely comfortable with technology but have an expectation that it will be a central feature of the way that they learn. This is not merely a question of the way that courses are delivered. Technology shapes the whole perspective about learning of the modern student. At the same time it is probably too simplistic to assume that there is a division purely based on age and that the gap between digital natives and digital immigrants cannot be bridged (Helsper and Eynon 2009). Yet, important though the issue of technology is for student learning, there is also something greater at stake here. It relates to the place of contract law and more broadly private law within the law school curriculum.

More than forty years ago traditional private law scholarship came under sustained attack from the Critical Legal Studies movement in the United States. These ideas were popular at a number of leading law schools and created a good deal of excitement at the time. Much of this scholarship was aimed at demolishing orthodox private law scholarship. Although there were some adherents of this view in the United Kingdom and in other parts of the Commonwealth, this approach never really took root in those jurisdictions. In recent times a more constructive dialogue with private law doctrine is discernible even in the United States (see Goldberg 2012). Private law subjects like contract law remain a big part of the compulsory part of the law curriculum everywhere. Nevertheless, there is a grave threat to private law as an academic discipline in the United Kingdom and similar jurisdictions which, whilst significantly different to the threat it has faced in the United States, is no less pernicious. It actually goes to the heart of contract law pedagogy. The threat is less about whether the subject is taught than the importance which is attached to it by both students and scholars. Contract law as a key part of the curriculum is at risk, less because of a concerted attempt to undermine its worth than as a result of neglect.

In a law school curriculum in which appreciation of economic, political and social context has come to play an increasingly important part, black letter contract scholarship has increasingly been marginalised. Good doctrinal scholarship is potentially very rich. Hogg, Morgan, Campbell and Bigwood in this volume all demonstrate how this kind of approach can make a worthwhile contribution to legal scholarship and, allied to this, make a vibrant contribution to the law curriculum. The reasons why this black letter approach risks being squeezed out are both various and complex. This type of approach towards pedagogy is difficult. It makes heavy demands on the lecturer and the student. Outside of the leading law faculties it is difficult to recruit academics who can and will teach the private law subjects. There are fewer generalist scholars than there used to be. Early career hires generally know more and more about less and less than they once did. This isn't really anyone's fault but rather it is partly a consequence of requiring a PhD in order to enter the academic job market. A failure to think systematically about the pedagogy of the subject is also partly to blame. There isn't very much written on the pedagogy of law teaching. As long as eighty-five years ago Joseph Beale made a plea to think more seriously about the teaching of the subject of law (Beale 1933). Subsequent responses to Beale's plea have left us with still a lot to do. Within the itself fairly limited class of pedagogical literature about law, almost nothing has been written specifically on the subject of contract law.

The decision to teach the subject in the traditional method involves making a pedagogical choice. There is nothing wrong in teaching in this way where the decision is a conscious one. However, all too often this is the line of least resistance. This is a shame. There are real benefits in teaching in a traditional manner. Roberts and Capper highlight a few of the benefits and suggest ways in which this approach to teaching might be strengthened. Getting students to read and think about cases is what being a lawyer is all about. The only way to gain proficiency in this skill is to actually do it, and then to do it some more. However, modern students other than the most able and bloody minded are unlikely to persevere doing this on their own. The typical student is quite different from their equivalent twenty-five years ago. These differences should not be exaggerated by casual use of the rhetoric of millennials or the snowflake generation, but they should not be ignored either. It has been documented for a long time that law students find the transition to university difficult (for example see, Silver 1968). Given that most law students will not have studied law before, these difficulties are understandable. But a shift in student perceptions has undoubtedly occurred. Modern students are generally a more diverse body with a different set of expectations than their predecessors. Modern students see themselves as consumers and their teaching a product (Woodall *et al* 2014).

Good pedagogy needs to be mindful of students but not a slave to them. This is only part of the story. Looking to the future the bigger task is to reinvigorate contract law teaching as a central part of the law curriculum. Contract law is truly foundational. The other private law subjects make little sense without having studied contract law first. Contract law or a closely allied form of it, whether in gift transactions or barter, is fundamental to the way that every society and its economy operates (seminally demonstrated in 1925 by Marcell Mauss 2008). Contract lawyers have for the most part been too slow to defend their discipline. Many of those who now teach the subject do not see themselves as contract lawyers. Their scholarly interests lay in other directions and contract law is what is sometimes referred to as their service teaching. There is little incentive to do things differently. Whilst there is a very vibrant contract law scholarship in the United States, elsewhere the subject has a lower profile in institutional research agendas. Research in private law is difficult and time consuming. Both of these factors put it beyond the reach of many law academics. It is so much easier to engage with the latest trendy fad or theory.

Those who teach contract law are not blameless. In many institutions the subject is tired. Many contract courses still for example spend a great deal of time on the old postal rule. As Brownsword shows, this can leave the subject looking irrelevant. Part of the problem is that contract law is too narrowly perceived and has tended to be taught in one way and that way is not particularly interesting. As the contributors here show, the status quo need not be a given. Contract law is in fact a rich tapestry. Wheeler, Gudel, Bix, Cartwright, Hyde and Wragg all give completely different insights and yet at the same time they are discussing the same subject. In the introduction it was suggested that it was necessary to rescue contract law pedagogy from the nineteenth century. As well as showing what is possible, the essays in this volume are a call to arms. Contract law is too important a part of legal education, our legal systems and society to be allowed to wither.

References

Beale, J., 1933. Legal Pedagogy, or What Have I, *Notre Dame L. Rev.*, 8, 402.

Gledhill, K. and Livings, B., 2016. *The Teaching of Criminal Law: The Pedagogical Imperatives*. Routledge, London.

Goldberg, J., 2012. Pragmatism in Private Law, *Harv. L. Rev.*, 125, 1640.

Helsper, E. and Eynon, R., 2009. Digital Natives: Where Is the Evidence? *Br. Educ. Res. J.*, 1–18.

Mauss, M., 2008. *The Gift*. Routledge, London.

Silver, L., 1968. Anxiety and the First Semester of Law School, *Wis. L. Rev.,* 1201.

Woodall, T. Hiller, A. and Resnick, S., 2014. Making Sense of Higher Education: Students as Consumers and the Value of the University Experience. *Stud. Higher Educ.*, 39, 48–67.

Index

Taylor & Francis Group
an informa business

Taylor & Francis eBooks

www.taylorfrancis.com

A single destination for eBooks from Taylor & Francis with increased functionality and an improved user experience to meet the needs of our customers.

90,000+ eBooks of award-winning academic content in Humanities, Social Science, Science, Technology, Engineering, and Medical written by a global network of editors and authors.

TAYLOR & FRANCIS EBOOKS OFFERS:

- A streamlined experience for our library customers
- A single point of discovery for all of our eBook content
- Improved search and discovery of content at both book and chapter level

REQUEST A FREE TRIAL

support@taylorfrancis.com

Routledge
Taylor & Francis Group

CRC Press
Taylor & Francis Group

For Product Safety Concerns and Information please contact our EU representative GPSR@taylorandfrancis.com
Taylor & Francis Verlag GmbH, Kaufingerstraße 24, 80331 München, Germany

www.ingramcontent.com/pod-product-compliance
Ingram Content Group UK Ltd.
Pitfield, Milton Keynes, MK11 3LW, UK
UKHW011004180926
475701UK00004B/548

* 9 7 8 0 3 6 7 6 6 2 5 8 5 *